SIX BILLION AND MORE

SIX BILLION AND MORE
HUMAN POPULATION REGULATION & CHRISTIAN ETHICS

SUSAN POWER BRATTON

WESTMINSTER/JOHN KNOX PRESS
LOUISVILLE, KENTUCKY

Book design by Dovetail Art and Design

First edition

Published by Westminster/John Knox Press
Louisville, Kentucky

This book is printed on acid-free paper that meets the American National Standards Institute Z39.48 standard. ∞

PRINTED IN THE UNITED STATES OF AMERICA
9 8 7 6 5 4 3 2 1

Library of Congress Cataloging-in-Publication Data

Bratton, Susan.
    Six billion and more : human population regulation and Christian ethics / Susan Power Bratton. — 1st ed.
        p.   cm.
    Includes bibliographical references and index.
    ISBN 0-664-25186-2

    1. Birth control—Religious aspects—Christianity.   2. Population policy—Religious aspects—Christianity.   I. Title.   II. Title: 6 billion and more.
HQ766.25.B73   1992
261.8'36—dc20   91-40419

FOR ZANE AND PACO

that they might grow up in a better world

CONTENTS

FOREWORD

"**A**nd God blessed them, and God said unto them, Be fruitful, and multiply, and replenish the earth." (Gen. 1:28, KJV). With these well-known words, the Creator lavishes blessing upon earth's creatures. Through this joyful blessing, God calls forth their fruitfulness, provides blessed impetus to their biological and ecological development, and divinely empowers them to bring fulfilling completeness to the earth.

If we read the Bible with ourselves in mind, we naturally see this blessing as ours. And it is. But it is not ours exclusively. It was given before we came. It was first given thus: "And God created great whales, and every living creature that moveth . . . and every winged fowl after his kind: and God saw that it was good. And God blessed them, saying, Be fruitful, and multiply, and fill the waters in the seas, and let fowl multiply in the earth" (Gen. 1:21–22, KJV).

That *other* creatures are so blessed, and blessed first, is not only humbling for us but also critically important. The populations of creatures—in their wondrous variety of kinds—are expected by their Creator to bear fruit through God-given means of reproduction; they are expected to develop biological and ecological interrelationships; they are expected to bring fulfillment of the Creator's intentions for the good creation.

God's blessed expectation for the populations of *other* creatures helps put our human population into context. We, *and they*, are

9

blessed. We, *and they,* are to reproduce, develop our kinds, and fulfill the earth to its God-intended completeness.

But God's blessed expectation for people goes further than for other creatures, and this, too, helps put human population into context. For our kind, we read, "And God blessed them, and God said unto them, Be fruitful, and multiply, and replenish the earth, and subdue it: and have dominion over the fish of the sea, and over the fowl of the air, and over every living thing that moveth upon the earth" (Gen. 1:28, KJV). Thus we humans are given not only God's joyful blessing that calls forth our fruitfulness, provides blessed impetus toward our development, and divinely empowers us to fulfill the earth, but also something more. God's blessing also graciously gives us the gift of dominion—and this in a peculiar godlike way. Our greater blessing is that we are given the blessed joy of reflecting the Creator's joyful delight, loving care, and persistent keeping of all creatures. We humans mirror the One who, as the scriptures tell us, ". . . sendeth the springs into the valleys, which run among the hills. They give drink to every beast of the field: the wild asses quench their thirst. By them shall the fowls of the heaven have their habitation, which sing among the branches. He watereth the hills from his chambers; the earth is satisified with the fruit of thy work" (Ps. 104:10–13, KJV). We are blessed with enjoying, caring for, and keeping all God's creatures.

Our human species thus is provided meaningful context by the scriptures: (1) Our own population joins with the populations of the other creatures God has made, participating one with another in the blessed expectation of reproducing and increasing our kinds, biologically and ecologically developing our kinds, and fulfilling the earth to its God-intended completeness, and (2) our own human kind enjoys this blessed expectation not only ourselves but also for the populations of all God's creatures.

It is here that we come to our present profound difficulty. Increasingly we people are occupying the land to the exclusion and extinction of the *other* creatures. This leads us to ask, "Does our God-given blessing of stewardship of creation grant us license to deny creatures God's blessing of fruitfulness and fulfillment? May we take this blessing of reflective rule to negate God's blessing to the fish of the sea and the birds of the air?"

We have come to a time when the impact of humankind—our exploding number multiplied by the power each wields and the defilement each brings—not only denies the creatures fruitfulness and fulfillment but also extinguishes increasing numbers of them from the face of earth. We add field to field, expending forest, prairie, wetland, and savannah in the process. We add house to house, consuming fields with sprawling cities and suburbs as we grow. With this expansion the creatures are pressed to the margins; many are driven to extinction. Many of our kind are moving headlong toward loneliness—toward a loneliness that comes when only people occupy the land.

Today, we human beings and our works are spilling over land and landscapes, displacing and submerging the other creatures, denying most of them fulfillment of the blessing, "Be fruitful, and multiply, and replenish the earth." God told Noah to bring into the ark two of all living creatures, male and female, to keep them alive (Gen. 6:19). Clearly, every kind of creature is valuable in God's eye. Clearly, it is God's will that the creatures' fruitfulness not be extinguished. Clearly, our attitude is one that should mirror the Lord's.

It is for people who respect the need for assuring creation's fruitfulness—who embrace the fullness of God's creation blessing—that this book is particularly important. It is important because it grips the dilemma that we have been avoiding: our self-deceptive labeling of the explosive growth of our kind as "fruitfulness" and "progress," even as it consumes the fruitfulness and progress of the *others* and eventually even *ours*. Ours is a progress so human-centered and human-directed that it leaves out the other creatures. It is one that fails to reflect God's care for all creatures, one that deprives them the realization of God's blessing.

The path through this book is one we all might wish to sidestep for just one more generation. We people might not want to look at our exploding number and the per capita consumption and destruction by which this number is multiplied. But it is by such growth and multiplication that we have begun to empty the earth of its creatures. Ours has become a narrow progress that diminishes and denies fruitfulness to the rest of creation, one that ultimately destroys what we are given to rule. Such "progress" makes a mockery of our dominion blessing, for by destroying the subjects we rule, we are destroying our ruling also. By not ruling our own appetites, we ultimately cease also to rule creation.

While we might wish to postpone addressing the issues of this book, creation cannot afford the wait. The creation is expectantly waiting for the coming of those who affirm God's blessed expectation for God's creatures. Amid the distant echoes of Isaiah, "Woe unto them that join house to house, that lay field to field, till there be no place, that they may be placed alone in the midst of the earth" (Isa. 5:8 KJV), we hear a groaning but expectant creation. It is standing on tip toe, with neck outstretched, waiting for the coming of the chil-

11

dren of God. The creatures are waiting for the glorious freedom to enjoy God's creation blessing: "Be fruitful, and multiply, and replenish the earth." May Susan Bratton's book begin the trek across the difficult ground we now must tread as we seek to affirm and fulfill God's creation blessing!

CALVIN B. DeWITT

Au Sable Institute
June 28, 1991

ACKNOWLEDGMENTS

I would like to thank Dr. Calvin DeWitt of Au Sable Institute, Carol Holst of the Ministry for Population Concerns, and Dr. William Power of the University of Georgia for reading and commenting on the draft manuscript even though they may not all be in complete agreement with my theses. Dr. Cynthia Thompson and Rev. Harold Twiss of Westminster/John Knox Press offered assistance and useful comments at various stages of the project.

1

THE CROWDED COSMOS

On July 11, 1987, the human population of our productive and often troubled planet reached 5 billion. *The Futurist* magazine, selecting the world's most common given and family names, dubbed the five billionth child Mohammed Wang in advance of his natal day.[1] Other journalists, desiring a real infant, joined the United Nations secretary general in welcoming a little Yugoslav named Matej Gasper, delivered at 8:25 A.M. on the Day of the Five Billion.[2] Matej, presumably having no preconceived notions about life on earth, assumed the honor without protest.

The exact time when there were, for the first time in history, 5 billion people simultaneously residing on the face of the earth was at best an estimate, and there was no doubt another baby born elsewhere, perhaps without the benefit of a hospital or a clock, was actually the five billionth human. The critical reality underlying the media event, however, is the unrelenting growth of the world's population. According to the United Nations Population Fund, by the year 2000 the newborns of 1987 will be joined by yet another billion people.[3]

Demographers, who study population structure and processes, think that through early human history, population increased slowly. Estimates vary, but a best guess at the Stone Age population of the earth is about 5 to 10 million. With the development of metal tools and other technologies, populations expanded. By the time of Christ's birth, the great ancient civilizations had produced sophisticated agricultural systems and transportation networks, and the world's population had grown to between 200 and 400 million (or about the combined size of the contemporary populations of the United States and Canada). By the beginning of the agricultural and industrial revolutions, about 1650 A.D., the world's population was still only about 500 million. In preindustrial times, the overall rate of human population growth was probably less than one tenth of 1 percent a year, and there were decades and perhaps even centuries when growth was negligible.[4] Historically, while human population was growing in one region, perhaps due to a series of favorable agricultural years, it was often falling in another as drought, poor harvests, disease outbreaks, or local wars decimated both rural and urban communities.

Europe was the first to experience the effects of industrialization and initiated the increase in world population growth rate that still dominates world demographics, even though the population of Europe itself is now almost stable. By 1800 the world population growth rate had risen to four tenths of 1 percent a year, and by 1920 it had exceeded 1 percent. Superficially, 1 percent seems like a low level of population growth, but population expansion acts much like compound interest on a bank account, and a small annual increase may become a large increment if it continues for a generation. From 1940 to 1950 world population grew at a rate of 1.3 percent per year. At that rate the world population could *double* every forty-five years.[5]

The great world population explosion began about 1950 and by 1970 had reached a peak growth rate of 2.2 percent. Even though the population growth rate has now fallen below 2 percent, the number of humans added per year is still enormous.[6] In 1987 the United Nations estimated there were 86 million more births than deaths, or an additional 235,000 people arriving a day.[7] An expansion of population equivalent to that of all human history prior to 1650 can now occur in less than a decade.

Despite the massive social, economic, and environmental impacts of such unprecedented changes in human numbers, Christians have only sporadically approached population processes as matters of ethical concern. A number of religious organizations, such as the American Scientific Affiliation (an organization of evangelical scientists), the United Presbyterian Church, and the World Council of Churches, have conducted discussions or produced general statements and position papers on human population growth or its environmental impacts,[8] yet very little academic theological material has been published on the subject. The issues generated by population change might superficially appear to be in the realm of sexual ethics, but the many fine books available on Christian sexuality usually limit their discussions to the choice of partners, the role of marriage, and other personal ethical decisions. The number and timing of children in Christian marriage is generally considered a matter of individual preference, although some denominations emphasizing "traditional family values" follow the simple reproductive formula of "more is better." Christians prefer to deal with sexuality in the sphere of the family or of interacting individuals rather than discuss and evaluate the behavior of entire societies. With the exception of abortion politics, Protestant Christianity has avoided wrestling with reproductive ethics and, by default, has allowed other cultural forces, including economics, to make most of the decisions.

Ironically, Christian bioethics has also fallen short on population questions. Christian medical ethics, for example, has investigated birth control and reproduction in relation to the rights and needs of individuals but has tended to avoid questions of international magnitude. The emphasis has been on the birth and death of persons and not on the economic and social factors that ultimately control the differential between the rates of birth and death, and thus the population growth rate. Christian environmental ethics is a new and relatively undeveloped field of inquiry, which is unfortunately still focusing on the complaints of anti-Christian critics (and all too often apologizing for past Christian failures).[9] Although Christian environmental ethics recognizes the need to tackle problems of international scope, it has produced only a handful of commentaries on specific issues such as population growth, pollution, and land degradation.

Christian social ethics, as one would hope, has made the greatest effort to investigate social and economic issues on community, national, and international scales but has viewed population as a subset of the problems surrounding poverty. Social ethicists, primarily trained in the humanities, may not feel comfortable with the scientific aspects of population issues and may be reticent to trespass into the territory of sexual ethics. Christian studying women's roles in the church discuss reproductive ethics, but again, deal primarily with the rights of the individual. One can only conclude that the unnatural separation between personal and social ethics that has so plagued Western Christianity in the last century has blocked serious discussion of human population regulation, a subject where the personal and the social are inseparable.[10]

Unfortunately, population issues often arise subtly in topics of critical concern to the entire Christian community. One sometimes hears Christians complain, for example, that giving more food aid to starving people is only going to make the situation worse because the disadvantaged "won't stop reproducing." A population process, real or imagined, becomes an excuse for not aiding the poor. Christians thus allow a population issue to influence contributions to missions, without ever bothering to discuss population growth itself and without determining whether anything can or should be done about it.

The purpose of this book is to introduce Christians to the social, economic, environmental, and spiritual problems created by massive shifts in human numbers and to develop a Christian ethical framework for determining "rights and wrongs" in dealing with human population regulation. The book is also intended to encourage Christians to apply Christian values to population issues at the personal, community, national, and international levels. Without serious study and organized discussion of the problems, members of Christian denominations lack the background and theological discipline to attempt to influence government policies and to determine the appropriate role of family planning in Christian community life and missions. This volume is also intended to move Christian environmental ethics away from general statements and defenses of biblical creation theology and to direct Christians toward concrete analysis of the most serious threats to human welfare and environmental integrity. While this presentation is neither technical nor scientific, it will use the best available figures on population change and will draw upon materials written by professional demographers, economists, ecologists, and sociologists. The reader should recognize that some of the sources quoted, however, may not be in agreement with the general tenets of Christian ethics or with the conclusions presented here.

IS POPULATION A PROBLEM?

Prior to establishing some principles for developing a Christian population ethic, we have to ask ourselves a simple question: Is demographic change really a problem, and if so, why? In environmental and economic circles, the "population explosion" has been raising controversy for over forty years. Many ecologists and environmental activists view population growth as the single greatest threat to the future of the planet. More people means more land abuse, more soil erosion, more water and air pollution, and more forest destruction. Ecologists see the earth and its separate geographic regions as limited systems that cannot house infinite numbers of humans. When the limits, or the *carrying capacity*, of the environment are exceeded, the available natural resources can no longer support the human population, and both human suffering and resource destruction are the sad results. In his 1968 book *The Population Bomb*, ecologist Paul Ehrlich presented unregulated population growth as a primary source of food shortages and predicted that within a decade world hunger would be worse (and he was right).[11] More recently, ecologists have implicated human overpopulation as a major culprit in the clearing and burning of hundreds of thousands of acres of tropical rain forest and in the devastating spread of the North African deserts into more fertile grazing lands. The ecologists, who see the well-being of humankind as dependent on the well-being of the earth, worry that the ever-expanding human population will damage the very source of human livelihood and harm the earth's ecosystems in ways that will be difficult or impossible to repair.

In the scientific community, the pessimism of the ecologists is to some extent countered by the optimism of the agriculturalists, who believe that new technology can partially relieve the resource limitations. Advocates of the "green revolution," a series of agronomic advances that have vastly increased crop yields in some parts of Asia and Africa, suggest that further technological improvements are possible and that many agricultural systems worldwide are falling far below their potential to feed the growing multitudes. The ecologists usually respond by pointing out that the green revolution, which requires capital investments and new expertise, has not stopped world hunger, and even if better methods of farming are implemented, present population growth rates in many of the poorer nations can quickly make even major improvements in food resources insufficient. Population growth is making it more difficult for the green revolution to catch up with world nutritional needs. Long-term solutions to world hunger are not simply technological, they are also social.

The ecologists, who find that new environmental problems are arising faster than old ones are being solved, pose some difficult questions about human population expansion. How many people can the earth support? How is population growth related to famine and starvation? If the population explosion causes increased pollution and land abuse, what sorts of measures may be taken to reduce human pressure on fragile environments? How do we fairly determine an environmental human carrying capacity for a nation or for a region? It is wrong for humans to damage the environment through rapid population growth?

Many social scientists agree with the ecologists that population is currently a serious problem, while others believe concerns for human population expansion have been overstated. On the one hand are the pro-growth economists, such as Lord P. T. Bauer of the London School of Economics. Lord Bauer argues that "rapid population growth has not inhibited economic progress either in the West or in the contemporary Third World."[12] Countries with high or very dense populations, such as the Netherlands or Hong Kong, are often quite prosperous. Population growth can stimulate innovation and economic development. Rise in personal income can accompany population growth, as can rapid material advancement. Further, children are not necessarily an economic burden. They will ultimately make an economic contribution, probably exceeding the cost of raising them. Perhaps more important, having children is a form of "psychic income, which is clearly a major component of human satisfaction."[13]

On the other side of the economic argument are the economists and sociologists who see population problems as integrally related to poverty. Birthrate is often a function of social class and income level. In many countries poor women have, on the average, more children than do women from the middle and upper classes and often do not have the resources to adequately care for their large families. As of this writing, per capita food production is falling in Africa, while the population is steadily growing. If all the additional children are to be fed, either technological and social change must revolutionize African agriculture or nations already heavily in debt must import more food. Population growth in some regions of the Third World is so great that already overcrowded school systems must be expanded to meet the flood of school-age children. Unfortunately, in urban slums and isolated rural areas, where many children are still not enrolled in school due to lack of space, rapid population growth is likely to exacerbate the existing inadequacies of the educational systems. Illiteracy and lack of technical training keep poor people trapped and underemployed in the unskilled labor market.

Rapid population growth is also related to high rates of infant and child mortality. Particularly in poor families, infant mortality increases dramatically as family size increases. The youngest children in large families are more likely to be malnourished and are therefore more subject to disease than their older siblings. Birth spacing is often a problem. A woman already weak from caring for a newborn infant may find that both her own health and that of her children is threatened by yet another child, conceived before she has had an opportunity to recover from the previous pregnancy. In regions where health care is very limited or inaccessible, childhood diseases and parasites spread unchecked by inexpensive vaccines or simple sanitary improvements such as piped water. Families discouraged by the death they see around them have more children, hoping to raise one or two to adulthood.[14]

Social scientists have generated a whole series of "population" questions concerning human welfare. Does population growth cause poverty and human suffering, or does it tend to relieve it? What are the best population regulation policies for the developing nations? How do health services and education relate to family planning? To what extent does family planning improve child welfare? Relative to family planning, what is the best way to aid the poor and disadvantaged?

To add to the conflicting views concerning the desirability of human population regulation, population trends are quite variable worldwide. While parts of the Third World are still experiencing terrific rates of population growth, several of the most developed countries are gradually slipping into population decline, and other nations, such as the United States, are expected to stabilize their populations or begin a decline within the next two to three decades. Human numbers in environmentally stressed sub-Saharan Africa continue to grow at 3.1 percent per year,[15] yet industrialized West Germany's population is declining by 0.2 percent a year and is expected to stabilize at 52 million, which is 15 percent below its 1986 population of 61 million people.[16] The nation of Kenya is growing at a remarkable 4.2 percent a year and is expected to increase its population from 20 million to 111 million before stabilizing— a 455 percent growth rate, or a projected increase of 90 million, which is tremendous for a single country.[17] Meanwhile, all of Europe is projected to grow by only 6 percent between 1985 and 2025, causing a population change from 492 million to 524 million (an increase of only 32 million for an entire continent).[18] While some industrialized regions are worrying about a "birth dearth" and are closing empty primary schools, some less developed regions are struggling to construct enough educational buildings and to find the money to pay for more teaching staff.

In the era of modernization following World War II, one fifth of the world could be easily classed as developed, and the remaining four fifths could be easily classed as developing. In the 1990s it will probably be more realistic to divide nations into those with low rates of population growth and improving living conditions and those with currently or recently rapid population growth and declining living conditions. In 1986 slow-growth regions, with grow rates of less than 1 percent, included Western Europe, North America, Eastern Europe and the Soviet Union, Australia, and New Zealand. East Asia (primarily China and Japan), with a population growth rate of 1 percent, was quickly entering the ranks of the low-growth regions. High-growth regions, with rates exceeding 2 percent, included Southeast Asia, Latin America, and the Indian subcontinent. Both Africa and the Middle East must be considered very high growth regions, with population expansion reaching 2.8 percent annually in 1986.[19]

Although there is no exact correlation between population growth rates and increases or decreases in personal income by nation, the general trend during the 1980s was for those nations having lower rates of population growth to experience some improvement in income per person. Nations with higher rates of growth were likely, in contrast, to have declining incomes. Nigeria, for example, had a population growth rate of 3 percent in 1986, and per capita income had fallen 28 percent between 1980 and 1986. Kenya, with a population growth rate of 4.2 percent, experienced an 8 percent decline in per capita income during the same time period. Pro-growth economists are quick to point to the exceptions, like India, with a population growth rate of 2.1 percent and a 14 percent increase in per capita income. Among Asian countries, however, Japan, with a low 0.7 percent population growth rate, and China, with a 1 percent rate, accomplished remarkable income increases of 21 percent and 58 percent, respectively. Lester Brown, director of the Worldwatch Institute, has projected that once some of the poorer countries begin a decline in per capita income and food production driven by an increase in population, they will find it extremely difficult to gather the capital necessary to continue the process of development and to care for their underfed populace.[20]

In a world divided into nations and various economic coalitions and cartels, population growth appears to be widening the gap between wealthy and financially prosperous nations and those with low gross national products and accumulating debts. The problems are much more complex than the necessary tailoring of population policies to the circumstances of individual nations. The collapse of national food supplies and declining economic resources spawn refugee and immigrant populations. Phenomena such as illegal immigration from Mexico and Central America into the United States are related to economic and population regulation policies, not just within governmental units but between nations. Further, the countries with declining or slowly stabilizing populations are those most scientifically able to develop new birth control technologies and the most economically able to provide international aid to encourage family planning. Those with the fastest growing populations often have the poorest existing health services and the least ability to initiate new population regulation programs.

Many experts in population issues believe that the half of the world that has already reduced population growth will have to help the other half which has not. This interaction will require dialogue between nations with very different population problems and social concerns. A West German businessman living in a country with great educational and professional opportunities for his two daughters will have to understand the needs of a Central African farm woman struggling to feed her four children. While the businessman worries that the increasingly aging German population will not be supported in their retirement by a declining number of young workers, the African women will evaluate her need to have one or two more children just to be certain she has a son to care for her if she lives to old age. As the West German picks up his morning newspaper and frets over the impact of chemical and nuclear pollution on his daughters' health, the African woman draws her last portions of corn out of a pot and contemplates the impending bad harvest and the declining physical condition of her youngest child.

In a world filled with nations and local populaces who prefer to act in their own immediate self-interest, communication between groups facing different problems and living in different social environments is often negligible. Can the West German and the African woman speak to each other? Can they work together to solve worldwide problems? Can the economically prosperous understand the problems of those struggling to improve their livelihood? Can the nations with low population growth communicate with those with burgeoning censuses?

SOCIAL PROBLEMS AND INDIVIDUAL ETHICS

Not all the controversies concerning human demography center on environmental degradation and the economics of social class structures. Questions concerning personal ethics and individual rights in regard to having children continue to trouble international policy formation. During the 1980s the debate over the morality of abortion became a politically virulent struggle, influencing governmental funding for population control programs not directly affecting the status of the unborn.

Although regional human populations may certainly stabilize and decline without abortion serving as a major means of population regulation, many organizations lobbying for population control advocate abortion not only as a woman's "right" but also as a safe way to reduce the number of children arriving each year and an important

23

means for obtaining zero population growth. In contrast, the anti-abortion lobbies feel the "rights" of the unborn child are primary and take precedence over all other concerns, including the population explosion. Groups pursuing *antinatalist* policies (those encouraging low birth rates) usually advocate permitting abortion to terminate unwanted pregnancies. While there are few groups internationally that are *pronatalist* as such, anti-abortion organizations often tacitly take that position. Rather than specifically favoring higher birth rates, however, these groups favor fewer fetal deaths. The antinatalist lobby, which is oriented toward solving problems related to overall societal trends, thus finds itself contesting groups that are anti-abortion or anti–birth control and therefore much more interested in the response and ethics of individuals than in average population growth rates. The two sides emphasize different aspects of reproductive ethics and therefore communicate poorly with each other.

In 1974, at a United Nations–sponsored International Conference on Population held in Bucharest, the United States took a strong antinatalist position, urging other countries to slow population growth through family planning. Ironically, the position "was attacked by many countries of the political left in the Third World, especially—although not exclusively—socialist Marxist states," who argued that "economic development would lead 'naturally' to fertility declines and what was really needed were transfers of capital and technology."[21] In 1984, at the International Conference on Population held in Mexico City, the administration of President Reagan broke with former United States policy on providing financial and technical assistance to other nations in human population regulation by proposing that "population growth is, of itself, a neutral phenomenon . . . not necessarily good or ill."[22] The antinatalist United States policy of the 1960s and 1970s was considered "demographic overreaction," and local population problems were seen as "evidence of too much government control and planning, rather than [evidence of] too little."[23] Mixed with Reaganomics, the 1984 policy took a strong anti-abortion stance. Although United States family planning funds had not been used to pay for abortions during the previous decade, the 1984 policy stopped any federal aid for family planning to "nongovernmental organizations which 'perform or actively promote abortion as a method of family planning' (regardless of the fact that no U.S. funds are used for that activity) or to nations that support abortion unless they set up 'segregated accounts which cannot be used for abortion,' or to the United Nations Fund for Population Activities unless it can offer 'concrete assurance' that no U.S. funds will be used for abortion and that the fund supports neither abortion nor coercive family planning programs."[24] As a result of this policy change, United States funding for international family planning programs "fell 20 percent between 1985 and 1987, from $288 million to $230 million."[25] Withdrawal of United States support from the United Nations Fund for Population Activities alone affected 340 million couples in sixty-five countries.[26]

Jodi L. Jacobson of the Worldwatch Institute suggests that the Reagan administration, in response to the "demands of the religious right, . . . further discouraged the development of effective contraceptives and their distribution in the Third World."[27] She also suggests that declining United States interest in population issues has inhibited research and development of new birth control technologies and, with Lester Brown, proposes that "public ambivalence toward contraception and abortion in the United States is eroding support for the government sponsored research" that could compensate for private industries' reticence to spend time developing new birth control technologies.[28] Whether American Christians know it or not, their ethical struggles in dealing with abortion, sex education in public schools, contraception for teenagers, and other related issues have carried over into the international population arena.

The United States is not alone in its ethical concerns. Many nations have confronted not only abortion but also the potential conflict between the rights of individuals and couples and the needs of the state in the implementation of potentially coercive politics of population control. Among the controversial methods of reducing births are forced sterilization of both men and women, payment for sterilization, and forced abortion. During the 1970s a population reduction program in India included sterilization of people who were either involuntary participants, were threatened with loss of salary, or did not understand the procedure. A political backlash in India and the protests of other nations eventually halted the coercive tactics, and the program shifted toward voluntary compliance. Government activities forwarding one-child families in China not only discourage women who would like more than one child from having more than one but also may dictate abortion. Since Chinese families have long selected for sons rather daughters, critics of the "one child per family" policy suggest that the severe limitation on family size has encouraged some couples to abort female fetuses or actually dispose of newborn females so they will not "waste" their single child allotment on a daughter. This type of fatal sex discrimination would occur far less frequently were families potentially larger. Many personal rights issues are far more subtle than these dramatic cases, and as

Lord Bauer has noted, in the least developed countries even "advice, education and persuasion in practice shade into coercion," especially where financial or social rewards fall to the compliant.[29]

Those interested in personal morality and individual rights are asking the most difficult question of all: How may populations be justly regulated? Are there times when societal goals take precedence over the needs or desires of an individual or of a family? Do some family planning programs and population regulation policies violate the rights of the individual or encourage immoral acts? How can the welfare of women and children best be protected?

DEVELOPING A CHRISTIAN POPULATION ETHIC

Determining the rights and wrongs of human population regulation presents numerous challenges to Christian faith in a technologically and politically complex world. As an international and basically missionary religion, Christianity needs an ethic that provides guidance, not just for a local denominational congregation but for Christians worldwide. A Christian ethic for human population regulation must have the following characteristics:

First, the ethic must bridge the personal and the social. Reproductive ethics for the individual family and for the local Christian congregation must correspond to reproductive ethics and policies for nations and must acknowledge world concerns.

Second, the ethic must link courtship and sexuality not only to reproduction but also to the social and economic factors driving human population growth. Western culture already associates sex, money, and power but is very unwilling to admit that right action concerning one might be tied to right action concerning one of the others.

Third, the ethic must be effectively cross-cultural. It must be robust enough and flexible enough to encompass the problems of the African farm wife and the West German businessman.

Fourth, the ethic must be spiritually basic enough to adapt to changing social and economic conditions. The population explosion is a recent phenomenon, as is population decline (without warfare, disease, or famine) in Western Europe. Within the next two decades, world population trends may change radically. Emergencies may arise, and old difficulties may disappear. The ethic needs to look ahead and not remain locked in solutions to former problems. It also needs to be based on general spiritual principles rather than specific case histories.

Fifth, the ethic must value the individual. One of the commonest deficiencies in a social or environmental ethic is neglect of the individual person. The ethics of human population regulation must consider the rights and feelings of human beings, particularly women and children.

Sixth, the ethic must be just, and it must consider the needs of the poor and the disadvantaged. Pursuit of justice and care of the poor are basic principles of biblical ethics and therefore a high-priority concern for reproductive and population ethics.

Seventh, and perhaps most important, the ethic must be based on Christian values, not just on contemporary public (or middle-class) opinion. Christian reproductive ethics must be within the spirit of Christ's teachings and Christ's mission. The ethic needs, however, to reach beyond what the Bible and Christian traditions say about the social pressures and cultural values of other eras and find out what the Bible tells us about God's will for humankind, in biblical times, now, and in the future.

In order to fairly investigate the ethics of human reproduction, we must combine a knowledge of contemporary population trends with an objective analysis of both biblical teachings and the lessons of Christian history. The next chapter will briefly outline basic population processes and will explain why human populations have changed so radically in the past few decades. Chapters 3 and 4 discuss biblical approaches to reproductive values and Christendom's historic struggles with population problems. Chapters 5 and 6 investigate environmental concerns and the impact of "biological" thinkers on population ethics. Chapter 7 discusses the effects of population decline in industrial nations, while chapter 8 reviews the population problems of developing nations, particularly those in Africa. The final two chapters look at the responsibilities of Christian communities in dealing with demographic change and discuss the more difficult ethical issues, including the use of coercive methods of population control and the role of abortion in regulating human population growth.

QUESTIONS FOR REFLECTION

1. Over two or three generations, the population of a region may double or triple, or it may start to decline. Thinking back to your parents and grandparents, what kinds of reproductive values did they have during their childbearing years? Did they value a large or a small family? How were their values different from yours? Why have or haven't the values changed between generations?

Has Christianity played a role in these value changes (or the lack of them)?

2. What, if any, impact have recent demographic changes in your nation or region had on your local church or on the membership of your denomination? In what ways has your congregation or denomination been making an effort to anticipate demographic shifts and adjust ministries accordingly? Are there ways in which demographic predictions could be used to plan future ministries and church programs?

2

WHY POPULATIONS
RISE AND FALL

If the human population of the earth grew so slowly for thousands of years, why has it suddenly expanded beyond all previous imaginings? And with some countries experiencing a baby boom, why are others worried they will soon be nations of old-timers? If population growth can accelerate, is there anything that can slow it down? The academic demographers who try to answer these questions usually drown themselves in mathematics. For our purposes, we can avoid most of the statistical tedium of professional census taking and look for the general social and economic patterns that determine current population trends. The first task in developing an ethic for human population regulation is understanding population processes.

Today, if we take the *crude birthrate*, or the total number of births per thousand people, and compare it to the *crude death rate*, or the total number of deaths regardless of age or sex per thousand people, we will find that since 1940 the crude birthrate in most developing nations has risen slightly or remained about the same. Meanwhile, the crude death rate has drastically declined. Thus *fertility*, or the ability to produce children, has remained constant or risen slightly, while *mortality* has fallen dramatically. Recent population growth is therefore not due to families' suddenly deciding to have more children—the number of babies produced per woman has remained relatively constant or increased just slightly—it is due to a smaller percentage of the population dying each year than in previous decades. This lower death rate generally affects all age classes. Far more babies survive infancy and the critical early childhood years. Mortality levels have also been lowered for adults, and in many countries life expectancy has greatly increased.

In the United States during the frontier era, if a woman had six children, two might die in infancy, one might die at age six of a childhood disease, and one might be injured in a farming accident and die of the ensuing infection. If only two children grew to adulthood and married, they would just replace their parents in the reproducing portion of the population. The women herself might die in childbirth or succumb to disease before her children were raised. Whole families perished in outbreaks of typhoid, cholera, and yellow fever. Today, in the United States, if a woman has six children, chances are she will raise all of them, and she herself will live to a ripe old age. Human *life span*, the length of time a human can potentially live, has always been a few more than a hundred years and thus has changed little in recent centuries. Human *life expectancy*, the average number of years a human can expect to live (usually calculated from birth), has increased dramatically with the onset of the industrial era. Human life expectancy in the United States rose from 47 years in 1900 to 73 years in 1980, while the crude death rate fell from 17.2 people per thousand per year in 1900 to 8.7 in 1980.[1]

We must carefully consider, however, how these population processes have operated historically and how they now operate in different cultures. In Western Europe and the United States, the major acceleration of population growth rate actually preceded the major advances of modern medicine. Changes in technology, economics, and material culture, the spread of colonialism, and the availability of new lands in the New World originally spurred the great outpouring of young Anglo-Saxons, Scots, and Germans into industrial cities and on to the Americas. The agricultural revolution of the eighteenth century not only brought improved farm equipment and land management strategies but also incorporated new high-productivity crops such maize and the potato. The potato became such a staple for northern European peasants that some authors credit it with much of Europe's population growth during the eighteenth and nineteenth centuries.[2]

A rise in European population and the depletion of natural resources in the heavily settled Old World agricultural landscape probably stimulated both the industrial revolution and European colonial ventures. Environmental historian Richard G. Wilkinson has suggested, for example, that the high price of fuel wood in Great Britain encouraged the use of coal for heating and cooking, which in turn encouraged the development of steam power to pump water from deep mine shafts (as the shallower veins were dug out). The expense of keeping draft animals on pasture in a nation where local agricultural self-sufficiency was slowly breaking down encouraged the development of canals, railroads, and other innovations in transportation. Even with major changes in farming methods, England became a major importer of wheat about 1760 and thus had further motivation to maintain a political stranglehold on neighboring Ireland (a net exporter of grain) and to develop control of international sources of food and raw materials. Wilkinson remarks that with an increasing population using every square inch of tillable land and every remaining woodlot, England's "formidable group of [technological] innovations should not be regarded as the fruits of society's search for progress, but the outcome of a valiant struggle of a society with its back to the ecological wall."[3]

Ironically, if population growth stimulated technological advances, the new labor-saving devices in turn encouraged further population growth. The industrial revolution followed quickly on the heels of the agricultural revolution and brought with it a demand for labor, including that of women and children. As manufacturing began to dominate agriculture, the new economy left the villages and began to center in consolidated industrial cities. In England, one of the first countries to experience an "industrial" population explosion, the annual population growth rate bounded from 0.48 percent in 1745 to 1.35 percent in 1800. Anthropologists Marvin Harris and Eric Ross hypothesize that this rapid change in growth rate was in response to several factors, including earlier marriage than on the farm (women who marry young tend to have more children through their lifetimes), a decline in infant and child mortality, and the availability of employment for children in the ever-expanding factory system.[4] England's colonial empire was to a large extent the ultimate source of these changes, as it fed the mother country with raw materials from all parts of the globe and provided markets for her ever more wealthy manufacturers.

Today many Third World countries with high rates of population growth are not industrializing nearly as rapidly as England was during the second half of the eighteenth century. The developing nations are acquiring modern infrastructures, however, such as paved highway systems, which help move food and other necessities from place to place and improve living conditions for at least part of their populace. Access to modern prophylactic medicine, even if it is just typhoid shots, antimalarial drugs, and antiseptics, has done much to lower crude death rates. England, in her first fits of modern population growth, however, had none of the modern medical technologies. Vaccination wasn't invented until 1798, when Jenner experimented with an improved preventative for smallpox. Proper cleaning of injuries and of surgical equipment wasn't practiced until the late nineteenth century, after Pasteur introduced the germ theory and Lister taught doctors the value of sterilization.[5]

In England population growth initially accompanied urbanization, industrialization, and tremendous economic expansion. Today in the developing countries, population growth is not necessarily associated with national economic improvement. We should also note that developing countries cannot support an increasing population or solve a food crisis the way England did historically. Conquering a third of the world to find timber for building ships, starches for making puddings, and tariff-free markets for profitably selling manufactured products is not a realistic possibility for contemporary Zaire or Haiti.

DEMOGRAPHIC TRANSITION

What happened to England's rising rate of population growth? In 1986 the natural rate of population increase in the United Kingdom was back down to 0.2 percent, well below the 1.35 percent rate of 1800. Modern demographic theory suggests that as nations develop, they go through a process called *demographic transition.* The classic concept of demographic transition holds that after a period of declining death rates and fast population growth, societies begin to compensate by decreasing their birthrates. Economists have noted that, to date, only industrialized nations appear to have completed this transition, going first through a period of population growth and then slowly beginning to balance their populations (usually at much higher density) by reducing birthrates to equal the lower death rates. This association of demographic transition with industrial development has led to the hypothesis that only developed countries with healthy economies could undergo demographic transition. The process is not that simple, however.

In England, "after the early 1800s, a general rise in population growth was paralleled by increasing mortality among the working class, especially in urban districts."[6] Child labor was commonplace, and many children started work in the textile factories before their ninth birthdays.[7] Average life expectancy actually fell in these new urban centers, and many of the deaths were children under five. A citizen of the town of Preston in Lancashire, England, had a life expectancy of 31.7 years in 1783 and of only 19.5 years by 1841.[8] Fertility peaked in England in 1815, just as wages reached a low point. Despite the fact that child labor laws were still rudimentary and unenforced at this point, fertility began to fall. Harris and Ross suggest this transition was not due to falling birthrates, at least for the working class. Urban conditions were unsanitary, and the poor were overworked and underfed.[9] Charles Dickens was hardly overstating the deplorable conditions when he described orphaned young Oliver Twist holding out his bowl and timidly asking for more gruel.

Child mortality increased, as mothers slaving in factories ceased to breastfeed their infants and left their younger children in the care of friends or older siblings (or no one at all) during the working day. Abandonment of newborns and other de facto forms of infanticide may also have increased as mothers found themselves unable to properly nurture their babies. Women of the middle and upper classes appear to have purposefully limited the number of their offspring, but in general, the transition began because of urban misery.[10] Of ethical note are the activities of nineteenth-century Christians, such as members of the Society of Friends or of the newly formed Salvation Army, who took a leading role in eliminating child labor, providing health and social services for the urban poor, and sponsoring legislation to improve living and working conditions in urban slums.

This early English industrial transition was unlike both the later transition in England and the processes that have lowered birthrates in modern industrial nations such as the United States and Japan. In England, from the late nineteenth century onward, the birthrate did decline. In the United States, despite unhealthy conditions in factory districts through the early twentieth century, overall infant mortality has continued to decline while life expectancy has continued to rise with industrialization. Families are, however, electing to have fewer children. The factors responsible for this change include the reduction of child labor (including on the farm) and the contemporary practice of leaving children in school through their teenage years. Having a large family thus has little if any immediate economic benefit for the parents. The cost of raising children and sending them through college, in fact, discourages middle-class families from having too many. Children in modern industrial societies are very expensive to raise. Estimates vary, but most middle-class United States couples can expect to spend over $100,000 to raise a single offspring. Top-notch health care, educational vacations, living in the "right neighborhood," extra bedrooms, and good schools may cost in excess of $300,000 per child.

Contemporary women sometimes wish to pursue their own careers, and family economics frequently force married women to work outside the home. A job away from the house discourages large families. In countries with social security programs, children are no longer needed to care for their parents in old age, and a large family could, in fact, interfere with a comfortable retirement as older parents would find themselves paying for one child after another to enter a university or technical college. Medical advances in birth control technologies allow women to continue sexual relations with a much reduced probability of conception. Literacy rates in the industrialized nations are higher than elsewhere, and educated women are more likely to understand and practice birth control. Educated parents are also more likely to pursue education for their children, and the passage through high school and college requires a prolonged period of parental care and financial support. With improved health services, children are more likely to survive, and this encourages parents to have fewer since there is less risk of losing a child.

We should recognize that the lowering of birth rates in the United States was a slow process, dependent neither on a relatively complete switch from an agrarian to an industrial economy nor on the development of modern family planning. In 1800 the average number of children produced per woman was 6.9. This had fallen to 4.3 by 1880 and to 3.3 by 1920 (all before the invention of the birth control pill). During the Great Depression of the 1930s, fertility per woman fell to a low of 2.1 then rose again during the postwar baby boom to reach 3.6 children per woman in 1960. By 1980 this had fallen again to 1.9 children per woman.[11] Economic and technological improvements have thus been related to both increases in birthrates (the baby boom) and to declines (the recent "baby bust"), but the overall trend in the United States has been a long-term decline in birthrates and an increase in life expectancy.

FERTILITY DECLINE IN DEVELOPING NATIONS

Economists and demographers once suspected that industrialization and development of a financially secure middle class were necessary for demographic transition to occur. In recent years, however, countries such as Sri Lanka, Indonesia, Thailand, Cuba, and the People's Republic of China have experienced fertility declines without massive urbanization or greatly accelerated socioeconomic development. Although these countries do not have particularly high per capita incomes, they all have made major efforts to provide social services to all regions or social classes within their countries. They have well-organized family planning services and public health care systems, as well as school systems accommodating economically disadvantaged students and accepting both boys and girls. Particularly important are the developed communication and transportation infrastructures, which help spread new ideas and information (such as use of contraceptives) and allow medical and educational services to penetrate into remote areas.[12]

Sri Lanka, for example, has had a much greater fertility decline than India despite similar low levels of per capita income. Sri Lanka has "provided food subsidies, free education, and free health care" and has established schemes to "provide security for wage earners and to protect the tenure of small farmers."[13] Government support has spread good-quality health care into the rural areas and so lowered infant mortality that in 1970 Sri Lankans lost forty-two infants per thousand born, while migrant workers in the medically advanced United States lost sixty per thousand. The spread of health services increases the availability of contraceptives and family planning, while decreased infant mortality encourages women to have fewer children since the first few born are more likely to survive.

Sri Lanka has also emphasized education. In 1970 over 40 percent of young Sri Lankans aged fifteen to twenty-four were still in school, and 83 percent were literate, "compared with 29 percent in India and 32 percent in the developing nations on the average."[14] Almost as many girls as boys enroll in primary and secondary schools (this is not the case in other Third World nations where limited educational facilities place an emphasis on educating boys). Increased educational and job opportunities have encouraged women to marry relatively late, at an average age of twenty-five, and a desire for smaller families reduced fertility 30 percent between 1953 and 1970. In the case of Sri Lanka, one suspects the provision of health services and low infant mortality, in combination with educational opportunities for women and relative financial security (independent of the number of children raised), have helped to lower the birthrate. Equal availability of services to both urban and rural populations and to upper- and lower-class families has also helped to deter rapid population growth.[15]

A second example of fertility decline without industrialization or tremendous economic improvement is the state of Kerala in India. Although Kerala is hardily the wealthiest of the Indian states, its birthrates have dropped much more rapidly than the rest of India's. Kerala has instituted land reform, which has helped to guarantee land tenure for small farmers. Kerala also has well-distributed health care facilities providing easy access to medical services, has built many new homes for the poor, and provides free schooling through high school. Like Sri Lanka, a high percentage of children, including girls, attend school. The state provides free, nutritious school lunches for all children whose parents request the service. Between 1965 and 1974, as these services became available, Kerala's birthrate decreased twelve points from thirty-nine per thousand to twenty-seven per thousand, while the remainder of India retained a birthrate of thirty-eight per thousand.[16] Although it is difficult to prove that better social services and more equal distribution of resources caused the decline in fertility, the circumstances clearly suggest that *greater social justice and equality initiated a demographic transition.*

OTHER CONSEQUENCES OF POPULATION GROWTH

As populations rise and fall, not only do the total numbers of individuals increase and decrease but the age structure of the populations also change. When populations are growing via reproduction, births exceed deaths, so the age structure favors the younger age classes. In developing countries such as Kenya or Mexico, where population has increased greatly over the past three decades, a very high proportion of the population is constituted by children under fifteen years of age. In the early 1980s demographers estimated that 45 percent of the population of Africa was under 15, while only about 23 percent of the population of the United States and Europe fell into this younger age class.[17] Africa, thus, had roughly three times as many dependent children per adult as the industrialized West. As these children begin to enter the reproductive age groups, which are often younger in developing countries (many girls will have their first child at ages 15 to 18), they in turn will add more offspring to their national censuses. A population that is very young will have more trouble reducing fertility than one that is older because such a high proportion of the population has yet to marry.

The opposite type of process occurs in populations that are stabilizing or declining. As birthrates go down and life expectancy increases, the population becomes older on the average. This is presently happening in the United States and western Europe, where economists are concerned that there will not be enough younger workers to support the increasing number of retirees in the present social security programs. In 1900 only 4 percent of the population of the United States was sixty-five years or older. In 1950 it was 8 percent, and by the year 2000 it will be about 13 percent. If present trends continue, 20 percent of the United States population will be over sixty-five by 2050.[18]

When populations are growing via immigration, the alteration of age structure may not favor the very young. In the nineteenth century, for example, many of the new arrivals to the United States were single males old enough to travel by themselves. Immigration laws may select for certain types of people, such as able-bodied men or professionals with skills, which in turn influences the impact of immigration on population structure. Immigration not under direct government control, such as illegal immigration from Central America into the United States or the immigration of political refugees, may also select for or against certain age groups (the very old may be less willing to leave home and the very young may be less likely to survive the trip), but few accurate figures are available on the impact of these types of migration on the population structure of the countries gaining or losing these groups.

MISCONCEPTIONS AND POPULATION CHANGES

Perhaps one of the most dangerous misconceptions held by many people, including Christians, is that human populations are primarily resource limited. Many of us were introduced in high school biology class to the *Malthusian model,* where a population of rabbits, deer, or bacteria breeds like crazy until it uses up all its food. The population then crashes due to starvation. In nature, the common wisdom holds, populations of a given organism cannot do this because they are controlled by disease, predators, and parasites. Wolves help to keep the deer in check. The more fawns the deer have, the more fawns the wolves eat. The deer herd thus may increase in a wet year, when there is more forage, and may decline in a bad winter, when there is less, but it is the wolves who ultimately keeps the deer from eating themselves out of house and home.

Human population processes are much more complex than this. A country such as West Germany, with very adequate food and housing resources, can have a declining population, while a developing nation with less adequate support can have a growing one. Further, when seventeenth-century England was at the point of serious resource limitations, it managed to overcome them with improved technology (and an unfortunately large number of imperialist ventures). Human populations with very similar per capita incomes can have different levels of fertility. One developing nation may be succumbing to a major population explosion while another is vigorously encouraging a declining birthrate. Human populations are subject to economic, political, and social factors in a way that animal populations are not. Education alone can initiate a change in human fertility. Humans can look to the future and project the need for more or fewer children and have for hundreds, if not thousands, of years been able to increase or decrease birthrates through social means. Historically, many human populations have been relatively stable for long periods of time and have not necessarily damaged the natural resources on which they relied. Humans can, if they wish, regulate their populations themselves and do not have to depend on the "wolf" to do it for them.

A second dangerous misconception, generated by economists rather than by biologists, is that economic growth is necessary to demographic transition. If we assume this, then we must immediately concede that any conscious governmental or social attempt to influence Third World population structures is worthless. Although improved economic conditions will often stimulate beneficial changes in population growth rates, a number of developing nations have proven that well-executed government programs and greater and more equitably distributed social services can, by themselves, make a difference. To assume that human populations must be regulated by war, disease, and famine is to assume that human beings cannot make sound, responsible, moral decisions about the course of their own lives.

QUESTIONS FOR REFLECTION

1. In nineteenth-century industrial England, mortality rates, particularly child mortality, rose as a result of conditions in urban slums. The children affected were primarily from poor working-class families. Did anyone have a moral responsibility to attempt to counter such a trend, and if so, who? To what extent should the national government, the municipalities, or the churches have taken action? England at the time was a society divided into a hierarchy of social classes. To what extent should the upper classes and factory owners (who often lived away from the factory areas) have taken responsibility for the welfare of their workers?

2. In the United States today, migrant farm workers and families living in urban slums have higher mortality rates, particularly infant mortality rates, than the rest of the nation. Does anyone

have the responsibility to counter this trend, and if so, who? To what extent should the national government, the municipalities, or the churches take action? To what extent is obtaining proper pre- and postnatal care for expectant mothers a responsibility of the pregnant woman herself, and to what extent is it a community responsibility?

3. In the case of the English industrial revolution, population growth may have stimulated a more vigorous national economy and innovations such as steam engines, which have resulted in great social benefits over the years. To what extent, if any, were the additional deaths and poor conditions caused by overcrowding and resource limitations justified by the accelerated economic development? Do the benefits of the industrial revolution to present and future generations of British citizens in any way justify the suffering of the first factory workers? How?

3

ABRAHAM'S SEED:
THE BIBLE AND REPRODUCTION

The poetic admonitions to righteousness and the ethereal prophetic narratives of the Holy Bible may seem at first to be literary light-years away from the plodding mathematics of modern demographers. Yet by delving into our scriptural heritage, we may be able to turn the wisdom and spiritual understanding of the past into guideposts for our own present and future action. In order to develop a Christian population ethic, we need to search the Holy Scriptures for values and teachings concerning not just procreation but also the worth of children, our obligations to future generations, and the reproductive role of biblical personages relative to their relationship to God. Biblical texts about immigration, refugees, the dispossessed, poverty, material wealth, justice, land tenure, and human health also provide a platform for choosing the most loving courses of action in a world greatly divided by economics and political systems. As we examine these materials, we will have to reflect on their meaning, both to the ancient reader and in our own contemporary Christian context, and avoid superficial interpretation in favor of extracting the most basic biblical lessons about the value of human reproduction.

Summarizing material from biblical books written during the various phases of Israel's history requires sensitivity to the social and theological environments fostering the writings. The Hebrew people lived first as desert herders, then as slaves in Egypt, then as a roaming wilderness band. What was initially a single extended family grew into a group of related households and eventually into twelve tribes. Even as they settled into the Promised Land and established the kingdoms of Israel and Judah, the size of the nation and priorities for raising children slowly changed. Conquered first by the Assyrians and Babylonians and later by Alexander the Great and his Macedonian army, the Hebrew people survived occupation, exile, and family disruption. Unable to rule their own homeland, the people of Israel ultimately dispersed throughout the Roman Empire. The ability to maintain family and community, even in a strange city, became a cornerstone of Judaism and a key to its survival.

Growing out of Jewish rabbinic traditions immersed in Greco-Roman culture, the New Testament expresses family and procreative values quite socially distant from those found in the beginnings of the Old Testament. Polygamy, for example, was a common family structure for the patriarchs, such as Abraham and Isaac, but had disappeared by the time of Christ. Hellenistic Jews did not have as many children as Solomon had. The Old Testament speaks to the nation of Israel, whereas the New Testament accommodates Greek and Roman family structure and is directed to both Jews and Gentiles.

In interpreting material centuries old, we must remember that the Western nuclear family was unknown in biblical times. The Hebrew family at the time of Christ, for example, was a patriarchal organization incorporating the entire male lineage. Sons and their wives tended to stay in their parents' households or live next door. Groups of relatives all lived in one town or in one district. Thus Judean and Galilean households were very unlike the small, ever-roaming United States family, moving every five years and leaving grandparents and cousins behind.

The reader from a Western cultural background will find that the Bible provides insights into how some non-Western peoples perceive reproduction and children. Although no contemporary culture has all the characteristics of Abraham's family camp, today's African pastoralists and Arab farmers organize their households in a very Old Testament fashion. The rural African's desire for long life and many children and sons to inherit may easily exceed that of Abraham. The clearly recognizable differences between modern Western and ancient Middle Eastern cultures, in fact, suggest that sociological and anthropological study is an appropriate precursor to theological and ethical interpretation of biblical texts concerning human reproduction.

Although many of the same population processes that operate today were in force in biblical times, a population explosion equivalent to the contemporary phenomenon could not have occurred. In the ancient world, local populations fluctuated with war, famine, and plague but did not double or triple simultaneously worldwide. While population was rising in one place, it was often falling in another. Agricultural and technological innovations spread slowly, and real advances in medicine and health care were few. Regional population growth threatened food supplies or resulted in poor agricultural practices and soil erosion, but these problems never reached global or even continental proportions. The modern reader, either from an industrialized and wealthy nation or from a largely rural, less developed country, must understand the biblical events and teachings in their original cultural context before attempting to apply them to today's problems, so greatly removed in space and time.

BE FRUITFUL AND INCREASE

The Bible offers far more ethical imperatives (thou shalts and thou shalt nots) concerning marriage and sexual acts than it does concerning procreation. Perhaps to make up for the dearth of specific instructions, Christians have sometimes interpreted a passage in the first chapter of Genesis as a population imperative for all humankind. When arguing against birth control or in favor of large families, Christians often confidently cite God's instructions to Adam and Eve in Genesis 1:28 to "be fruitful and increase [or multiply] and fill the earth." (w)[1] The passage is certainly a mandate for reproduction, and a superficial application to family life suggests that Jews and Christians should have as many children as possible. This strongly pronatalist interpretation has, in fact, inflamed environmental critics of Christianity, who have accused the Judeo-Christian tradition of encouraging human overpopulation and propagating the belief that humans have the right to displace all other creatures from the cosmos.

In order to understand this controversial passage, it must be read in context. In the creation narrative, the first living organisms generated by God's Word are the green plants. God said in Genesis 1:11 (w): "Let the earth sprout forth . . . And so it was." Then, in Genesis 1:20–22 (w), God said:

> Let the waters teem with living beings, and let birds fly above
> the earth across the vault of the heavens. And God created the
> great sea monsters and every living being that moves, with which
> the waters teem, each of its kind, and every winged bird, each of
> its kind. And God saw how good it was. And God blessed them
> saying: Be fruitful and increase and fill the waters in the seas, and
> let the birds increase on the earth.

In comparing the two creative acts, that of making the plants and that of making the swimming and flying animals, it is notable that God blesses the fish, birds, and sea monsters but does not bless the plants directly. God then creates the land animals and proceeds to create "humanity according to his image . . . as male and female" (Gen. 1:27, w). The passage about human increase now rests in its full context: "And God blessed them (saying): Be fruitful and increase and fill the earth and make it subject to you" (Gen. 1:28, w).

Although set in the imperative, "be fruitful and increase" is actually, as the Genesis texts clearly indicate, a blessing, and it is a blessing shared with the animals, including the sea monsters. The difference between humankind and the other creatures thus does not fall in the realm of reproductive rights (humans are, instead, differentiated from other creatures by their creation in God's image). As Old Testament scholar Walter Brueggemann has noted, the call to "be fruitful" is immediately answered by the land animals in Genesis 1:24, "not because of coercion but because creation delights to do the will of the creator."[2] Fruitfulness and increase were never intended to be relentless marching orders but were a call to living organisms to grace the earth with the beauty of God's handiwork.

God's blessing is therefore not an ethical imperative, nor is it a way to please God by reaching to excess. Instead, this great blessing is something "God has ordained into the processes of human life."[3] While the blessing does impart generative power and fertility, its intent is reproduction in balance, springing joyfully forth to produce the well-being God continues to weave into the entire created universe. The blessing is part of what makes the creation "very good" and very beautiful in the eyes of God. Human population growth has no mandate to damage or desecrate the cosmos, nor is it God's intention, although the act of childbearing itself is painful (Gen. 3:16), that human reproduction be a source of societal sorrow and suffering.

BARRENNESS AND BLESSING

In the Old Testament, fertility is a very important theme. The longing for human offspring and the desire for productive herds on well-watered lands weave through the narratives of the patriarchs. Conception and birth were largely mysteries to these nomadic pastoralists, and they accepted them as outworkings of God's providence and blessing.

On the surface, the Old Testament promotes reproductive values much like those of today's Middle Eastern agricultural societies. Roland de Vaux, in his work on the social institutions of ancient Israel, notes that "to have many children was a coveted honour, and the wedding guests often expressed the wish that the couple would be blessed with a large family."[4] When a servant fetches Rebekah to take her to marry Isaac, Rebekah's mother and brother bless her, saying, "You are our sister, may you increase to thousands of thousands" (Gen. 24:60, w). Barrenness, in contrast, was a great trial or perhaps even "a chastisement from God."[5] Sarah (initially called Sarai), Rachel, and Leah all suffered loss of self-esteem because of their initial inability to produce children. When Abimelech took Abraham's wife Sarah, Yahweh closed "every womb of Abimelech's household" (Gen. 20:18, w) to indicate divine displeasure at the situation.

De Vaux also suggests the Old Testament texts "show that the Israelites wanted mainly sons, to perpetuate the family line and fortune and to preserve the ancestral inheritance. Daughters were held in less regard; they would leave the family when they married, and so the strength of a house was not measured by the number of daughters."[6] Evidence for this can be found in Abram's complaint to God that Sarah's childlessness was leaving him without an heir, and in Psalm 127:3–5, which declares:

> Lo, sons are a heritage from the LORD,
>   and the fruit of the womb a reward.
> Like arrows in the hand of a warrior
>   are the sons of one's youth.
> Happy is the man
>   who has his quiver full of them!
> He shall not be put to shame
>   when he speaks with his enemies in the gate.

Rather than assume, however, that expression of cultural values is the predominant reproductive theme of the Old Testament, we must analyze some of the key passages in terms of how Yahweh interacts with fertility and the production of offspring. In introducing Abraham (called Abram at the beginning of the story), Genesis 11 immediately states, in the midst of Abraham's genealogy, that his wife Sarah is barren. Despite this sterility, as God guides Abraham away from his birthplace in Ur of the Chaldeans to the land of Canaan, God promises, in Genesis 12:2–3 (w), "I will make you into a great people and I will bless you and make your name great so that you will be a blessing. I will bless those who bless you and execrate those who curse you. And all the families of the earth are to bless themselves in you."

Here, Yahweh leads Abraham away from barrenness into the land of promise. The release requires pilgrimage and change and, most important, trust in God.[7] The Hebrew root of the word "to bless" means the "power of fertility, growth, [and] success,"[8] and it appears five times in this passage. The blessing, which could be limited to immediate circumstances, is much more than the arrival of another generation or a male heir. It becomes part of a future promise and initiates the participation of Abraham's household in holy history. The blessing is not one-sided, and Abraham is not its sole recipient. Abraham's descendants are not just to secure Abraham's inheritance and to forward Abraham's pleasure. The blessing is interactive— Yahweh will bless *all the families of the earth* through Abraham's line. God's purposes and desire to benefit all humankind subsume Abraham's personal and clan concerns. The power of God's blessing "is effective on the environment through and beyond the one blessed."[9]

After the blessing, Abraham travels to Canaan and thence to Egypt because of a famine. Returning to an area in what is now Israel, Abraham and his brother's son Lot, both wealthy in livestock, find that "the land could not support them both living together, for their possessions were too great" (Gen. 13:6, w) and that their herders were in conflict with one another. In one of the oldest recorded human encounters with environmental carrying capacity, responsible Abraham gives Lot the option of taking the best grazing territory by saying, "Look, the whole country is there before you! Let us part company. If you go left, I will go right; if you go right, I will go left" (Gen. 13:9, w). Observing "how well watered the plain of Jordan was" and that it "was like the garden of the Lord" (Gen. 13:10, w), Lot chooses the rich river valley, while Abraham turns west to the land God has selected for him in Canaan.

These passages make it clear that Abraham and Lot still had the option of relieving overcrowding by moving into new territory. Ironically, childless Abraham had so many herders and cattle that he could not share an expansive and barely settled landscape with his own relatives. As Walter Brueggemann has recognized, the matter of dividing up wealth and resources produced a conflict between "the *power of promise* and the *ideology of scarcity*." Unlike most of us, Abraham was not possessed by a fear of not having. He avoids fighting with Lot by trusting in the promises of God.[10] Lot, doing what superficially appears best, unknowingly courts disaster as he and his family move toward what is now called the Dead Sea and become enmeshed in the fate of Sodom and Gomorrah.

After Abraham separates from Lot, God again blesses Abraham. Yahweh promises, "The whole land which you see I will give to you and your descendants forever. I will make your descendants like the dust of the earth; if anyone can count the dust of the earth, he can count your descendants" (Gen. 13:15–16, w). In ancient times, if a lineage were going to occupy the land, they had to people it. Human numbers and resource security went together (a situation almost the opposite of today's population dilemmas). This second blessing not only tied Abraham's progeny to the Promised Land, it also made them the means of maintaining ownership.

As the story of Abraham progresses, it becomes a miracle not of reproduction but of faith. Despite God's two promises to provide offspring, nothing happens. In Genesis 15 Abraham protests his lack of heirs to God. The word of the Lord informs him that he will have a son and descendants as many as the stars in the heavens. Abraham "believed Yahweh, and he accounted it to him as righteousness" (Gen. 15:6, w). Both Abraham and his wife are entering old age, and their reproductive ability is now past, yet Abraham believes God's promise. Abraham abandons the hopeless physical reality and accepts God's future and God's promise through faith.[11]

The narrative moves into doubt again, as Sarah, convinced she can no longer conceive, offers her maid Hagar to Abraham as a substitute for herself. Hagar bears Ishmael. Yet God speaks to Abraham again and tells him to expect ninety-year-old Sarah to produce an heir. This promise is set in the form of a covenant: Abraham is to become the father of a multitude of nations, and his descendants will possess the land of Canaan forever. In return Abraham will circumcise all the males of his household as a sign of their relationship with Yahweh. The promise is fulfilled, and Sarah gives birth to Isaac.

To interpret the story of Abraham primarily as an argument for pastoralist social values and the blessings of large families is to miss the point. Abraham and Sarah never reach the cultural ideal, undoubtedly commonly held during their era, of having a large family. The promises of God are fulfilled through a single son born to them very late in life. The first of the "fathers" of Israel never received the immediate benefit of having armies of children romping about his tent. What Abraham gleaned was faith and the promise of not just a fertile but also a holy future, and of a continuing relationship of his offspring with God. The next generation, that of Isaac, goes through a very similar process where Rebekah is initially barren but finally delivers just two sons. Again, the promises are fulfilled through one child, Jacob. In these narratives, Abraham's trust in God ran counter to what his cultural background told him had to be the case—one must have many children to have a reproductive future. Abraham believed God, and one son was enough.

Christians often generalize the promises in these texts—of off-spring as many as stars in the heavens or as the dust of the ground—to a blessing desirable for all who believe in the God of Israel. The issue here, of whether large families are a blessing of God, must be approached with theological caution. Although in the context of the time many children were certainly a source of great joy (and were also very useful around the family camp, since they could herd sheep and goats almost as soon as they could walk), the greater blessing was to have the child of the promise, even if it was only one child. Fertility, as expressed in Genesis 1, is an ever-flowing bounty of God. To be interested in nothing but fertility, however, is a characteristic of idolatry, particularly the worship of the Canaanite god Baal. God's providence, as expressed in the Old Testament, is not just to an individual person or to a single family. What God was providing through Abraham to all the families of the world was not multitudes of relatives; it was Abraham's understanding of God and Abraham's faith—this, and not sexual prowess, was what made Abraham's lineage unique.

PATRIARCHAL PRIORITIES?

Lest we begin to believe the spiritual always supersedes the emotional and personal side of having children in the biblical narratives, we should investigate God's dealings with the women in the Old Testament. In the story of Abraham, Sarah and Hagar are major figures, who can, like Abraham, hear and understand the voice of Yahweh. God's care for and interest in these women and their offspring is expressed in several ways. First, if God's only purpose were for Abraham to have a son, then Abraham could have continued to produce children through Hagar and could have accepted Ishmael as his heir. God chooses instead to bless Sarah and provides her with a child in old age. The Old Testament never limits the value of women to their role as "baby-makers." If it did, women would be discarded and replaced by someone else if they were barren. Yahweh recognizes Sarah's love for Abraham and her need for a child of her own and blesses her through a mighty act.

In Genesis 16, when Hagar conceives, she looks down on her mistress Sarah. Sarah, in retribution, mistreats her, and Hagar runs away into the desert. Yahweh sends a messenger (an angel) to Hagar, who promises her, "I will multiply your descendants so that they cannot be counted. . . . and you will bear a son, and you will call him Ishmael, because Yahweh has heard your cry" (Gen. 16:10–11, w). The name Ishmael means "God hears," and the spring where Hagar spoke with the divine messenger is called Beer-Lahai-roi, which means something like "spring of the living one who saw me" (referring to God as the living one).[12] In these remarkable texts, God makes promises to a serving maid similar to those he has made to Abraham. God does not speak or act through Abraham but sends help and comfort directly to a pregnant, fleeing woman. Hagar, a victim of Abraham's wavering and lack of faith in God's promise, suddenly becomes the mother of a mighty nation. Whatever God's purposes in holy history, God's care and mercy are continually extended on a day-to-day basis to people who are not of high social status and who are not in complete charge of their own social circumstances.

It is also notable that through the social pressures of the times the Old Testament portrays faithful men of God as remaining dedicated to their childless wives. Genesis implies Abraham's intercourse with Hagar was a lapse of belief in God's promise. In 1 Samuel, Elkanah, who goes to Shiloh regularly to worship and sacrifice to Yahweh, has children by his wife Peninnah, while his favorite wife Hannah is barren. After the sacrifice at Shiloh, he allows his wives and children to join the feast (in the custom of time they might have waited until after the men had eaten) and gives Hannah "one portion of the face, for he loved Hannah, although the Lord had closed her womb" (1 Sam. 1:5, H).[13] The meaning of "portion of the face" remains unclear, but it is probably a very desirable piece of meat, or a piece large enough for two people. When Hannah weeps because Peninnah has provoked her over her childlessness, Elkanah tries to reassure her by saying, "Hannah, why do you weep? And why do you not eat? And why is your heart sad? Am I not more to you than ten sons?" (1 Sam. 1:8). Here the godly man cares for his wife even though she does not meet the reproductive standards of the culture. God ultimately hears Hannah's prayers in her trouble, and she bears a son, Samuel, whom she dedicates to Yahweh. Samuel, the son of the barren, grows up to be a great prophet and the man who anoints David king over all Israel. The Old Testament indicates that the desire for children should not undermine the marriage relationship and shows how a godly man, faithful to his barren wife, ultimately fathered a spiritual leader of Israel.

In an interesting example of an opposite sort of process, Jacob loves Rachel far more than he loves his first wife, Leah. God responds to the plight of Leah, for "when the LORD saw that Leah was hated, he opened her womb, but Rachel was barren" (Gen. 29:31). Leah bears four sons, Reuben, Simeon, Levi, and Judah (the latter of whom was the forefather of David and is listed in the "genealogy" of Jesus in both Matthew and Luke). Rachel, in frustration, gives her maid to Jacob. When Leah finds she can bear no more children, she also gives her maid to her husband. God eventually "remembers" Rachel, and she gives birth. Through the four women, Jacob sires twelve sons (six of them Leah's) and a daughter (also Leah's). In this case God reproductively favored a woman partially neglected by her husband.

THE PROBLEM OF POLYGAMY

Although the modern mind may associate polygamy with dancing girls and wealthy sheiks who can afford to keep harems for their personal pleasure, polygamy can also be a way for a man to produce a large number of offspring. Christians are usually very apologetic about the frequent practice of polygamy in ancient Israel and often have trouble explaining why God allowed so many great leaders and men of God to take more than one woman into their households. In Abraham's sexual relationship with his wife's maid, God clearly blesses rather than chastises the polygamist. God also blesses Elkanah with his two wives.

Abraham's entry into polygamy was in fact a response to his desire for a son. De Vaux reports that under "the Code of Hammurabi (about 1700 B.C.), the husband may not take a second wife unless the first is barren, and he loses this right if the wife herself gives him a slave or a concubine."[14] The husband remained free, regardless of his wife's fertility, to acquire a concubine, who did not have the same rights as a wife. The husband could not acquire a second concubine unless the first was infertile. The patriarchs do not appear to have followed as strict a code of behavior as that of Hammurabi, however. Jacob had children by two wives and by both their maids, while Esau had three wives.[15]

Through the history of Israel, monogamy was probably the predominant form of marriage. De Vaux suggests, however, that men might sometimes out of "self-interest" take a second wife and "thus acquire another servant," and that even more frequently a man might take a second wife out of a "desire for many children, especially when the first wife is barren, or has borne only daughters."[16] The taking of a second wife or a concubine was thus more frequently a response to reproductive insecurity than to sexual lust. Certainly, fear of barrenness and the desire for more children encouraged polygamy among the patriarchs.

The extended collection of wives and concubines was restricted to the very wealthy and may have been limited to specific periods of

Israel's history, such as the early monarchy. Although Walter Kaiser in his book *Old Testament Ethics* has attempted to prove that the Old Testament nowhere condones or officially sanctions polygamy,[17] there remain the dozens of historic texts where leaders such as David practiced polygamy and the priests or prophets made no attempt to exclude them from the cult or to rebuke them for violations of God's law.

What the Bible does subtly suggest is that attempts to produce offspring through additional wives or through serving women were often prompted by a lapse of faith and created family strife, as did keeping several wives or concubines. Sarah's forcing Hagar out of the house for the second time in Genesis 21 separated Abraham from his son Ishmael and caused great hardship for Hagar and Ishmael, who nearly died of thirst in the wilderness of Beersheba. There was great strife between the two sisters Rachel and Leah. Jacob's large family appears to have been more a product of the competition between his two wives than a conscious effort on the part of the patriarch to father the heads of twelve tribes. (Lev. 18:18, part of the Mosaic law, forbids marriage between a man and his sister-in-law while the sister who is his first wife is still alive; thus a household such as Jacob's would not have been allowed once the nation Israel established residence in Canaan.[18])

During the period of the kingdom, the polygamous household of prolific King David spawned immoral behavior and internal family conflict, ultimately descending into bloodshed and bitter revenge. Old Testament scholar Hans W. Hertzberg suggests that the enumeration of David's sons in the texts of 2 Samuel show "David's blessing" and are an indication that "in this respect, too, the king is great and powerful."[19] The glorious side of having many children through many wives is countered, however, by the story of David's eldest son, Amnon, who fell in love with his half sister Tamar. (There were many half siblings in David's household.) Amnon rapes Tamar, then rejects her. Absalom, Tamar's full brother, tricks Amnon into coming to a feast and kills him to avenge his ill treatment of their sister.

In Amnon's disreputable behavior there is a reflection of the same sensuality displayed by his father when the lustful king sees Bathsheba bathing on a nearby roof and arranges to sleep with her while her husband is away at war. The prophet Nathan's response to David's sin represents an important undercurrent in the thought of Israel. In 2 Samuel 12 Nathan suggests that David has behaved like a rich man who has taken a poor man's only lamb, referring to Bathsheba's husband Uriah who only had one wife. Nathan's rebuke is not aimed just at sexual sin; it also poses a question about just distribution of reproductive opportunities and resources, including those belonging to the family. David, who already had so much, was the man who overstepped the bounds and took from one who had only one wife and only one route to procreation.

The Bible's subtle negative reaction to polygamy continues into the reign of David's heir. Solomon, Bathsheba's son, assumes the throne. To secure his position, he has his elder half-brother Adonijah killed. Adonijah had asked Bathsheba to petition Solomon for his deceased father's concubines. The control of these women would also confer his father's social status on Adonijah, thus making the elder son a further threat to the throne.

Solomon goes further than any other biblical figure in removing the institution of marriage from its stated role in Genesis 2:24 of a man and a woman becoming one flesh, as the "wise" king comes to love "many foreign women" (1 Kings 11:1). Taking seven hundred wives and three hundred concubines, he uses arranged marriages as a route to international alliances and political power. In the story of Solomon's household, the listing of sons has lost its importance, as has the individual personality of any of his children except for his heir, Rehoboam. Solomon's love for Yahweh, which gave the wise king the ambition to build the temple, is slowly displaced by love not only for many women but also for their gods.

The historian who wrote this chronicle of the reign of Solomon was certainly trying to suggest to the reader that enough is enough. Solomon had lost a valuation of marriage and of children and an understanding of God that his ancestor Abraham strongly displayed. Walter Brueggemann suggests Solomon made a tragic exchange:

> All these efforts in the sexuality of politics and the politization of sexuality are ways to secure one's own existence, to retain initiative for one's own life. And the upshot is to eliminate the transcendent Lord and any principle of criticism. Solomon's new alternative loves have reduced life to something manageable, predictable and administrable. To love God means to yield before One who is an overwhelming holy mystery. It is to trust but not to control. Conversely, to have these modest divided loves is to love only as much as we can manage and so to be in control.[20]

We can now review the development of polygamy in the lineage of Abraham. Abraham himself took a second woman because he feared he would not have a son by his wife. Although Jacob took a second wife because his father-in-law tricked him into marrying the elder daughter first, the addition of sexual intercourse with his wives' maids was in response to reproductive competition between Rachel and Leah. In the life of David, polygamy has moved from a solution to reproductive insecurity to a symbol of social status and power and, ultimately, an excuse for lust. For David's sons Adonijah and Solomon, the harem becomes purely a means to political and social power, and, in the case of Solomon, the final route to spiritual apostasy. For Solomon, the deep knowing of a wife is gone, as is any real pleasure in most of his children. Ironically, Solomon's many offspring could not maintain the kingdom intact, and in the next generation the nation split into Judah and Israel, leaving the Davidic dynasty sinking in a sea of political and spiritual problems. What God could do with one son of Abraham who inherited faith in Yahweh God could not do with a hundred sons of Solomon who worshiped foreign gods.

THE KINGDOM OF LITTLE CHILDREN

Like the Old Testament, the New Testament strongly affirms the value of children. Mary submits to God and bears the Messiah. Christ himself, in some of the most commonly quoted passages in the New Testament, finds that the people are bringing their children to him so he "might lay hands on them and pray" (Matt. 19:13). The disciples rebuke the people, which causes Jesus to become indignant and say, "Let the children come to me, do not hinder them; for to such belongs the kingdom of God. Truly, I say to you, whoever does not receive the kingdom of God like a child shall not enter it." Jesus then takes the children in his arms and blesses them, "laying his hands upon them" (Mark 10:14–16).[21] In the various versions of this story in the Gospels, Christ teaches his disciples a lesson about their own worldly view of what is important (the disciples reject children as less important than adults because children have no social status of their own) and about the characteristics of the kingdom. The child, in fact, becomes the model for the ideal disciple, the one who "must receive the present proclamation of the kingdom of God with a childlike attitude of complete dependence to enter into the eschatological [coming] kingdom."[22]

Christ displays an open love for children. In the ancient world, where fathers often had life-and-death control over the fate of their offspring and infants (especially baby girls) might be abandoned if unwanted, Christ's "tenderness in taking [children] into his arms and blessing them through prayer and laying on of hands"[23] superseded parental and cultural prerogatives. If the Old Testament rejoices in children as gifts of a caring and merciful God to a chosen people, the

New Testament rejoices in children as beloved heirs of an eternal kingdom.

Christ further affirms the intrinsic worth of children in his healing and teaching ministry. Showing deep concern for parents as well as their offspring, Christ answers Jarius's desperate call to heal his daughter by taking the girl's hand and raising her from her deathbed (Matt. 9:23–26; Mark 5:35–43; Luke 8:49–56) and responds willingly to a father's request to free his son from seizures (Matt. 17:14–21; Mark 9:14–29; Luke 9:37–43). When a Syrophoenician woman petitions Jesus, crying, "Have mercy on me, O Lord, Son of David; my daughter is severely possessed by a demon" (Matt. 15:22), the irritated disciples suggest, as they did when the children came to him, that Jesus send her away. Christ responds first by stating he was sent to the "lost sheep of the house of Israel" and suggests that Gentiles are not yet to be included in the kingdom by remarking, "It is not fair to take the children's bread [ministry meant for the nation of Israel] and throw it to the dogs [the Gentiles]" (Matt. 15:24, 26). The woman wisely replies that "even the dogs eat the crumbs that fall from their masters' table" (Matt. 15:27), and Christ, praising the great faith of this Gentile, heals her daughter. The action declares that the doors of the kingdom are open to all children, not just those who are direct descendants of Abraham.

Christ acknowledged the continuing importance of progeny to their parents, even in adulthood. Ancient Palestine had no social service agencies, and a widow, lacking the financial support of a husband, had to depend on the productivity of her mature male offspring. When the widow of Nain lost her only son, she lost all she had left in the world, including her daily bread. On encountering the funeral party, Christ has compassion on her and says to her, "Do not weep" (Luke 7:13). Raising the man from his bier, Christ indicates the ministry was as much to the mother as to the son by giving the man back to his mother.

Another very moving example of this type of concern is found in John's description of the crucifixion, where in John 19:26–27 the dying Jesus, seeing "his mother and the disciple whom he loved standing near, . . . said to his mother, 'Woman, behold, your son!' Then he said to the disciple, 'Behold , your mother!' And from that hour the disciple took her to his own home." The Hellenistic reader of the Gospel would have recognized the real economic and household responsibility Christ was asking John to assume. Today, throughout much of the Third World, parents, particularly women, must still depend on their surviving progeny for support in old age.

Just as in biblical Palestine, having an adequate number of children remains a social necessity.

In the New Testament, children were incorporated into ministry, as was the case with the boy who offered his five barley loaves and two fish for the feeding of the five thousand (John 6:9). Children traveled with the crowds following Jesus and were brought into the the first gatherings of Christian believers. Acts 16:15 states that Paul baptized Lydia "with her household," and Acts 16:33 presents Paul and Silas baptizing their jailer "with all his family." Both of these passages suggest that children or adolescents participated in the sacrament and became part of the early church.

A PROMISED LAND WITH NO LAND LEFT

In summarizing the New Testament narratives concerning children and families, it would be difficult to overstate the spiritual importance and worth of children. The New Testament affirms and extends the values found in the Hebrew Scriptures. Christ ministered frequently to the young and called them into the kingdom of God—a call to which they joyfully responded. The New Testament diverges greatly from the Old Testament, however, in the role given to reproduction and the raising of offspring in the lives of God's chosen leaders and in the role of God's chosen people, which in New Testament terms includes the entire church. Much of the history in the Old Testament deals with spiritual inheritance within family lines. The story of Abraham sets the precedent, and the theme continues through the era of the kings and into the exile. Messianic prophecy repeatedly utilizes the motif of the "new David" or the "son of David" or the "shoot of Jesse," implying that Israel is to be redeemed by an heir to the greatest of her rulers. The Gospel of Matthew, often thought of as the Gospel written for a Jewish audience, begins with a genealogy of "Jesus Christ, the son of David, the son of Abraham."

The New Testament repeatedly presents Christ and his disciples, including new members of the infant church, in terms of family relationships, yet there is almost no information presented on wives and offspring. The Scriptures present no evidence Christ or John the Baptist were ever married, although we know disciples like Peter must have been (Christ healed Peter's mother-in-law—Matt. 8:14; Mark 1:30; Luke 4:38). The Scriptures do not report any of the apostles as having children (although they probably did). The four Gospels describe the relationship of Jesus to his parents and report the activities of several sets of siblings, including James and John, Peter and Andrew, and Mary, Martha, and Lazarus. The next generation, however, is not even mentioned.

This pattern is further developed in the ministry of Paul, who discusses his decision to remain unmarried and gives advice on the subject in 1 Corinthians 7. While encouraging matrimony to prevent temptation to immorality, Paul exhorts those who are unwed and able to contain sexual desires "to remain single as I do" (1 Cor. 7:8). Paul expresses an unmarried ideal when he states, "I wish that all were as I myself am" (1 Cor. 7:7). Paul's position is clearly founded in the relationship between marriage, with its associated household responsibilities, and ministry. Paul proposes, "The unmarried man is anxious about the affairs of the Lord . . . but the married man is anxious about worldly affairs, how to please his wife, and his interests are divided. And the unmarried woman or girl is anxious about the affairs of the Lord, how to be holy in body and spirit; but the married woman is anxious about worldly affairs, how to please her husband" (1 Cor. 7:32–34). These passages represent a remarkable shift from Judaism, where the entire nation was the progeny of Abraham, the Temple was in the hands of the hereditary Levitical priesthood, and the anticipated kingdom would blossom when a descendant of David returned to the throne in Jerusalem.

To understand this change in emphasis between the Old and New Testament reproductive values (and to avoid extreme interpretation of the Scriptures), we must analyze the social and theological setting of "infant" Christianity. Gerd Theissen, in his *Sociology of Early Palestinian Christianity*, proposes that socioeconomic factors encouraged the development of "wandering charismatic ministers," such as Christ and his disciples, who "left their ancestral homes, breaking more or less abruptly with established norms."[24] Judaism at the time of Christ was marked by the Diaspora. Jews, often without financial means, were emigrating to nations outside Palestine. Unlike the Babylonian captivity, they were not deported en mass but scattered themselves throughout the Roman Empire. Related to this international movement were the activities of resistance fighters, attempting to oust the Romans and their puppet rulers, the Herods, from the Jewish homeland. Many of these rebels or "robbers" were dispossessed farmers or those who were poor or in debt. Begging and other behaviors related to poverty or lack of land for food production are well documented in the New Testament and contemporary documents.[25]

Aside from social and political stresses, there were environmental stresses during the early Christian era. Both Josephus and the authors of the New Testament report famine in the Levant during the first century B.C. and the period during which the Christian church arose. In the Greco-Roman world, particularly in the semiarid, unpredictable climates of the Middle East, food shortages were commonplace and were of considerable political and economic importance. Serious famine was less frequent, but when it occurred, the collapsing food supplies could cause high levels of mortality and major displacement of rural and urban populations. Famines also generated political unrest, such as food riots. Collapse of the food supply could be preceded or followed by disease epidemics, which raised the number of fatalities. Although accurate figures are rare in Greco-Roman records, ancient historians report 200,000 people died as the result of famine and disease in Utica and Carthage in 125 B.C.[26] In the region surrounding Edessa and Antioch a major famine about 500 A.D. produced 15,000 dead from the lodging house at Edessa alone in a period of five months.[27] Considering the size of Hellenistic cities, a very large percentage of the regional populations must have been affected by events such as these.

The city of Rome itself had recurring food crises, including those in 41 to 36 B.C., 23 B.C., 18 B.C., 5 to 9 A.D., 19 A.D., 40 to 41 A.D., 51 A.D. and 64 A.D.[28] Mark 13:8 sees contemporary famine as a sign of the birth-pangs of Christ's coming kingdom, and Acts 11:28 reports that the prophet Agabus foretold a great famine "all over the world," which took place in the days of Claudius. Other ancient sources verify the occurrence of "food crises in Egypt, Syria, Judea, and Greece" in 45 to 47 A.D.[29] In response to this life-threatening situation, the disciples in Antioch responded to the needs of the brethren who lived in Judea by sending relief to their elders via Paul and Barnabas.

Theissen suggests the Jews were dealing with "a degree of overpopulation in Palestine."[30] About the time of Christ, Josephus, the Jewish historian, states that the Galileans "have always been very numerous"[31] and that there were 240 cities and villages in Galilee,[32] with 15,000 residents in "the very least of them".[33] The modern Jewish geographer Michael Avi-Yonah takes issue with Josephus's figures, however, since they imply a total population for Galilee alone of 3 million. Avi-Yonah also rejects Josephus's estimate of 2,700,000 Jews making the Passover pilgrimage to Jerusalem as "absurd" but suggests that Josephus was assuming that every Jew in Palestine made the pilgrimage every year, and this represents the total Hebrew population for the entire region. If one takes the estimates for the number of men mustered for military service and extrapolates from them the number of woman, children, and the elderly in the total population, Judah supported 250,000 people in Nehemiah's time after the return from Babylon and 500,000 in Hasmonean times when the Maccabees revolted against the Hellenists (about 150 B.C.). Josephus's figures for military service indicate that there were 750,000 Jews resident in Galilee in 66 A.D. The Jewish population of Palestine shrank considerably, however, after Bar-Kochba's war and the destruction of the Temple about 70 A.D.[34]

Further information can be gleaned from archaeological surveys, which estimate there were three times as many villages in Galilee in the peak Roman period, and four times as many in the Roman-Byzantine period, as in 1900, when the population of Palestine was 700,000.[35] These ratios suggest a population between 2.5 and 3 million for all Palestine. During the life of Christ and the period of the early church, the region was much more densely occupied than in any other era prior to the modern period. Since the methods of agriculture used at the beginning of the twentieth century were relatively little changed from those of ancient times (and many farmers of 1900 were poor and underfed), one can assume the land was intensely utilized in New Testament times and may have been pushed to the limits of its productivity. An estimated 97 percent of Palestine was under cultivation during the Roman period, and when Herod had excess Jews to settle, he moved them outside their original tribal territories, suggesting that there was no room for them in their own ancestral lands.[36]

In the time of Abraham, there were new settlements to be established and new lands to be had. By the time of Christ, Palestine had reached or exceeded its human carrying capacity, and almost all arable land was in use. Excess population had no place to go but into the Roman legions or to the slums of the Hellenistic cities. Many residents of Galilee may, in fact, have experienced a dilemma common in the modern Third World—if they didn't produce several offspring, then all their children might die and there would be no one to care for them in old age, but if they did produce several offspring, then they might not be able to feed them all, and if several sons lived to adulthood, there would not be enough land to support all of them. Further, the Jews had become a minority group, under the thumb of Roman authority. A small nation in a nest of superpowers, they had little chance of invading surrounding lands, even if they managed to free themselves from the Roman oppressors. Further expansion of the Jewish people, at least in their homeland and nearby territories, was very unlikely. The high population densities of Palestine may not have been found in the entire Roman world, but the frequency of famine and immigration and the high concern for the landless and displaced poor in the New Testament (and its frequent use of imagery concerning food) imply that population and the basic availability of commodities were problems for the entire Middle East, and throughout the socially indifferent cities of the empire. The lack of New Testament emphasis on producing more children is thus not surprising, considering the conditions of the age.

THE CROWDED OLD KINGDOM
AND THE SPACIOUS NEW ONE

Judaism, in the first centuries A.D., was an ethnic sect based on family lineages and tied to a specific region. Although the Jews had always accepted "God fearers," those who believed in the God of Israel, into the congregation, an outsider could not become part of a tribe or a member of the Levitical priesthood. The proselyte was forever excluded from entering the inner court of the Temple or serving with the priests in the Holy of Holies. With the establishment of the Christian church, the chosen of God were no longer limited to the biological seed of Abraham—anyone could become a Christian in the fullest sense. An emphasis on progeny's assuming leadership might, in fact, have been damaging to the growth of the early church, as it would have favored Jews or Galileans and concentrated power in the hands of a Palestinian leadership. The New Testament emphasizes holiness and spiritual maturity rather than family background as the prerequisites for responsibility or office.

Christianity was a missionary religion from its beginnings. Encouraged by the well-developed Roman road and sea lane system and fostered by the scattered communities of the Jewish Diaspora, the new sect depended on an apostolate relatively free from family responsibilities and able to travel. Paul was the ideal evangelist, ready to journey to Corinth, Macedonia, or Rome and to remain as long as the mission required. The New Testament repeatedly emphasizes the potential size of the harvest or the number of sheep without a shepherd and the lack of willing laborers to carry out the evangelistic mission. The aspiring young disciple could produce far more new Christians by remaining single and traveling the empire than by staying home and raising children. The New Testament presents no evidence that its affirmation of celibacy was in direct response to high population densities accompanied by poverty and urbanization. Yet burgeoning populations and the presence of displaced immigrants throughout the Roman world influenced the early church's style of evangelism and ministry and probably encouraged a leadership free from family responsibilities.

The New Testament attitude toward childbearing was greatly influenced by the eschatology of the early Christians. Most thought Christ's return to earth was imminent and that the new kingdom would arrive any day. The destruction of the Temple in 70 A.D. was convincing proof that the end times were in progress, and the stress of plagues, famine, and Roman military intervention strengthened the first believers' expectation of a worldwide cataclysm. In 1 Corinthians 7 Paul finishes his exhortation for the unmarried to remain so and avoid the affairs of the world by writing, "For the form of this world is passing away" (1 Cor. 7:31). He also suggests that "those who have wives should live as though they [have] none" (1 Cor. 7:29), because he is expecting Christ to return within their generation. In the later passage Paul is neither discouraging sexual relations nor forbidding the conception of children but rather is directing the Corinthians toward spiritual goals and away from a preoccupation with mundane matters.[37]

A number of the prophetic passages in the Gospels and in Revelation predict future tribulation, and some directly employ images suggesting the distress of mothers with young. Describing the destruction of Jerusalem, Mark 13:17-19 reads, "And alas for those who are with child and for those who give suck in those days! Pray that it might not happen in winter. For in those days there will be such tribulation as has not been from the beginning of the creation which God created until now, and never will be." Revelation 12:1 uses the allegory of a "woman clothed with the sun, with the moon under her feet, and her head crowned with twelve stars" to symbolize the early church. "She [is] with child and she [cries] out in her pangs of birth, in anguish for delivery" (Rev. 12:2), when a dragon appears and attempts to devour the child, forcing the woman to flee into the wilderness. Although such passages are not directly antinatalist, they associate childbearing with social disruption and dissociate it from a glorious national future.

The early church did not perceive its task as building a two-thousand-year dynasty or as constructing the religious and social foundations for European culture. They saw themselves as calling others to be prepared for stressful events in the next few decades and the coming of an eternal kingdom where they "neither marry nor are given in marriage, but are like the angels in heaven" (Matt. 22:30). Abraham's need for a son to establish a holy nation was no longer relevant. The new kingdom was not of this world, and no heirs were needed to receive a place in it.

WOMEN SANCTIFIED BY CHILDBEARING

The New Testament contains no directives concerning the number of children desirable for a married couple. The apostolic letters, however, exhort children to obey and respect their parents and exhort parents not to "provoke your children to anger, but [to] bring them up in the discipline and instruction of the Lord" (Eph. 6:4). (Col. 3:21 reads, "Fathers, do not provoke your children, lest they become discouraged.") The pastoral epistles of Timothy and Titus require an elder of a church body to have a well-disciplined and properly managed household. All these passages are an extension of basic Hebrew attitudes toward the young and emphasize not family composition but family relationships.

An exception, and one of the more socially and theologically problematic texts in the New Testament, is 1 Timothy 2:9–15, which reads:

> Women should adorn themselves modestly and sensibly in seemly apparel, not with braided hair or gold or pearls or costly attire but by good deeds, as befits women who profess religion. Let a woman learn in silence with all submissiveness. I permit no woman to teach or to have authority over men; she is to keep silent. For Adam was formed first, then Eve; and Adam was not deceived, but the woman was deceived and became a transgressor. Yet woman will be saved through bearing children, if she continues in faith and love and holiness, with modesty.

If taken at face value, this text not only enrages Christian feminists, it also disturbs faithful followers of Luther and Calvin, since literal interpretation suggests that women receive salvation from their sins through the physical act of having children rather than by God's grace. Some biblical interpreters do not believe Paul actually wrote 1 Timothy, and therefore this text. Other interpreters, who think Paul penned the letter to a younger apostle, argue this passage is a later gloss since it seems to disagree with other Pauline writings. Leonard Swidler considers the passage to be among those ambivalent about the role of women in the church and "perhaps the most negative of the New Testament in its attitude towards women."[38] For Swidler, who assumes Paul was not the author, the purpose of the text is exclusion of women from ministerial functions, and they "are relegated to pious motherhood to gain salvation,"[39] a directive reflecting rabbinical teachings of the time. Whatever the authorship, a literal interpretation conflicts with Paul's admonition to single girls in 1 Corinthians, that an unmarried woman "is anxious about the affairs of the Lord, [and] how to be holy in body and spirit." Salvation according to Romans or 1 Corinthians does not have to do with one's marital status, much less with bearing children.

The translators of the *New International Version* of the Bible try to resolve the problem by translating the text "But women will be kept safe through childbirth, if they continue in faith, love and holiness with propriety." This implies that having children can help divert women from sinful behavior (which again conflicts with Paul's exhortation to remain single). Evelyn and Frank Stagg in *Woman in the World of Jesus* suggest that salvation refers not to release from sin but to "personal fulfillment, or vocational fulfillment, not in teaching [in the church] but in the home."[40] Commentator Luke T. Johnson suggests the passage disallows women a public teaching role but allows them "a role in educating their children in virtue."[41] Other interpreters consider the passage to be metaphorical and best rendered " 'Yet she will be saved by childbearing (or the birth of a child), namely the Messiah. While Eve was deceived and became a transgressor, it is from her progeny that the child, the Messiah has come."[42] *The Living Bible* translates the passage "So God sent pain and suffering to women when their children are born, but he will save their souls if they trust in him, living quiet, good and loving lives." This rendering reflects God's punishment inflicted on Eve in Genesis 3:16, where Yahweh declares, "I will greatly multiply your pain in childbearing" and concurs with the thought of theologian Paul Jewett, who proposes that women "will be brought safely through the threatening experiences of motherhood, if they, i.e. women, continue to live a life becoming a Christian name."[43]

Perhaps it is best for our purposes to view the text as a strong affirmation of childbearing as a spiritually legitimate vocation for women. It is the only statement of its type in the New Testament and implies that the church was not concerned about total numbers (low or high) but rather was wrestling with the vocational role of women in the church body. Children are thus further affirmed as valuable and worthy of a woman's full-time attention. This cannot, however, negate other calls, including passages concerning older widows also found in 1 Timothy and the previously cited encouragement to single women to completely devote themselves to service to God.

THE REPRODUCTIVELY UNFIT
AND THE SOCIALLY UNSUPPORTED

In investigating how a culture or social group deals with reproduction, one must look not only at those who have children but also at those who do not or cannot. Further, some members of a community may be reproductive or economic liabilities—extra mouths to feed with little to add to the future or well-being of the community. In the ancient world, those who were reproductively unfit included eunuchs, the diseased (particularly those with illnesses of the reproductive tract), and the aged. Those who were economic liabilities included the very poor, lepers, the blind, the crippled, orphans, widows, and people who were dispossessed through loss of their land or business.

In the Old Testament, those who are visibly reproductively unfit are excluded from worship at the Temple either by direct and continuing prohibition, in the case of eunuchs, or by remaining unclean because they have a discharge or skin lesions. Holiness before God was thus partially a matter of the physical state of the individual (just as circumcision served to fulfill the covenant with Yahweh). Deuteronomy 23:1 declares, "He whose testicles are crushed or whose male member is cut off shall not enter the assembly of the Lord." The prohibition is even broader for service as a priest. In Leviticus 21:17–20 God instructs Moses to "say to Aaron, None of your descendants throughout their generations who has a blemish may approach to offer the bread of his God. For no one who has a blemish shall draw near, a man blind or lame, or one who has a mutilated face or a limb too long, or a man who has an injured foot or an injured hand, or a hunchback, or a dwarf, or a man with a defect in his sight or an itching disease or scabs or crushed testicles." A priest may not marry a divorced woman, a widow, a prostitute, or any but a virgin daughter of Levi, in order to secure the purity of the priestly line. The law in Leviticus 21 and 22 also forbids sacrifice of animals that are blemished, imperfect, or castrated, just as castration of animals was forbidden to the nation Israel in general as an act against nature.

A Hebrew with both normal genital discharges, including semen and menstrual blood, and diseases generating flows was unclean and temporarily banned from the assembly. Further, things they wore or people or things they touched became unclean. Thus if someone had continuing uterine bleeding or a venereal disease, he or she was effectively excluded from Hebrew society. A woman remained unclean during and for seven days following menstruation.[44] The extended period of menstrual uncleanness would tend to limit the participation of women in the social and religious life of the community since anyone they touched would become unclean. Prohibition of intercourse during menstruation would encourage sexual intercourse during ovulation and thus increase rates of conception, although the association of women with "pollution" or ritual uncleanness in some cultures may actually serve to discourage casual intercourse and thus

62

reduce birth rates overall. Interestingly, and for reasons that are not understood, women were also considered unclean for a period after childbirth. Whatever the religious motive, this ritual period of isolation may have protected the mother and, coincidentally, the child from disease and is common among other cultures.[45]

The concern for reproductive soundness and male virility found in the Old Testament disappears in the New, as Jewish laws of ritual purity and the concept of uncleanness are abandoned. The addition of Gentiles to early Christian congregations necessitated some modifications of the ancient customs, but the changes also grew out of differing concepts of holiness and spiritual inheritance. The Hebrew religion was bound by blood relationships, whereas early Christianity was not. Further, by the time of Jesus' ministry, the law had often become a hindrance to loving or charitable action, and superficial passion for the law often disguised hypocrisy.

The woman who had had a hemorrhage or a "flow of blood" for twelve years who touched the robe of Christ was reproductively unclean. Although according to Leviticus she had also polluted Jesus, he ignored her social affront. Christ not only healed her, he called her "daughter" and praised her for her faith (Matt. 9:20–22; Mark 5:25–34; Luke 8:43–48). For Christ, "uncleanness" was a corruption of the heart, not a discharge. The healing of this ostracized woman separated physical maladies, and reproductive disorders in particular, from questions of spiritual purity. Christ's discussion of celibacy in Matthew 19:10–12, also justifies reproductive unfitness for the servant of God. In teaching his disciples, Jesus says to them, "Not all men can receive this saying, but only those to whom it is given. For there are eunuchs who have been so from birth, and there are eunuchs who have been made eunuchs by men, and there are eunuchs who made themselves eunuchs for the sake of the kingdom of heaven. He who is able to receive this, let him receive it." Here, lack of reproductive activity or ability is portrayed more as a circumstance of life or a calling and if anything is a sign of holiness.

Although there is some question whether the Greek word translated as "eunuch" in Acts 8:27 actually implies castration rather than just a position as a court official,[46] the Ethiopian chamberlain baptized by Philip by the desert road became the first to carry news of Christ to Africa. The very fact that a word suggesting loss of sexual function (and a practice that was anathema to the Jews) is used to describe this important disciple indicates that the early church had little concern for reproductive fitness. The baptism of the eunuch also fulfills a prophecy of Isaiah 56:3–5 concerning the coming kingdom and ties the Hebrew Scriptures to New Testament values:

Let not the foreigner who has joined himself to the LORD say,
  "The LORD will surely separate me from his people";
and let not the eunuch say,
  "Behold, I am a dry tree."
For thus says the LORD:
  "To the eunuchs who keep my sabbaths,
  who choose the things that please me
  and hold fast my covenant,
I will give my house and within my walls
  a monument and a name
  better than sons and daughters;
I will give them an everlasting name
  which shall not be cut off.

This text clearly speaks of a spiritual inheritance.

Both the Old Testament and the New Testament make frequent reference to the needs of the poor, widows, and orphans. The aged were generally respected in Israel, as is true of most Middle Eastern cultures. A widow, however, could easily find herself without a source of support. The Old Testament requires in Deuteronomy 25:5–10 that if a man has left no sons, his brother must marry the widow and thus produce an heir that will bear the dead man's name. This also provides support for the widow. Relatives cannot have cared for everyone in Hebrew society, however, because Leviticus 19:9–10 instructed farmers not to glean their fields and vineyards themselves and to leave the corners uncut so that the widow, the fatherless, and the sojourner might harvest food. Deuteronomy 24:22 directly reminds the people "that you were a slave in the land of Egypt," and this is why such charity must be provided. Deuteronomy 26:12–13 also provides that every third year the tithe of the produce of the land should be given to "the Levite, the sojourner, the fatherless, and the widow." The New Testament makes care of the poor and dispossessed a major characteristic of the righteous life. The story of the rich man who rejects starving, dying Lazarus, or of the rich man who dies with his barns full, makes the case for those who need a selfish motive (such as salvation from hellfire) to prompt a charitable act. The Old Testament thus excludes those who are reproductively unfit from the assembly while providing support for those who might be an economic liability. The New Testament welcomes both the reproductively and the economically unfit into the new kingdom.

FROM SHEPHERDS TO SUBURBS

Now, how do these biblical values apply to contemporary Christian life? The Old Testament tells us reproduction is a blessing and presents a generally pronatalist stance (although one's interest in fertility should never overshadow one's faith in God). The New Testament confirms the value of children while placing no emphasis on procreation as a means to multiply the church. Rather than call the New Testament and Paul's exhortation to celibacy antinatalist,[47] it would be more appropriate to deem the general tone of the Gospels and the epistles "non-natalist." Having children is good and a godly pursuit, and not having children serves the Lord. No conflict exists between these two roles, since either can be the individual's true "calling." Early Christianity did not consider spiritual status contingent on reproductive status.

Christ's and Paul's teachings set a standard that is difficult for many people to accept, however. Children are to be treated as worthy of the kingdom, yet the rank or worth of an individual Christian is not elevated by having lots of them. Most people are more comfortable with giving children some "earthly" value, such as increasing one's social status as a proof of one's virility, or improving one's economic position by providing financial security in old age, or having a necessary heir to take over one's land or one's profession. The Christian parent has something that is, on the one hand, very important—the responsibility to care for the heirs of the kingdom. Yet, on the other hand, no earthly heirs are necessary to guarantee one's place by Christ's throne. Perhaps one of the reasons Christendom has had difficulty articulating a population ethic is that individuals seeking spiritual status for themselves have, at different times in church history, held either the celibate or the very prolific reproductive state to be the ideal. Through the Middle Ages, celibates were "more holy than thou," while with the rise of Protestantism, middle-class family life became the "most spiritual" response.

Some caution must be extended in applying the biblical texts about reproduction out of their original social context, or in quoting the Old Testament without looking at the New. A case in point is God's promise to Abraham to bless the patriarch with offspring as numerous as the stars in the heavens. Although procreation remains a means of raising the people of God, Christ broadens the methodology when, in a resurrection appearance, he commands his disciples to "make disciples of all nations" by baptizing them and by "teaching them to observe all that I have commanded you" (Matt. 28:19–20). Old Testament laws restricting the reproductively unfit are overridden by the New Testament emphasis on faith as the criterion for entering the kingdom, as opposed to parentage or physical characteristics. This change is integral to Christian theology, since the New Testament expresses a missionary zeal reaching far beyond the households of the remaining Israelites. The growth of Christianity, unlike the growth of the Hebrew people, did not depend on begetting children. Christians begot new Christians through spreading God's word and by bringing the love of Christ to those who were not of their own household. A non-natalist stance was, in fact, an important factor in the early success of Christianity in evangelizing the Roman world.

Despite the winding turns of history, the Bible offers basic values that remain a useful foundation for ethical discourse on reproductive issues:

First, reproduction in all of creation is a blessing of God and should be a great joy for humankind.

Second, having many children is not a substitute for faith in God. A household full of heirs cannot compensate for apostasy or rejection of God's will. The future rests in Christ, with or without procreation. Fear of scarcity, including scarcity in childbearing, inhibits faith, and the rush for plenty can divert one toward Sodom or toward false gods.

Third, children are to be highly valued, both as members of a family and as citizens of the new kingdom. God's concern for them and their position in the kingdom of Christ supersede parental prerogatives that might allow them to be treated solely as material possessions, symbols of personal status, genetic or economic heirs, or sources of income or labor. Children do not have to be offspring of the "chosen" to have a place in the kingdom; thus children of non-Christians are as valuable to Christ as the children of Christians (e.g., the Syrophoenician woman's daughter). Children have inherent worth before God, unrelated to their age, economic status, or parentage.

Fourth, the reproductively unfit are as valuable to God as the reproductively fit. The unfit may have a special spiritual calling. The economically disadvantaged and people who are potential social liabilities also have great value before God. Widows and orphans are, in fact, God's special concern.

Fifth, the primary means through which the kingdom grows are spreading the gospel, baptizing, and teaching (and acts of love and charity), rather than birthing. A child born to Christian parents does not automatically inherit the kingdom, the way a son of Benjamin or Judah inherited the land. In Christianity, God's chosen must also choose God.

Sixth, the New Testament presents no specific directions concerning the production of greater or lesser numbers of children. Some women will find motherhood fulfilling, others will have a different calling.

QUESTIONS FOR REFLECTION

1. How do the social and economic conditions confronted by the early church compare with those faced by your congregation? What are any differences that might influence your community's attitudes toward human reproduction?

2. Try to identify one biblical value for human reproduction not listed above, and find some texts to support it.

3. If the New Testament does not provide specific directions concerning the number of children that might be desirable for a couple or a community, what are some New Testament passages concerning personal, economic, or social ethics that might provide some guidance?

4. Think of some biblical passages not discussed in this chapter that deal with population issues, such as the prevalence of famine, the desire for children, or the protection of mothers with infants. (Due to the limitations of space, this chapter did not, for example, extensively discuss the prophets or the history of Israel after Solomon.) What do these passages suggest about reproductive ethics?

5. If the New Testament is non-natalist, what implications does this have for the role of women in the church? How would a change from a pronatalist to a non-natalist approach to human reproduction be tied to changes in female roles between the Old and New Testaments?

4

THE BLACK DEATH
AND THE NEW JERUSALEM

Perhaps one of the most damaging delusions Christians have about human population regulation is that a majority of the problems are recent. American Protestants are especially apt to visualize their ancestors living in a spiritually idyllic environment where family life was central and happy, respectful children gathered around the dinner table on the farm. Western Christians also tend to see themselves as being "above" the food shortages and child mortality of the Third World, and wonder why these poor people don't think the problems through and stop having so many babies—as if a good Euro-American could never wind up in the same circumstances. The truth is that Christians, including those of Western European heritage, have long faced population-related issues, from devastating food shortages in the late Middle Ages to increased mortality rates resulting from urbanization. Christian responses to population crises and to long-term reproductive trends have sometimes been immediate and appropriate—biologically, economically, and ethically—and sometimes not.

Church historians have spent relatively little time investigating the environmental aspects of Christian theology, and population historians have spent relatively little time investigating the theological aspects of population changes. Academic literature dealing with past Christian ethical responses to population regulation is therefore very limited. We can, however, investigate the historic and sociological literature on demographic trends through the last two thousand years, and even if we are not always able to determine what Christians thought about population changes, we can at least determine what they did about them under stressful circumstances.

PLAGUE AND FAMINE IN CHRISTIAN EUROPE

As the power of ancient Rome declined, Europe became increasingly Christian while social and economic superstructures deteriorated. During the first centuries of the Christian era (late antiquity), population remained at high levels, then fell as the grip of the old empire loosened or was wrenched away by the Germanic tribes. Environmental hazards such as famine that had troubled the first Christians remained part of the status quo in a social millieu that was less organized and less able to deal with regional disasters than the Imperial Roman world had been. Population historian Josiah Russell estimates that the population of Italy was 7.4 million at the time of Christ, 4 million in 500 A.D., and only 2.5 million, or about a third of Augustinian levels, in 650 A.D. The population of France and the Low Countries, similarly, was about 6 million at the time of Christ and had fallen to 3.5 million by 650 A.D.[1] Despite a decreased density of humans, which should have left more farm acreage per person, we can hardly assume the people of the Dark Ages were adequately fed or free from disease. The decay of well-managed Roman agricultural and transportation networks meant less efficiency in food production and distribution. A devastating plague beginning about 540 A.D. suppressed European population growth for over two hundred years.[2] By 1000 A.D., the population of Europe had returned to the levels of 1 A.D., showing little net increase for a millennium.

During the following centuries, Europe experienced a pre-industrial era population explosion, where human numbers increased two to four times.[3] Russell estimates the population of France and the Low Countries grew from 6 million in 1000 A.D. to 19 million in 1340 A.D. In the British Isles population expanded from 2 to 5 million during the same time period.[4] This era ended with a series of catastrophes, some regional and some continental in scale. Major famines struck northern Europe from 1309 to 1315, and famine devastated the Low Countries from 1315 to 1317, causing 5 to 10 percent mortality. Traveling from the Near East in Mediterranean shipping, flea-infested rats brought bubonic plague to Europe in 1348. The Black Death is thought to have killed a third of the inhabitants of Europe. The plague also suppressed population growth by reducing birthrates among the survivors, presumably as a result of disease-induced weakening and the disintegration of families.[5] The initial outbreak of the Black Death was followed by several other epidemics. General population decline continued until about 1440, when Europeans numbered about 50 percent of pre-plague levels.[6] Then populations began to increase once more but did not necessarily cease growing as they returned to their former densities. The populations of Italy and England, for example, shot well past pre-plague numbers.[7]

The trauma of the fourteenth century had both social and environmental roots, as did the later disease outbreaks and food shortages. World climate has always fluctuated, and an extended period of cooling in the late Middle Ages may have caused a general decline in grain productivity and therefore in economic conditions throughout Europe. There was bad weather about 1300, including heavy rains and flooding. Another major interval of famines and plagues struck in the late sixteenth and early seventeenth centuries (although nothing as severe as the Black Death of 1438).[8] Cold, wet conditions caused famine, associated with an outbreak of plague, in Sweden from 1596 to 1603. Similar events occurred about the same time in England, Spain, and even Constantinople.[9] Curtailed only by the agricultural revolution, recurring food crises continued to threaten the populace of agricultural Europe until the nineteenth century.[10]

In addition to coping with climatic variations, the Europeans of the Middle Ages may have reached their environmental carrying capacity, at least relative to the agricultural methods of the times. Historian Lewis Spitz reports that in fourteenth-century Europe

> the exploitation of arable land had been pushed about as far as it could go. The marginal lands provided a less certain return, and formerly fertile lands were becoming eroded or impoverished for lack of fertilizers, by disregard of fallow periods, or because of inadequate rotation of crops. It was not possible to wrest new tillage from the forests, for those that remained were needed by the poor and were being exploited for metallurgical "factories" in industrial areas. There was as yet no scientific seed production or any radical technological breakthrough that would make for higher yield on a limited acreage. . . . Potatoes, with their high yield per square foot of land, were, of course, not yet known.[11]

Constant worry over the adequacy of the harvest and the possibility of serious shortages characterized village life in early modern Europe. The frugal peasants had already cut all the forests, drained all the wetlands, and plowed under most of the meadows. They had less livestock than their forebears, and even manure for fertilizing fields became scarce.[12] New acreage was unavailable, and the inheritance systems attempted to protect the integrity of the family holdings (usually by primogeniture—undivided inheritance by the eldest son, a custom that became increasingly common through the Middle Ages).[13] Population processes in preindustrial Europe were closely tied to the productivity of the land, so that "changes in the price of wheat corresponded closely with the changes in the number of conceptions, burials, and marriages."[14] Economically secure post–industrial era Christians should not underestimate the power of food costs to regulate childbearing, nor should they underestimate the intensity of preindustrial European food crises. Past famines in the Christian West have been so severe that people were reduced to eating straw, bark, grass, and dung, and, in the worst events, even corpses, in an effort to survive.

WHETHER TO MARRY AND WHEN TO MARRY

If both overpopulation and sudden population decline greatly influenced the lives of preindustrial Europeans, did the Europeans develop any social or ethical responses to mitigate the negative aspects of these phenomena? Did the Christian church play any role in their reproductive practices and ethics? And how well did the teachings of the church (at first the Roman Catholic Church, and later the Protestant sects) correspond to what the populace actually did? Slower population growth during some periods and accelerated population growth during others suggest that Christian marriage customs and childbearing and childrearing practices have varied, historically and geographically.

Before the development of our contemporary contraceptive technology, human beings could modify birthrates, and child survivorship by

1. Manipulating the onset and frequency of sexual intercourse: Later marriage tends to reduce the number of children a woman will have, as will reducing the incidence of intercourse while she is sexually active. Complete renunciation of sexual activity, of course, produces no offspring.
2. Varying the duration of breastfeeding: Women are much less likely to conceive while lactating, thus delaying weaning for two to three years will usually delay conception of another child.
3. Providing differential care to fetuses or children: Abortion is a very ancient practice, as is infanticide. Unwanted children can

71

also be abandoned or neglected. A preference for males over females can result in inadequate feeding, abandonment, or outright killing of female infants, and thereby a reduction in the rate of population growth.

The first Christian culture practice that comes to mind, when one begins to investigate how the Christians of previous generations may have regulated populations, is celibacy. Influenced by the ascetic communities of the desert fathers, monastic orders arose in both the Roman Catholic and the Eastern Orthodox churches. After a long theological battle, the priesthood in the West also became celibate (at least ideally—caring for priests' children was a continuing problem for the medieval church). It remains to be seen, however, if celibacy was ever a very socially flexible or fundamental means of population regulation.

Historian Peter Brown, in his book *The Body and Society: Men, Women and Sexual Renunciation in Early Christianity*, presents a thorough overview of early Christian arguments for and against complete sexual renunciation.[15] We should note, first, that population control was not an important early argument for celibacy, although some ancient opponents of the practice thought sexual renunciation would undermine family life and the production of children for the state. The fight for a sexually "untainted" priesthood was won by Platonism and Greek philosophical ideals, not by fear of overpopulation. Second, although the monastic movements began at a time of relatively high population densities, the first great flowering of monasticism in northern and western Europe was during a period of relatively low or declining population, about 400 to 800 A.D. Third, the number of adults choosing the celibate vocation varied geographically and by social class. Christians under vows of celibacy may not have exceeded 5 percent of the population in many regions.[16] By the High Middle Ages, many monastic establishments would not accept the children of the poor (except perhaps as laborers),[17] even though the poor were more likely to be stressed by famines and economic depressions and therefore were more likely to have extra mouths to feed.

Although further historic analysis would be highly desirable, we can assume the availability of monastic communities did have some impact on population structure. Many children were abandoned at the doors of monasteries and churches and were taken in and raised as part of the community. Parents might also "donate" their children, a practice called oblation. The Roman Catholic Church eventually ruled that such children had no obligation to stay, once they became adults, but many did choose the celibate life. Prior to the development of strict rules of primogeniture, placing excess off-spring at a monastery became an easy way to avoid inheritance squabbles or fragmented estates. Some of the abandoned or dedicated were crippled or handicapped and thus did not have to be cared for at home. As placement of younger sons in monasteries became less popular, placement of daughters continued for the wealthy classes. This certainly reduced the availability of eligible single women, although by the twelfth century openings in convents were hard to come by.[18]

A more important method of population regulation for Christians, particularly in western Europe, has been adjusting the age of marriage. The Roman Catholic Church and the major Protestant denominations have always enforced monogamy (itself a mild form of population control), but the average age of marriage and the percentage of the adult population remaining unmarried have varied widely through Christendom. Typically, marriage customs in the West have been influenced as much by economics as by church doctrine. Christianity, unlike some other religions, does not prescribe an age for first marriage and does not require marriage for entry into adult standing in the community. Christianity also affirms the reproductively unproductive, thus maintaining considerable flexibility in marriage and childbearing strategies.

Although modern Western Christians tend to think of themselves as marrying late in comparison with their ancestors, this is not necessarily the case. The average age of first marriage in the English village of Colyton, for example, was twenty-seven from 1560 to 1646, and a delayed thirty for women from 1647 to 1719. Mean age of first marriage actually began to fall after 1720 and reached a youthful twenty-three by the early 1800s.[19] The reproductive difference between marriage at twenty-three and thirty is easily two children, and perhaps more. The fertility of Colyton would thus have fallen during the Reformation, then risen again during the early industrial era.

We can follow changes in the age of marriage and the correlated changes in fertility through the history of Europe. In the early medieval period, European age of first marriage was typically in the middle to late twenties.[20] In the era of great population growth from about 1000 A.D. onward, marriage, especially for women, was earlier, often in the teens.[21] Families tended to delay marrying off their children as population densities increased, but after the devastating plague in the fourteenth century, the age of marriage probably temporarily lowered in Europe.[22]

As the population recovered and all the farmlands were once again occupied, the peasants developed a social system where the children would not marry until they inherited the parents' house and land or they were otherwise economically independent. Long apprenticeships were common for tradesmen. A son often stayed in the paternal home until the parents died; he was then able to start a family of his own. "Family survival" concerns then largely determined the choice of a mate. It was said of the residents of a seventeenth-century French village "they do not worry about the bride's pretty face, they ask only how many sheep she will bring into the family."[23] These cultural patterns postponed marriage until well past puberty and discouraged marriage during periods of economic depression. In some cases, a large number of single adults, sometimes 20 percent of the mature village residents, were left unmarried (but not necessarily cloistered).

The Protestant Reformers, while conducting a war against promiscuity, secret marriage, and illegitimacy, maintained some amount of social flexibility in their teachings on age of marriage. Lutheran Johannes Benz proposed a legal age of twenty-five for both sexes, a recommendation quite in line with the practices of the wealthier families of the early 1500s. Luther, however, "fearing for the mental and moral health of men unmarried after age twenty and women not married between fifteen and eighteen, urged marriage at a much earlier age."[24] These first Protestants were often urban bourgeois who could educate and find employment for several progeny. Historic demographic data testify, however, that Protestant marriage strategies were influenced by the same fluctuations in local economies that regulated their Roman Catholic neighbors.

With an increase in urbanization and industrialization in Europe, the demand for labor grew, and inheriting land became less important. At least regionally, the age of marriage often decreased, elevating the number of children a woman could potentially bear and encouraging the large families of the early industrial era. It should be noted that in the case of both rising and falling age of marriage, the cultural patterns did not always shift as quickly as would have been desirable, especially when populations were expanding at a greater rate than the food or farming resources would support.

Twentieth-century commentators, discussing late marriage and sexuality, often imply that the recent tendency for North American Christians to marry later than they did just after World War II results in temptation to sexual immorality. This is probably true, but it is worth noting that late marriage has not necessarily been historically associated with high rates of illegitimate births. Population historian E. A. Wrigley suggests "where early marriage was widely countenanced, extra-marital intercourse was often also common and the percentage of illegitimate births rather high, whereas if a community set its face against early marriage, illegitimate births were nevertheless usually few in number."[25] In the past, economic necessity acted as a considerable social restraint.

Historic Christian attitudes toward marriage have several implications for reproductive ethics. First, one of the major "legitimate" population controls was integrally tied to local economies rather than to direct ethical response or to church doctrine. Western Christians are used to marrying when they can support themselves, rather than at some set age or in response to a set ritual. Second, Western Christianity is just completing a shift from controlling birth rates primarily through adjustment of the age of marriage and changing the proportion of single adults in the community to controlling birth rates via contraception within marriage.[26] Some of the Western unwillingness to articulate population issues in theological terms may arise from this change. The contemporary Christian, with more traditional Christian values weaving through his or her memory, may be somewhat embarrassed that limitation of population is occurring simultaneously with sexual intercourse. Third, Western Christians may not communicate well with Christians from cultures that have never used late marriage or the maintenance of a "bachelor population" as culturally approved methods of population regulation. The Western Christian may think of African or Asian peoples who marry off their children at puberty as "less developed," when in reality the differences in customs reflect very different histories of population growth and regulation, and different family structures as well as different economic concerns.

SKELETONS IN THE CLOISTER?

After the time of the apostles and martyrs, the church began to assume a different posture in regard to human population regulation. The Roman Catholic hierarchy moved to restrict the paths for marriage and sexual intercourse. Church leaders attempted to eliminate various forms of marriage to near relatives and also banned polygamy and concubinage, while greatly restricting the conditions for divorce or annulment.[27] Many of the flock objected to the elimination of marriage to cousins because it was "attractive and a better preservative of inheritances than exogamy,"[28] but the faithful also understood that "the law of charity obliged Christians to seek in marriage an alliance with those to whom the natural ties of consanguinity did not bind them, so that the bonds of relationship and affection might be extended through the community of Christians: the sexual relation was to be legitimated by the social relation it created."[29] This restriction of marriage options would have depressed fertility slightly, as would Christian disapproval of fornication and illegitimate offspring.

In regard to procreation within the limits of marriage, however, the Western church chose a generally pronatalist stance. Early church fathers adopted an ethic influenced by Jewish writers such as Philo and by Stoic Greek philosophers. In the second century Justin declared, "We Christians either marry only to produce children, or, if we refuse to marry, are completely continent."[30] Clement of Alexandria, one of the most respected fathers of the early church, agreed that Christian husbands should "use their wives moderately and only for the raising up of children."[31] This "sex for procreation" ethic is grounded in a very ideal concept of interpersonal relationships that distinguishes love from sexual desire and values continence as being holier than sex within marriage. Like the pursuit of perpetual chastity, the ethic was not related to any defined population policy of the church fathers (and encouraging chastity while also encouraging procreation could hardly be deemed a consistent approach to human population regulation.) The earliest postbiblical writers on Christian marriage show no concern for swelling the Roman legions, improving Christian social standing, or even filling the portals of heaven.

The attitude of the church fathers toward the status of the human population is clearly expressed in the writings of Tertullian about 200 A.D., who suggests the world is already full:

> Everything has been visited, everything known, everything exploited. Now pleasant estates obliterate the famous wilderness areas of the past. Plowed fields have replaced forests, domesticated animals have dispersed wild life. Beaches are plowed, mountains smoothed and swamps drained. There are as many cities as, in former years, there were dwellings. Islands do not frighten, nor cliffs deter. Everywhere there are buildings, everywhere people, everywhere communities, everywhere life.
> . . . Proof [of this crowding] is the density of human beings. We weigh upon the world; its resources hardly suffice to support us. As our needs grow larger, so do our protests, that already nature does not sustain us. In truth, plague, famine, wars and earthquakes must be regarded as a blessing to civilization, since they prune away the luxuriant growth of the human race.[32]

A number of early theologians, among them Jerome, agreed that the world was fully populated yet insisted on "the procreative requirement in intercourse."[33] The early church recognized the "luxuriant growth" of the human race as a problem yet considered maintaining sexual purity and producing "quality" Christians more important endeavors than regulating population. The fathers encouraged Christians too spiritually "weak" to remain celibate to marry for the purpose of procreation.

Augustine of Hippo synthesized the theological opinions of his predecessors and concluded that sexual intercourse and procreation were good, while lust was not. "Good sex" was therefore for producing children, not for personal pleasure. The learned saint, who prior to his conversion had fathered a child by a woman he did not marry, suggested that since the world was "full," procreation was not "a duty of human society" and was not as necessary as it once was. Augustine, like most of the early theologians, did not think the return of Christ was served by having more offspring.[34] Nor were the purposes of heaven achieved by pronatalist tactics. In interpreting Augustine and his age, social historian David Herlihy writes:

> . For the number of saints had been fixed from eternity and
> could not be altered by human behavior. "The number of saints,"
> says Augustine, "will be perfect, none fewer, and none greater."
> In a widely shared view, the saints would exactly replace the
> number of fallen angels. In lauding virginity over marriage, and
> childlessness over parenthood, the Christian fathers had to face
> an evident consequence; if all men adhered to their counsels, the
> human race would not last a generation. This would be,
> Augustine responds, entirely a good thing. It would indicate the
> number of saints had reached its predestined size, and the City of
> God had become perfectly populated. The Christian fathers
> refused to concede that there was any social or religious value in
> sheer numbers of people.[35]

Theologically, Augustine extended past the "marriage is good, chastity is good" stance of the apostle Paul, and converted it to an antinatalist "chastity is vastly better." In justifing sex in marriage, Augustine also added to Paul, who, when instructing married couples to offer each other their conjugal rights, did not state that sexual intercourse was solely for the purpose of having children. Paul did teach that intercourse within marriage deterred temptation to sin, but did not delete the possibility of pleasure as a motive. When the fathers made procreation the only "holy" motive for intercourse, they moved church teaching on sex in marriage from a non-natalist to pronatalist stance, ironically while devaluing sexuality. Christians thus received a mixed message on procreation. Reproduction was good or bad depending on personal circumstances. The state of the world or even of the church was not an issue.

Later theologians modified the thrust of these first Christian arguments for procreation. Thomas Aquinas, for example, takes the position "the preservation of the species as a natural good obtained by intercourse."[36] Although this is a minor shift in emphasis, Aquinas thus acknowledges an increase in human population as potentially beneficial, because it is part of God's ordained cosmic order. Unfortunately, in the hands of less scrupulous clerics, the church's blessing of procreation in marriage could be utilized for economic and political ends. A large landholder, the established ecclesiastical hierarchy joined the feudal lords in encouraging reproduction in the peasant classes. Rising urban populations in early modern Europe also increased church prosperity.[37] Although the churchmen who introduced Stoic values into Christianity were apparently free of worldly motives for encouraging reproduction, theological pronatalism was (and is) easily tempted by the value of human service and the wage-limiting properties of excess human labor.

CONTRACEPTION AND THEOLOGICAL FOUNDATIONS

Perhaps the most important reproductive consequence of the thought of Justin, Clement, and Augustine is condemnation of contraception, at least by interference with sexual intercourse. Justin forbade intercourse during pregnancy on the grounds that a child was already conceived so further sexual activity was "indulgence in appetite.[38] Others who accepted the Stoic ethic would necessarily have regarded intercourse as sinful when contraception was employed because it prevented conception. A number of early Christian writings forbid the use of contraceptive drugs, as well as abortion, infanticide, and child abandonment. Some of the condemnations were directed against Gnostic practices, where potentially contraceptive sexual acts such as oral intercourse had become part of their religious ritual. An anti-Gnostic discourse was, in fact, the first Christian document accusing anyone of the sin of Onan. According to Genesis 38:9, Onan went into his deceased brother's wife and "spilled his semen on the ground"—that is he practiced coitus interruptus.[39]

Augustine, in a text condemning married couples who seek only the "pleasures of the flesh," closely associated infanticide, abortion, and contraception:

> They give themselves away [as shameful], indeed, when they go
> so far as to expose the children who are born to them against

78

their will; for they hate to nourish or to have those whom they feared to bear. Therefore a dark iniquity rages against those whom they unwillingly have borne, and with open iniquity this comes to light; a hidden shame is demonstrated by manifest cruelty. Sometimes this lustful cruelty, or cruel lust, comes to this, that they will even procure poisons of sterility [*sterilitatis venena*], and, if these do not work, extinguish and destroy the fetus in some way in the womb, preferring that their offspring die before it lives, or if it was already alive in the womb to kill it before it was born.[40]

Although there can be no doubt that Augustine intended to discourage contraceptive practices, the modern reader should note that many ancient contraceptive concoctions, unlike modern drugs, caused permanent sterility and other physical damage and could justifiably be called poisons. Augustine also rejected the Manichean heretics' use of the sterile period (when a woman was not likely to be fertile) and of coitus interruptus.[41] Through the Middle Ages, Christian opposition to contraception, abortion, and infanticide was expressed both by civil laws and church canons.

One form of "natural" contraception, prolonged nursing of infants, was never contested by the established church. Continued lactation helps to prevent conception immediately after childbirth, and most medieval women probably knew it could be used to delay pregnancy. When the practice of hiring a wet nurse became popular with the wealthier classes, the fertility of noblewomen increased, as they could bear children yearly (which incidentally increased the risk of the woman's dying during or because of childbirth). An Italian nobleman of the fourteenth or fifteenth century might have ten or more children skipping about his palazzo, and if one wife died, he could marry another.[42] During this era, the upper classes had higher fertility than the lower classes (the opposite of nineteenth-century England) even though a child left with a wet nurse was more likely to die than one cared for by its natural mother. The Roman Catholic Church also condoned temporary sexual abstention, for religious and health reasons, not for population control. Both official and popular wisdom discouraged sexual relations during menstruation, Lent, pregnancy, and the period of nursing after childbirth.

What the religious establishment allows and what people actually do are often two different things. Circumstantial evidence suggests married couples did use some type of birth control, possibly coitus interruptus, well before modern methods were available. Analysis of baptismal records indicates that English villagers often ceased to produce offspring well before the end of their childbearing years, suggesting they attempted contraception after several infants had survived.[43] There is scattered evidence that abortion was practiced in Christian Europe, although it is difficult if not impossible to determine its importance in population regulation. A substantial body of information suggests, however, that infanticide was common. Archaeologists investigating cemeteries have found, for example, that the sex ratios during the Middle Ages were heavily skewed in favor of males. The normal ratio of males to females at birth is 105:100. For the period from 1 A.D. to 1500 A.D. the European average was 132:100 (for ages fourteen to thirty-nine). Assuming that Europeans were willing to inter their deceased adult females, differential mortality of women during the childbearing years could not account for the pattern (and the ratio for the forty- to sixty-year-old class rose to 193:100, or almost twice as many men as women). Although cemetery data do not actually prove the case, the best explanation is elevated mortality of young female children. In the period from 1000 A.D. to 1348 A.D. about 25 percent more girls than boys appear to have died in infancy.[44] Since no known disease is this sexually selective in young children, females must have either been severely neglected or consciously disposed of.

Historically, infanticide in Europe included blatant instances of drowning, striking, or burying children. Seeming accidents were probably much more common, however. "Over-laying" of mothers on the infants was so frequent in some areas that authorities forbade mothers to sleep in the same bed with their newborns. Neglect of unwanted children could result in accidental drowning, starvation, or death from disease. Those who were illegitimate, deformed, or sickly were much more liable to ill treatment. Children placed with wet nurses had a notoriously high mortality rate, and more girls were placed with wet nurses than boys. Although a few cases were tried in court, convictions for infanticide were few. The sympathies of the public and even of the church were with struggling mothers. The penance for "over-laying" was fasting on bread and water, and the length of the penance was reduced if the mother was poor.[45]

Prior to the keeping of hospital records and modern systems of registering births, it was relatively easy for a mother to dispose of a child without the notice of the magistrate, the police, or even the neighbors. Infant mortality due to intent or neglect continued as an important social phenomenon into the industrial era. During the "enlightened" eighteenth century, infant corpses were often seen lying in the streets or dunghills of large European cities. British newspapers of the 1860s report "the frequent finding of dead infants under bridges, in parks, in culverts and ditches and in cesspools."[46]

Famous Britons, such as Benjamin Disraeli, decried the callousness of the mothers and criticized the indifference of the police, who had become all too accustomed to decaying little bodies. Infanticide finally declined dramatically in the last quarter of the nineteenth century due to stricter legislation, better maternity and child care, increased use of contraceptives, and better-organized systems of adoption.[47]

John Boswell, a historian very willing to correct naive impressions of past Christian sexual mores, has published an extensive analysis of abandonment of children from Roman times through the Middle Ages. Boswell argues that abandonment was widely practiced, although he holds that it was not in general intended to kill the child. Abandonment was an ordinary procedure in the Greco-Roman world and was not considered a crime, since the father had the right to dispose of the child. In late antiquity abandoned children were sometimes sheltered by loving foster parents but more often became servants, slaves, or prostitutes. As Christianity took hold, the church hierarchy never tried to repress the practice and instead allowed or even required abandoned children to be placed on church doorsteps or at the gates of monasteries. Boswell finds that during the height of the monastic movement, abandoned children were usually well cared for, if not welcomed, by the monastic establishments, and many such children grew up to become pious servants of the mother church. Boswell hypothesizes that mortality from "exposure" was not as high as is commonly thought.[48]

On the other hand, Boswell may be underestimating the potential losses from the mere shock of leaving a newborn temporarily without maternal care. Abandoned children were more likely to come from poorer, ill-fed mothers and therefore may not have been healthy at birth. The abandoned were more likely to be ill, crippled, or the youngest of several siblings. Their mothers may not have initiated nursing, and the infants were likely to be undernourished and dehydrated by the time wet nurses were found. The abandoned were also more likely to have been female. Even if many survived, their mortality rate was almost certainly higher than that for infants lovingly received at the natal hearth. Infant mortality rates prior to the modern period were so high that if even a few of the abandoned children survived, no one may have noticed the fate of the others.

The scheme as practiced by the church through the early to the High Middle Ages offered a solution to a continuing social problem. Families unwilling to divide an inheritance would seek to rid themselves of excess offspring, as would families who could not feed the children they had. The monastery or convent was a "spiritually safe" harbor for the child for whom there was "no room at the inn." If the children survived, abandonment redistributed them from those who had too many or could not raise them to those who had no children of their own, needed servants, or required more recruits for the spiritual life.

As the monasteries declined in numbers and financial power, the established church adopted a new strategy for caring for abandoned infants—the foundling hospital. Beginning perhaps in the twelfth century, the institution was well-developed by the fourteenth. No effort was made to find the persons depositing children, and some hospitals hid the identity of the parent or servant leaving the child by providing a special revolving door where the culpable adult could not be seen. Mortality was tragically high. At one late medieval Italian hospital 20 percent died within the first month and another 40 percent within the first year. At another similar institution, 25 percent died in the first month, and another 40 percent within a year. At the latter institution, only 13 percent lived to age six. This exercise in "Christian charity" continued into the nineteenth century, with appalling death rates. In one French district in the eighteenth century, 91 percent of infants and 86 percent of all children admitted to foundling hospitals died. In Paris during the same era, 77 percent died before age twelve. In small French towns, with even more poorly managed facilities, losses might approach 100 percent. Disease was almost impossible to prevent in such establishments, and everything from typhoid to tuberculosis took its toll.[49]

Abandonment, particularly when it decayed into de facto infanticide, almost certainly acted as a mechanism of population regulation. In Toulouse, France, in the late eighteenth century, for example, abandonment swept away over 20 percent of the children born and sometimes separated 25 percent from their natural mothers. In the poorer parts of the town, abandonment approached 40 percent, although it was still a significant 15 percent in the richer neighborhoods. In eighteenth-century Paris the rate was similarly between 20 and 30 percent. In nineteenth-century Florence it reached an astonishing 43 percent, or almost every other child.[50] If one adds infants never reported and estimates the overall potential deaths, abandonment must have been one of the more important eighteenth- and nineteenth-century means of population regulation. Exact figures may never be available, but where abandonment was widely practiced, it may have doubled overall infant and childhood mortality rates. Despite public awareness that homes for children and the "baby-farms" of unscrupulous nurses were death traps, the English Parliament did not pass legislation regulating such institutions until

the first Infant Life Protection Act of 1872.[51] The marital and reproductive values of Christendom had fallen greatly short of the ideals
of St. Augustine.

TRADITION, HYPOCRISY, AND JUSTICE

Rather than criticize the church fathers for their importation of
Greek philosophy into Christian theology, we need to investigate
why the ideals of Christendom ended up at such a distance from actual practice. Justin, Clement, Jerome, and Augustine all held Christianity to be a high calling and were dedicated to the propagation of
holiness and the execution of the will of God. The emphasis on chastity worked well in the first Christian communities. Many women, in
fact, preferred celibacy because it released them from the restrictive
Roman patriarchal marriage. In late antiquity being a Christian was
not only voluntary, it was also dangerous. The persecuted Jewish sect
was for the spiritually strong and able. The followers of Christ were
"soldiers" or "athletes" for God, dedicated and self-disciplined. The
church strove for individual and community purity and left the social
problems of the age to exogenous solutions such as plague, famine,
and warfare.

The marital ideals of the fathers were not, however, well adapted
to an urbanizing Europe, filled with the illiterate poor and the cyni-
cal rich, many of whom were Christians because everyone else was.
People did not always have sexual intercourse for the purpose of procreation, nor, if they wanted children, did they always bear one that
suited the demands of the inheritance systems. Theologians made
little effort to try to meld lofty canons to ever-changing social pressures. The church of the Middle Ages, in pushing for personal holiness, remained blind to the role of economics and accommodated the
outfall of baby girls, younger sons, and illegitimate children by offering asylum, when the social institutions existed that could absorb the
extra offspring, and by looking the other way, when the social institutions failed.

Protestantism, less bound by tradition than Roman Catholicism,
departed from Augustine on the value of chastity and therefore on
the role of sexuality in marriage and the morality of contraception.
When Luther and his cohorts began to "empty the convents," they
also started a major reevaluation of continence as a route to holiness.
This in turn established the possibility of sexual intercourse for love
or pleasure rather than for procreation. Protestant arguments against
abortion and some means of contraception turn on the potential dam-

age to the fetus (or on the possibility of murder) and not on the sin of the parents in having intercourse without wanting a child. Lutheran theologian Carl Braaten writes:

> The sexual function of man and woman is not primarily to propagate the race but to serve each other. A married couple does not and ought not marry to have children, but to have each other. Sexual intercourse in marriage has a profound personal value in reflecting a human dimension of love which Christians have interpreted as the earthly analogy of the love of God. Because this is so, it is necessary for the church to make absolutely clear that it now rejects the teachings of some previous theologians who held that the only excuse for coitus in marriage was either to procreate or, if necessary, to satisfy irrepressible lust. Love and sexuality are primarily in the service of two persons whom God has joined together in a one-flesh union.[52]

Since Braaten considers parenthood a vocation, couples should be free to practice "any means of contraception which do violate the integrity of the love relationship in marriage and which are medically sound."[53]

Protestantism has, however, followed in historic church footsteps by shying away from the economic and social side of population regulation. Historically, Protestants as well as Catholics have tolerated abandonment and have ignored the population problems of the poor. Although nineteenth-century Christian reformers struggled to ban slavery, restrict child labor, and protect unwanted infants, twentieth-century theological commentaries on contraception usually center on individual rights or on the institution of marriage, not on the population problems of the underprivileged or even on international injustices to women and children. The dons of Protestantism have justified middle-class Presbyterians and Lutherans who use new technologies for limiting family size. Unfortunately, where poverty, cultural exploitation, class prejudice, sexism, or environmental damage stand as central issues, Christendom is still slow to respond and is still willing to look the other way.

We can draw several conclusions from the history of population regulation via contraception and infanticide in Western Christianity. First, the theology of the early fathers encouraged conflicting values concerning the production of offspring and moved away from the non-natalist New Testament position into a maze of pronatalist and antinatalist positions, contingent on sexual rather than economic or social circumstances. Personal purity, rather than community or family need, determined "right behavior." Second, church condemnation of contraception, abortion, and infanticide did not prevent the practices. As monasticism declined, the Christian community did not cope well with the multitudes of unwanted infants and slid into de facto infanticide. The early church's obsession with marital purity ignored social and economic realities, and though attempting to keep adults from personal sin, only weakly wrestled with the social structures causing high infant mortality. Third, the methods of population regulation historically employed in Christendom encouraged some degree of fatal sex discrimination. Paul's instruction in Galatians 3:28 that in Christ there is "neither male nor female" was disregarded in the case of infants and young children and was replaced with an economic model. Fourth, when Christianity became enmeshed in political and financial institutions and hierarchies, teachings that were biblically based or well intended became distorted. In the case of human population regulation, deviations in Christian doctrine or social convention resulted in human misery, neglect of the poor or disadvantaged, and abuse of the undefended.

CHRISTIAN DOMINION, SOCIAL DAMNATION?

Having looked at population regulation within the Christian community, we now need to investigate historic Christian attitudes concerning population issues between communities or nations. This is a very broad subject, and two major examples will have to suffice: (1) the relationship between England and her subject nation Ireland at the time of the Irish potato famine and (2) the relationship between Christian missionaries and settlers and aboriginal populations during the Age of Discovery. The relationship between European colonial powers and their colonies in Africa and Asia will be discussed in chapter 8.

The proximate cause of the Irish potato famine was a fungal disease that began after a long spell of warm weather in the summer of 1845. The starvation following the loss of only a single crop was, however, tightly tied to international politics. At the time of the famine the Irish were under British rule, and a large portion made their living from agriculture. Some of these were freeholders who owned their own small farms, but many were tenants on the larger estates (often owned by absentee British landlords). Forty-five percent of the holdings were under five acres. Thoroughly tangled in the British economy, Irish manufacturing was doing poorly in competition with British factories, and struggling to survive in an environment where England controlled the tariff regulations and the transportation networks (and wanted to protect her own industries as much as possible). The Napoleonic wars at the beginning of the century had raised the price of grain and encouraged Irish farmers to expand grain production for export while encouraging the Irish themselves to depend upon the potato. The need for farm hands stimulated population growth, but as the economy declined after the war, the population did not.[54] In 1800 there were an estimated 5 million Irish, and by the time of the Great Famine, 8.5 million. Interestingly, birthrates in Ireland and in England were similar during the period preceding the famine (the era of high mortality in British industrial centers is discussed in chapter 2). In 1841, for example, the estimated crude birthrate was 36.4 per thousand in Ireland and 36 per thousand in England.[55]

During the first year of the potato blight, the British moved to stabilize grain prices, bought some maize for emergency relief, and set up a relief commission, including the establishment of public works projects to help the unemployed. The next year the crop failure was complete and the relief efforts totally inadequate. The hungry abandoned their lands and moved out into the countryside or flooded into the public works camps. By midwinter of 1846, fever was rampant and killing far more Irish than was outright starvation. The British government, in response to the growing crisis, tried to get the Irish landlords to bear as much of the financial burden of the famine as possible. The landlords responded by evicting pauper tenants, casting families out of their homes and, if necessary, burning the cottages to get rid of them. The disaster continued until 1848. Estimates of famine-related deaths vary from 500,000 to 1.8 million, but recent demographic work suggests about a million fatalities, not counting deaths among the 1.3 million Irish who emigrated.[56] British response to the famine (or lack of it) created a bitterness in Irish hearts lasting to the present day.

The reaction by Christians, in actuality, graded from brutality to complete self-sacrifice. On one hand, the British government was unwilling to disrupt the profitable economic ties between the nations. During the famine years grain exports from Ireland to England continued, and the export of cattle actually rose. Although the exported grain would not have compensated for the lack of potatoes, it could have helped the starving populace.[57] Thomas Gallagher, in his popular account *Paddy's Lament: Ireland 1846–1847, Prelude to Hatred*,[58] quotes a number of British sources that explicitly pinned the blame for conditions in Ireland on either Celtic ethnic characteristics or on Roman Catholicism. *The (London) Times*, taking a racist bent, declared, "The Celt is less energetic, less independent, less industrious than the Saxon" and suggested that English effort and English law would have prevented such a situation from developing. The Irish farmer was "sucked in poverty which he is too callous to feel, or too supine to mend."[59] At at time when many Irish were weakened from malnutrition and fever (and they could not have converted their small plots to grain in any case), *The Times* accused them of being basically lazy:

> They have tasted public money, and they find it pleasanter to live on alms than on labor. The alternative raises no feeling of shame or self abasement. Deep, indeed, has the canker [of laziness] eaten. Not into the core of a precarious and suspected root—but into the very hearts of the people, corrupting them with a fatal lethargy, and debasing them with a fatuous dependence! . . . Thus the plow rusts, the spade lies idle, and the field fallow.[60]

The Irish found themselves trapped between landlords who were set on getting rents the peasant farmer could not possibly produce and a small army of well-paid and unsympathetic British civil servants who were ineffective in providing relief.

Even when they attempted to emigrate, the Irish suspected that the crown was against them. Irish who sailed on American ships found themselves better treated and in more sanitary conditions than the poor "Paddies" who ended up sleeping with filth and typhus on uninspected English lower decks.[61] Many of the British and the landlords were privately or openly thankful for the famine, either because it would get rid of poorer and low-productivity tenants, allow conversion of the land to more profitable cattle rearing, or still rebellion against British rule. One English university professor feared that the famine in Ireland "would not kill more than a million people, and that would scarcely be enough to do any good."[62]

The role of organized Christianity during the famine was a mixture of antagonism, blessing, and confusion. In 1846 starving Ireland was still under a tithe law, and monies were collected through the landlords to support the Anglican church, even if all the residents of a parish were Roman Catholic. Some Protestant ministers attributed the famine to providence (not to problems with land tenure or taxation), while the more violently anti-Catholic suggested it was God's judgment on the nation because of "popery." More than one rabid Protestant suggested the native Irish had brought the famine on themselves through "idolatrous worship of Romanism."[63] In gentle contrast to these attitudes were the activities of the Society of Friends (the Quakers), who although few in number in Ireland got down to the business of providing relief. English and American

Friends generously assisted their Irish members with funding for soup kitchens and grain shipments from the United States.[64] Irish historian Mary Daly summarizes the efforts and the foibles of the more charitable Christians:

> Increased sectarianism and allegations of souperism [Protestants proselytizing by means of charity] . . . disrupted local relief efforts, though many Protestant clergymen were actively involved in famine relief during those years. All grants given by the Society of Friends were locally administered by Church of Ireland [Anglican] clergy. Many of the clergy and their wives manned soup boilers, while catholic priests were constantly engaged in administering the last rites to dying people. Evidence of Church of Ireland involvement is best indicated by the fact that, in the year 1847, forty protestant clergy died from famine fever, while the famine also claimed the lives of many catholic clergy. Some relief work was carried out by joint co-operation between catholic and protestant clergy, but divisions were all too common both between clergy of different religions [denominations] and between influential local laymen. Applications of famine relief from individuals, rather than committees, were common, and . . . during the famine years, "Catholic-Protestant suspicions often led to the breakdown of this tradition of self-governing aristocratic method of government." This breakdown lessened the efficiency of local relief efforts and in the process probably cost lives.[65]

If Christians had ignored the gathering storm of increasing poverty and population, at least some tried to aid the stricken as a flood of starvation, fever, and despair swept over Eire. Unfortunately, denominational prejudices often undercut their efforts.

Historians, economists, and demographers have long argued over why the potato famine occurred and who was really at fault for the high mortality. The immediate physical cause is obvious, but why were so many people dependent on a single crop on such small holdings? One modern school of thought blames English economic manipulation. Ireland had formerly been a cattle-producing nation without a large excess rural population. England needed cheap food for her growing urban populace and ready markets for her industrial products. This shifted the agricultural emphasis in Ireland to export crops and created a need for labor for tillage. The potato was one of the keys to the transition as it allowed the crofter to live on a very small parcel of land while helping to raise wheat or pork for sale abroad. Initially, the high productivity of the potato and the availability of land produced an agricultural surplus, but eventually the system failed—just at a time when a transition away from grain production was economically desirable (from an English point of view).[66]

There can be little doubt that the attitudes of influential Englishmen toward the Irish reflected their attitudes toward the poor in general and their self-interest in perpetuating the existing economy. Irish historian E. R. R. Green comments bluntly, "The ministers of the crown who had to accept responsibility once the disaster occurred were callous and parsimonious and self-righteous. Yet these are the very qualities which Charles Dickens, for instance, found so distasteful in men of their class, and they were exhibited as much to the English as to the Irish poor."[67] Underlying British indifference to the unending rattle of carts removing stacks of coffinless corpses was a long series of arguments for and against the British Poor Laws and the appropriateness of relief for the poor.

The central figure in the original political battles was an English clergyman named Thomas Robert Malthus, who first published an essay on human overpopulation in 1798.[68] Malthusian principles, commonly invoked at the time of the potato famine, are still very prevalent in Western environmental and social ethics, as we shall see in the next three chapters. Malthus can be played as either a villain or a seer, but there can be little doubt he correctly identified a principle of population growth: Human and animal populations increase geometrically (i.e., they first double, then they quadruple, etc.) as compared to the slower, often arithmetical, increase of vital food resources. If humans reproduce at their maximum capacity, they will increase at a much greater rate than their crops and agricultural produce. Space, food, and water will eventually limit the human population. When the number of people has exceeded the carrying capacity of the land, famine will result and the population will decline, often radically. The Irish potato famine seemed a ghastly proof of Malthus's theory.

Malthus died in 1834, well before the famine, but he was aware of "the Irish question" and thought the Irish had two principal problems: the potato and rapid population growth. Malthus also suggested, however, that the style of taxation, specifically tithing, was undermining the Irish agricultural economy, and that application of a "single tax" (a set rate of land taxation that would give the farmer more opportunity to make a profit) would initiate land reform. Malthus held that the increasing rents and decreasing wages were trapping the farmer in poverty, just as British jealousies concerning trade were inhibiting the growth of the Irish economy. Malthus even proposed that giving the Irish peasants "all the rights and privileges of British subjects" would help to alleviate the political difficulties of the subject nation. For Malthus, greater equality for the Catholic Irish would help to counter the already serious population problems.

Unfortunately, the governmental powers of his time did not agree with him.[69]

Of greater influence, in actual English dealings with the Irish and with their own poor, were Malthus's opinions on the English Poor Laws. Malthus thought that public assistance to those in need, particularly on a long-term basis, discouraged people from working and encouraged further poverty. Regular funding for the poor stimulated the production of children for whom there were no jobs and thus cheapened the cost of labor. Particularly problematic were programs that provided increased cash support to families with larger numbers of children, which of course might encourage the unemployed to expand their families. Malthus favored the abolition of the Poor Laws in favor of private charity, which would be more discriminating in its distribution, more likely to discourage long-term dependence, and better able to determine who was worthy of assistance. For Malthus the proliferation of the poor would only reduce food supplies and weaken a nation's economy.[70] The Poor Law passed in Britain in 1834 reflected Malthusian thinking in that "it took effective power from local authorities [to provide relief] and increased the role of the workhouse. Poverty became regarded as more of a crime than a misfortune, and the cost to the nation of relieving poverty was henceforth to be kept as low as practicable."[71]

Malthus himself thought that the solution to overpopulation was moral restraint, particularly voluntary delay of marriage. (In his day it would have been illegal to publish a tract on contraception for public distribution, and Malthus, in any case, would not have found this morally acceptable.) Malthus held that "it is clearly the duty of each individual not to marry till he has a prospect of supporting his children; but it is at the same time to be wished that he should retain undiminished his desire of marriage, in order that he may exert himself to realize this prospect, and be stimulated to make provision for the support of greater numbers."[72] Sexual restraint was a virtue not because it met Greek ideals of personal purity but because it avoided misery and famine. Unlike Augustine, Malthus "recognized that human passions were a source of great happiness and were to be regulated by reason but not suppressed."[73] Marriage was, for Malthus, a pleasurable and desirable state, even if it had to be postponed for economic reasons. Thus this English clergyman's motives for recommending sexual restraint were utilitarian and showed no concern for Stoic values.

By the time of the potato famine, the British public largely concurred with Malthus but had little inclination to adjust the land tenure system. Malthusian thinking led, instead, to a fatalism about the event and a tendency to blame Irish woes on their own lack of restraint or initiative. This in turn deflated relief efforts and left the British of two minds concerning the crisis. The Malthusian message had always been that if overpopulation continues, famine or some other environmental disaster will act as the ultimate control. Once people accept this prospect and assume it is bound to occur, they are less likely to take remedial measures. The arguments that raged over Malthus's work in the eighteenth and nineteenth centuries have, for better or worse, continued to the present day.

NEW WORLDS, OLD PROBLEMS

A last example of historic Christian approaches to population issues is the interaction between Christian missionaries and settlers and aboriginal populations. During the Age of Discovery, European contact with indigenous populations invariably caused disruption of long-established patterns of fertility and mortality, for peoples as scattered as the woodland Indians of eastern North America, the islanders of Tahiti, and the isolated Maori of New Zealand. The usual impact of European contact with unsuspecting natives was a decline in fertility and an increase in mortality that led to radical population declines, often terminating only after the smaller tribes and bands were both genetically and culturally extinct. Long before agriculturally oriented settlers tried to claim native lands, explorers and Christian missionaries began the process by accidentally introducing European diseases to peoples who had not been previously exposed. Contagious nightmares like smallpox took such tolls that frightened indigenous communities, who had never experienced anything like the European plagues of the Middle Ages, would either capitulate to the "whites" or become so socially disoriented that cultural practices of long standing would fall by the wayside. The natives could therefore offer little organized resistance to the invaders from across the water. Settlers needing land followed the diseases with firearms and, in some cases, an open extermination policy. Economic pressures and competition for resources thus removed whoever was left of the dying races.[74]

The attitudes of the Christians who participated in this process were as varied as they were about the potato famine. Some, including explorers such as those on the Cook expeditions, realized the presence of the outsiders would be permanently disruptive, and they grieved the passing of native ways. A few, such as the more sensitive missionaries, lamented the demise of their "new friends" or "flocks." Some took advantage of the situation to counter the power of shamans and heathen religions. The Jesuits in the colonial Americas were hardly able to turn the tide of epidemics with their medical skills, but their "dedicated nursing of stricken villagers and the well-timed administration of a few placebos and cordials may have saved as many natives as did their constant prayers. Because the new epidemics commonly struck down whole villages, leaving no one well enough to fetch wood, water, or food for the sick or to shift them on their mats, the Jesuits and their servants cheerfully assumed these chores."[75] This introduced the faith into the villages and gave the Jesuits a chance to spread the idea that the catastrophic disease outbreaks were "God's just punishment of native sin, individual or corporate."[76] The demoralized natives fled their old religions and medicine men, while confessing that "all our ill luck comes to us because we do not pray to God."[77]

Some settlers believed Jehovah was acting in their behalf by sending pestilence. John Winthrop, the first governor of Puritan Massachusetts Bay, optimistically wrote in 1634, "For the natives, they are all dead of small Poxe, so as the Lord hathe cleared our title to what we possess."[78] Winthrop was a perceptive man; a plague among the Indians in 1616 to 1618[79] had removed much potential resistance to the band of Pilgrims arriving at Plymouth Rock. The theological perspective of the first colonists is not surprising, since the plague and smallpox still periodically marched through Europe and such disease outbreaks on the home front were attributed to corporate Christian sin. The Puritans do seem, however, to have been so involved in their own search for religious freedom that they were oblivious to the needs of the natives. These religious refugees never really considered the "uncivilized" Indians potential citizens of their very European holy nation in the wilderness.

It is notable that most of the Europeans took no direct responsibility for the demise of the indigenous populations and did not modify their exploratory plans in order to protect these "children of the forest" from the ravages of civilized plagues. The Europeans, of course, knew little of epidemiology and were not certain how the diseases were transmitted. Their evident lack of horror at the situation, however, betrays their own heritage. In their overcrowded and unsanitary cities, mass mortality was a periodic fact of life. The decimation of the natives helped to justify their occupation of Indian lands, just as the Black Death had helped to provide unoccupied patrimonies and stimulate population growth during the Renaissance and Reformation eras.[80] The New Jerusalem rose not on a holy hill but on the bones of the suffering tribes.

The demise of the indigenous peoples provided hundreds of thousands of acres of unoccupied land and helped relieve Christians arriving in the New World of resource limitations that had influenced European marriage and reproductive strategies for several centuries. Although it was hardly a free-for-all, the limitations of inheritance were not what they had been in the late Middle Ages. Pioneer families in frontier America could and did place excess children on farms and in businesses elsewhere, and population pressures stimulated the drive to open previously uncultivated lands. In some cases, filling the frontier was actually critical to personal safety, and more people were needed to clear fields, build roads, and swell the ranks of the militia. During the French and Indian War, for instance, citizens living at the borders of the British colonies had to protect themselves from attack on their scattered farmsteads—something much better accomplished by a group than by an individual.

Eventually the situation began to reverse, and resource limitations became more critical than defense, but solutions continued to be found in emigration rather than in population regulation. By the early 1800s, for example, New England had lost most of its big game animals and most of its virgin forest. Soil exhaustion was a problem for farmers, and "European pests and crop diseases had already begun to appear."[81] Rather than waiting till age thirty-five to marry, the disgruntled farmers and excess offspring just headed west to new lands. Even in the twentieth century, the New World solution to overcrowding is exploration for new resources (such as oil in the Arctic or in South America) or a quick family move to establish a new business or find a new job. This mentality tends to lead to "frontier" or "cowboy" ethics, which will be discussed in chapter 6.

Perhaps the greatest lesson of past Christian intercultural interactions is that when population catastrophe strikes, the ruling classes, those in political control, or even the religious leadership are quick to blame weather, providence, or even the judgment of God. Especially in cases where economic resources are at stake, the starving or ill may be cast as genetically inferior, lazy, stupid, sinful, or sexually promiscuous. There have been population crises where Christians have piously thanked God for the demise of other Christians, and population crises where Christians who would not consider committing any form of personal sexual sin have stood idly by while their neighbors have perished from famine and disease. There has also been a tendency for Christians to feel themselves called to minister to the victims of food crises and fevers but not necessarily to attempt to avert such disasters, possibly because the latter requires broad social action as opposed to assistance to individuals in temporary need. The

Christian approach to intercommunity or international population problems has historically been limited by ethnic, class, and denominational prejudices and by social condemnation of the unbelieving or the uncivilized. What natural disasters could not by themselves have accomplished, social indifference has easily achieved.

LEARNING FROM OUR PAST

Systematic Christian theology, almost from its postbiblical beginnings, fluctuated between pronatalist and antinatalist positions without recovering and maintaining the ministry-oriented non-natalism of the New Testament. In the historic cases presented above, Christianity has had difficulty tying sexual ethics to economic ethics and to social processes for establishing personal position, self-esteem, or inheritance. Population growth is never limited by sexual purity (except in instances where a large portion of a population renounces sex completely). The Irish at the time of the famine were probably among the most sexually conservative people in Europe. The average Irish farmer was faithful to his wife and fell well within Paul's recommendations for marriage, including offering conjugal rights. Biblical family life is a perfectly good way to produce lots of offspring.

The more basic issues in population growth concern scarcity and availability of resources including land, food, jobs, inheritance, and even people themselves (labor). To discuss population growth as if it were entirely the result of promiscuity or lack of sexual restraint is to not understand the process. A Christian method of population regulation that is ethically acceptable must not only encourage loving sexual behavior, it must share resources fairly. The New Testament sets very high ideals in this regard. Although the Bible does not relate its teachings on care for our neighbors and the management of our wealth directly to population regulation, both the Old and New Testaments discuss just distribution of food, money, social position, and even of marital partners (each person having but one spouse). The history of Christendom demonstrates that theology has usually seen itself as above or separate from economy; yet without a working partnership between the two, many of the gravest problems of human existence cannot be resolved. One of our quests, therefore, in developing a viable and humane ethic for human population regulation is to integrate theology and economy, sexual ethics and resource ethics, and personal social values and community into a spiritually sound yet practical approach to solving the actual problems presented by changes in human demography.

The history of population regulation in Christendom, with its ghosts of female infanticide, abandoned infants, and a million Irish expiring in a single food crisis, clearly indicates that Christians should be very concerned about population issues because they are so closely tied to God's call for justice for the defenseless, the poor, and the oppressed. Overpopulation breeds conflict and injustice as resource availability falls, spurring people to wrest limited necessities from one another. The reverse is also true. Injustice breeds over-population and population-related problems. Sexual and social discrimination and political and economic domination all encourage practices or conditions that deny parts of populations basic resources or cause excess mortality among selected groups, such as females, native tribes, or the poor. "Structural violence" may actually stimulate excess population growth, particularly where there are upper. and lower classes. Malthus considered only the responsibility of the individual in not having too many children. Control over the sexual act as such is indeed an individual matter. History tells us, however, that the responsibility for sharing reproductive and other resources goes far beyond the realm of individual control and must also be confronted on the community and societal level, because that is where so much of the economic power lies.

QUESTIONS FOR REFLECTION

1. Does your denomination have a pronatalist, a non-natalist, or an antinatalist position on procreation within the bounds of marriage? What is its position on contraception? Try to trace the development of your denomination's position on procreation historically. Has it originated theologically, socially, or economically? How is it likely to change in the next few decades?
2. How important is late marriage as a contemporary population regulation technique in Western culture? Can you describe any ways the practice has had any long-term impacts on Christian theology or social values?
3. Considering England's role as a colonial power at the time of the potato famine, what economic and social responsibilities did the English actually have to the Irish once the famine struck? What would the best "Christian" policy for England have been?
4. Can you identify some biblical passages that provide ethical guidance in the case of child abandonment? Try to use biblical values or the theological tradition of your denomination to deter-

mine the ethical validity or lack thereof of de facto infanticide as a means of population control.

5. Compare the practice of female infanticide in the Middle Ages to the contemporary possibility of selecting against female infants via genetic gender determination followed by abortion of female fetuses. Are the social and economic factors encouraging these practices similar or different? Can the same ethical arguments be made concerning both?

6. Contact between isolated indigenous peoples and "Europeans" is still occurring. If such contact encourages disease introduction, what are the ethical responsibilities of the "Europeans" concerning this? Are there times when contact should be delayed or should not occur? What responsibilities do Christian missions have in this regard?

5

THE STOLEN BLESSING: POPULATION AND THE ENVIRONMENT

Turning to contemporary issues, we will try first to understand the environmentalists and their distress over unrelenting human population expansion. Professional ecologists agree that human populations have a tremendous potential for growth. They also agree that if a human population gets too large, it will exceed its environmental carrying capacity. The result is often an environmental disaster, such as a famine. If that is the case, we might ask, why not let cultures that are foolish enough to do this go ahead and suffer the consequences? One reason, of course, is the great human suffering this causes, and the other is the impact of millions of humans on the environment itself.

Population expansion in medieval Europe, for example, resulted in more and more land being put to the plow. This ultimately removed much of the forest and wetland and locally extirpated many native animal species, particularly the larger ones such as brown bears and eagles. The big game, in fact, were either driven back to the untillable mountains or found refuge on the hunting preserves of the wealthy. In the British Isles some creatures, such as wild boar, disappeared. By the time St. Francis of Assisi was talking to wolves, they had become rare in the Italian lowlands, and Francis, unlike the monks of earlier eras, rarely met a deer or a wild boar.[1] One major environmental concern is that a growing human population needing more and more space will convert wildlands and the habitats of other species into developed property. Contemporary industry and agriculture so completely disturb the environment that many species are threatened with extinction, not just forced withdrawal to the Italian Alps.

A second environmental problem is that rapidly expanding human populations, in the process of exceeding their food and land resources, usually damage what resources they have. Sustainable rural populations, especially those without access to chemical fertilizers, rotate their tillage so that the same plot is not farmed year after year. This allows the nutrients and the organic matter in the soil to rejuvenate. As population increases, the need for food grows, and farmers drop these fallow periods and thus slowly wear out the soil. Eventually their crops fail, and they must either move on to new lands or, if none are available, face famine and poverty.

The same type of phenomenon occurs on grazing lands when populations begin to exceed the carrying capacity of the land. As more food is needed or more children are produced who want herds of their own, more cattle, sheep, camels, or goats are put out on pasture. Grasses, which are stimulated to grow by mild grazing pressure and can tolerate a moderate amount of trampling by livestock, are eaten down so quickly that the plants cannot recover. The density of the vegetation declines, and wind and water begin to erode the soil surface. Once lush meadows can be reduced to barren sand hills in less than a generation. After the population in the region declines, the land will not produce as it did before, and either far fewer people will maintain herds or those who do will remain in poverty. Population pressures can also encourage people to develop better farming and herding techniques, but often major damage occurs first.

A third environmental problem is that an expanding human population consumes ever-greater quantities of nonrenewable natural resources. (A nonrenewable resource cannot be regrown, although it can sometimes be recycled. Once it is used up, it cannot be replenished.) More people require more petroleum, more natural gas, more copper, and more building stone. Often resource harvest in an environment of expanding need is hurried, and there is less effort made to conserve for the future. Environmentalists fear that dense populations that are based on fast-growth economies based on petroleum will face future shortages as reserves close to the earth's surface are depleted. Petroleum prices will rise, creating a shortage of fuel and social disruption as nations try to adjust to other energy sources.

A fourth environmental problem is that larger populations produce more pollution. Bigger cities and more people mean more power plants and more automobiles. The recent waste crisis surrounding New York City is a sad example of the dilemma. As you run out of land, but keep increasing in size, what do you do with all the garbage? Dumping it in the ocean just sends it washing up on the beaches, or slowly poisons fish. More people on the land also means more soil erosion, which muddies and degrades clear running rivers. In densely populated regions, processing of human and animal waste is a major headache, and improper disposal can lead to outbreaks of disease or water contamination.

FUEL FOR FIRES, LAND FOR GRAIN

The depth and complexity of these issues can best be understood by looking at a few examples of population-related environmental problems. A straightforward case is fuel wood gathering in the developing countries. Many traditional cultures have never converted to fossil fuels (petroleum, natural gas, or coal) as a primary source of household energy and still depend on wood for cooking and heating. Although there are many different methods of wood conservation, cultures "in balance with the environment" do not collect more than local forests and shrublands can produce. Some cultures have maintained woodlots specifically for wood harvest, while others have moved their camps as wood was depleted, only to return when the forests have regrown. More than 2 billion people now rely on wood as their primary source of fuel, and at least 1.5 billion have trouble finding or purchasing enough. By the year 2000 an estimated 2.3 billion will have trouble obtaining wood, and over 350 million people will be coping with acute shortages. Some Third World households already spend two fifths of their cash income or more purchasing firewood.[2] These fuel-wood dependent cultures have not improved their life-styles so that they need more energy per capita, they have increased the number of households so that more people are depending on the same acreage of forests. If their populations increase further, the need and the competition for wood will intensify.

Aside from creating financial distress, the shortage of fuel wood has other unfortunate effects. One is that women, who are usually the wood gatherers, must spend much more time looking for and hauling wood. They may have to walk long distances, possibly two hours or more from home, and thus be away from their gardens and their children for extended periods of time, which harms both agricultural productivity and child care. It also greatly increases their daily workload. If the poorest people in a region cannot afford wood, they cease to cook every meal and cannot regularly boil water. This increases the risk of disease, especially for children, who are very prone to intestinal ailments. Further, once wood is in short supply, gathering of dead wood is replaced by cutting of live trunks and branches, which quickly depletes the ultimate source of the fuel. In the worst cases, slopes are stripped of trees and shrubs, which permits water and wind erosion to remove the soil and also increases the likelihood of flooding and mud slides, since forest vegetation helps to absorb excess rainfall. Increased fuel wood gathering is encouraging the spread of the north African deserts and accelerating the demise of hundreds of thousands of acres of grazing lands.

The gathering of fuel wood is also a critical element in an environmental problem of global scale—the destruction of the tropical forests. Through the entire equatorial region, from Brazil to Zaire to Indonesia, economic and population pressures are felling the most magnificent and biologically diverse forests in the world, while only minor efforts are being made to restore these complex ecosystems once they have been cleared and harvested. The tropical evergreen and seasonally dry forests are of much more than regional ecological importance. They harbor the great majority of the world's terrestrial and freshwater species, including everything from shy, brightly colored birds to diminutive unnamed beetles to formidable mountain gorillas. Unlike temperate broadleaved forests, tropical stands are slow to recover their original species composition after large-scale disturbance. Many of the creatures residing deep in what were once inaccessible jungle tracts have very local distributions and will be lost if an entire watershed or mountain range is cut. The threat of massive extinctions due to tropical forest destruction is a growing reality. By the year 2000 an estimated 20 to 50 percent of all species present at the beginning of this century will be extinct, and most of these will have been lost with tropical forests.[3] Although there is much argument over their role in stabilizing global climate, tropical forests are absorbing carbon dioxide entering the atmosphere from human burning of fossil fuels, and these forests protect thousands of watersheds and hundreds of thousands of acres of very fragile soils. Further, their produce, if well managed, can be of great value to humankind for many decades to come. The rain forests and monsoon forests are famous for their hardwood timber and other products including latex, nuts, fiber, and medicinal compounds.

The human pressures on tropical forests come from several sources. International firms based in Japan, Europe, or the United States are responsible for logging many of the more valuable stands. International economic interests also remove forests to make way for plantation agriculture, cattle ranching, and mining. Funding from corporations and organizations such as the World Bank often only starts the clearing process, however. Sometimes following the commercial logging, sometimes preceding it, armies of displaced peasant farmers, having no land of their own, advance on the remaining areas of virgin soils.

Forest farming via slash and burn methods is a very ancient farming technique, and has been practiced for centuries by the peoples of the Amazon and of central Africa, with little damage to the forests' resources. Traditionally, groups of families clear plots along river banks and then cut the trees and burn them to release precious ash into the otherwise nutrient-poor earth. After this temporary flush of natural fertilizer is exhausted, the farmers move on and start over, only to return to the previous site after many years have passed and the soils have been naturally restored. Today, with increasing population pressure, the traditional long rotations of forest clearing have been shortened, and there is more of an attempt to convert the land to perpetual agriculture. Many tropical areas now have three times the numbers of shifting cultivators as they had in 1950. In addition, subsistence peasants who have not traditionally farmed the forests but are unable to obtain land elsewhere are invading the forest frontier. Such "marginalized" peasants reduced Thailand's forests by 50 percent between 1960 and 1980. Lowland and seacoast farmers who move to the rain forest know little of the cropping methods and fallow rotations of the traditional forest agriculturalists. They thus attempt to put as much land into use as possible, completely removing the forest and preventing its recovery.[4] Forest farmers are difficult to count, but an estimated 300 million people clear forest plots annually.[5] "Each year more than 10 million hectares of mature tropical forest cover are converted to other uses," in addition to the clearing of 5 million acres of secondary forest and 12 million hectares of deforested agricultural lands.[6] Today there are so many fires burning in the tropical forest belt that the heat and smoke can easily be distinguished in photographs taken by satellites.

Population increase is a driving force behind this assault on the forests and may become worse before it becomes better because the populations of the equatorial nations have such a high proportion of children and teenagers who will eventually need land. The move toward new territories is not just stimulated by increasing head count, however. Land tenure systems make it difficult for peasants to own land and concentrate the best agricultural acreage in the hands of a few powerful families. Much like feudal Europe, in "tropical Latin America overall, a mere 7 percent of land owners possess over 90 percent of the arable land, by contrast with the United States, where the largest 7 percent of the farms account for only 27 percent of the farm land."[7] In Latin America the poorest one third of farmers control only 1 percent of the arable land. By the 1980s one of three Kenyan farmers had no land, with perhaps nearly as many "ranking as near landless."[8] The migrants to the rain forest often cannot obtain title to their little hand-cultivated plots, and even if they do, the red, well-leached clay will wear out quickly, and they will be moving on. Eventually, just as Europe ran out of frontier, the tropics will also, and the equatorial nations will have to cope with large numbers of poor settlers with no unoccupied forests to turn into temporarily productive gardens.

The haphazard management of tropical forests is tied to another key population issue, the availability of arable land. A recent publication of a Christian organization providing food for the undernourished proclaimed optimistically, "Only half the world's potentially arable land is under cultivation today."[9] This may be the case, but it depends on what one wishes to call arable, and how much land one wishes to remove from other purposes, such as providing fuel wood. In 1980 there were an estimated 2 to 2.5 billion hectares of arable land worldwide, and about 1.6 billion in cultivation.[10] Much of the remaining land that could be cultivated has shallow, dry, or very acid soils or is on steep slopes or in wet areas and would be better committed to grazing or forestry. The best lands are usually already under cultivation, precisely because they are the best lands.

To add to the problems, desertification and land abuse are making vast regions not just untillable but also totally unusable for any sort of agriculture. In the arid zones, 6 million hectares of land (an area twice the size of Belgium) disappear into the deserts each year, and an additional 20 million "become so impoverished they are unprofitable to farm or graze."[11] The virgin lands opened annually in tropical forests are less than half the area of the lands lost (and most of these new lands will also be abandoned after a few years). Poor irrigation practices, improper cultivation techniques, intensive use by livestock, and other land abuses are degrading at least 375 million hectares of cropland in the drier climatic zones alone.[12] The area of grain harvested worldwide increased 24 percent between 1950 and 1981 and then began to decline. By 1988 it had fallen 7 percent, and it remains just under 700 million hectares.[13]

As population increases worldwide, land shortages, especially in developing countries, will have to be confronted. Even now many of the poorer nations do not have new arable lands available (Haiti, for example, is not land rich), and although some still have substantial frontier zones, population growth in developing countries is hardly correlated to the relative richness of their untouched natural resources. Great opportunities exist for improving land husbandry and restoring damaged lands to fertility. Yet both of these strategies require capital and agricultural expertise. The question is not just the future quality of life and the security of land ownership for the Third World, the question is whether the next generation can and will be fed.

TOO MANY ROADS, TOO MUCH LIGHT?

Pollution is very much tied to consumption, which is in turn linked to the number of consumers. The more automobiles there are traveling the German autobahn or the United States interstate highways, the more carbon dioxide and nitrogen will be released into the atmosphere. The developed world has been having trouble with air pollution since the nineteenth century, and sewage disposal has harassed civilization ever since people consolidated into large villages and cities. Soil erosion and the associated siltation of water courses is as old as the plowed field and the great irrigated empires of Mesopotamia and Babylon. During the twentieth century, however, what were once regional or national problems have become international in scale.

The soot from English factories once rained down primarily on the British. Today, due to tall industrial stacks and myriads of automobiles, acid rain originating in Britain and Germany falls out in Scandinavia and kills Swedish forests. Chlorofluorocarbons rise from every region where refrigeration is used and accumulate in the upper atmosphere, threatening the ozone layer worldwide. Ironically, the first hole in the ozone "shield" appeared over Antarctica, a continent with little dependence on artificial refrigeration. Depletion of ozone will cause an increase in ultraviolet radiation, particularly at the higher latitudes, which in turn could cause a wide variety of problems including a major rise in the incidence of human cancer. Carbon dioxide from the combustion of fossil fuels, primarily in the developed nations, is accentuating the greenhouse effect and slowly raising the average temperatures at the earth's surface. This global change will affect both nations that are culpable and ones that have made little contribution to the problem. Climatic warming may increase desertification in Africa and may dry the interior of the North American continent, causing a loss of agricultural productivity. Most critical is a potential rise in sea level (due to the melting of the polar ice caps and the expanded volume of the slightly warmer sea water). Even a one- or two-foot rise could overwash many coastal lowlands, and a four- to seven-foot (one- to two-meter) rise is anticipated. Some low-lying countries, such as Bangladesh, already are having substantial problems with flooding, and a major increase in sea level would be catastrophic. Unlike Noah's flood, the guilty and the innocent will all float away together—the beach home of the upper-middle-class United States resident and the crops of a poor Asian farmer who has never had enough capital to buy a car will be equal prey for the sea.

Despite its relationship with population, we need to recognize that pollution is not a direct function of head count or household numbers. A high density of humans with a sophisticated sewage treatment system can avoid water pollution, while a low density of humans without septic tanks cannot. Chlorofluorocarbons can be replaced with other less destructive compounds. A nation can be adequately clothed and fed without burning excessive amounts of fossil fuel. Americans and western Europeans consume far more energy per capita than Kenyans or Chinese. In general, however, pollution is associated with population growth, especially accelerated growth.

Demographers are not certain at what level world population will stabilize. Present predictions are in the range of two to three times as many people as there are on the earth right now—or 12 to 16 billion people. Common sense tells us we cannot burn three times as much petroleum as we are burning now—there is not that much oil in the international reserves, even if we start digging much deeper wells and harvesting smaller and less accessible oil fields. Further, just providing fuel oil, coal, or firewood for the numbers of people potentially on earth in the year 2025 will greatly increase the levels of carbon dioxide in the atmosphere and increase the rate of climatic warming. We also will have to get rid of all the sewage, garbage, and toxic chemicals all these people will produce (many of them will be residents of megacities in developing nations), and we will have to decide how to provide them energy without greatly increasing atmospheric contamination. Either quality of life will have to diminish greatly, especially in nations without rich energy resources and advanced pollution control technology, or a superhuman effort will have to be made to prevent worldwide environmental degradation.

AM I CREATION'S KEEPER?

Most Christians would agree that we should love our human neighbors and that we have a responsibility to share resources among the human community. Some might hesitate, however, to consider the environment our neighbor or to be concerned about the resource "needs" of the natural world. When discussing the clearing of the tropical forest, many Christians would assume that if there are people who have no land (and there are many poor campesinos without other resources), that maintaining the integrity of the forest to provide for more careful harvest at some future time is not practical. Where children are starving, the forest must fall and burn.

One of the reasons we so quickly decide against maintaining the forest is that we see ourselves as fighting nature or as displacing it in order to survive. We blithely assume humans have dominion over creation and the right to take what they need for their homes and farms. We rarely stop to ask if this view is theologically correct, or what God's intent for the cosmos actually is (much less if cutting down the rain forest is really solving the social and economic problems of the migrating forest farmer). In making ethical decisions concerning the impact of human population growth on the environment, are we only concerned about shortages of food and fuel needed by humans, or are we concerned about the condition of the creation as well?

It may seem odd, in confronting pollution, extinction, and forest destruction, to return to the very ancient book of Genesis. Genesis, however, is where God's role as Creator and the origin of the cosmos are described. To cope with environmental difficulties, we must have a sound cosmology and a sound theology (or ecotheology) of our interactions with the natural world. We should notice first that in the Genesis creation narratives (chapters 1 and 2), Yahweh acts spiritually and personally to create the universe, although the world spawned by God's effortless word is distinct from God. Creation therefore is not part of God, but it reflects many divine characteristics. The spirit of God is instrumental in the original creative act and continues to interact with humans and the cosmos. If God withdraws the divine spirit, then every creature "must sink down in death."[14]

In Genesis 1:10, after the earth is separated from the seas, "God saw that it was good," and at the termination of the creation event in Genesis 1:31 "God saw everything that he had made, and behold, it was very good." The English translation misses the full meaning of the Hebrew word *tob*, which can mean both "good" and "beautiful"[15] and implies that God had a very favorable view of the original production. The declarations of creation's goodness also imply that creation has inherent worth—the cosmos has a value in its own right and a relationship to God, because God created it. This idea of inherent worth is enhanced by biblical passages describing God's continuing interaction with and love for creation, independent of human presence and need. Psalm 104:10–11, for example, tells us that God's providence keeps "springs gushing in ravines . . . supplying water for wild animals" and that Yahweh provides the rain for the cedars where the birds make their nests. The lions of the forest must claim their food from God, and God satisfies them in their hunger. The Creator takes joy in creation, appreciating even the monstrous sea creatures. The psalm ends by glorifying God and wishing, in verse 31, that "Yahweh find joy in what he creates" (JB).

Psalm 24:1 declares, "The earth is the Lord's and the fullness thereof, the world and those who dwell therein," and Psalm 104:24 concurs, stating, "the earth is full of thy creatures." In the Bible there is no evidence humans own the earth; it remains the property of God simply because God created it. When God speaks to Job from the whirlwind, God reminds Job that the power of creating from nothing and of completely understanding the purposes of creation remains with the Creator and is not a human prerogative.

In the Genesis narrative, when God creates the plants, they are not classified according to their potential for crops or their healing properties, which would relate them only to humans, but by the type of seed they produce, which relates them *both* to humans and to the animals that depend on them. When God fills the seas, the Creator says, "Let the waters teem with living beings, and let the birds fly above the earth across the vault of the heavens. And God created the great sea monsters and every living being that moves, with which the waters teem, each of its kind, and every winged bird, each of its kind. And God saw how good it was" (Gen. 1:20–21, w). These texts emphasize the productivity and the diversity of creation, again, independent of human need. God blesses this assortment of creatures, which includes little slimy worms and big sharp-toothed reptiles, by saying, "Be fruitful and multiply," just as God blesses the first humans.

In addition to the blessing of fertility, in Genesis 1:28 God gives human beings "dominion" over "the fish of the sea and over the birds of the air and over every living thing that moves upon the earth." The commission to rule, however, is limited by the human role as God's servant, or representative, on earth. Humans have an especially close relationship with the Creator and therefore a special responsibility to do the will of God. The Hebrew verbs used in the instruction "to subdue the earth and to take dominion" in Genesis 1:28, are *rada* and *kabas*, which carry a strong connotation of treading down or trampling.[16] There is no reason, however, to assume the author of the passage intended anything other than "the basic needs of agriculture and settlement."[17] The interpretation of Genesis 1:28

must also agree with the interpretation of Genesis 2:15, where God places Adam in Eden to "till it and keep it." The verb *abad*, translated as "to till," implies not only work but also service, and could be translated "to serve" or "to be a slave to." The word *shamar*, "to keep," might also be translated "to watch" or "to preserve."[18] God's power placed humans in Eden to serve and preserve the earth. God then allowed them to eat the fruits of the garden. Nowhere is it stated in the Bible that humans have any rights to subsistence above those of other creatures, and nowhere is it implied humans may do as they please with the earth. Humankind is always bounded by God's will, not just for the biped portion of the cosmos but for nonhuman creation as well.

We should also recognize that the Bible, particularly the Old Testament, treats the land as if it is to be shared by the people of God. Passages in Leviticus and Deuteronomy proclaim a jubilee year when Hebrew families would return to their original patrimonies, thus ensuring that the land could not fall into the hands of a few wealthy people. The ancient law also required farmers to allow travelers to eat from their fields and to permit widows and others in need to glean the fields at harvest time. The presentation of the tithe at the Temple supported the priests, and in every third year was also made available to the widow, the orphan and the sojourner.[19] Divine providence as expressed through creation was never intended to be the sole property of the strong, the wealthy, the competitive, or the powerful.

Biblical creation theology can help us to develop a Christian cosmology that can in turn serve as the basis for making ethical decisions about the interaction between human population growth and the environment. The above passages allow the extraction of several basic principles:

1. Creation has inherent worth before God and is enjoyed by God; therefore, any sort of unnecessary destruction or abuse of the environment grieves God.
2. The earth is the Lord's; therefore, Christian values should guide our use of the earth's resources, and we should honor what belongs to God. We should also willingly share the bounty of creation with our human neighbors.
3. God did not intend for humans to be in conflict with creation. The Christian ideal should be a peaceable kingdom where humans utilize the environment while they also protect and preserve it.
4. The blessing to be fruitful and multiply is a shared blessing.

Humans should not "steal" the blessing from the rest of creation and reproduce to such a great extent that they completely displace other creatures from the earth or greatly inhibit the ability of other species to reproduce.

5. God created a great diversity of species, which fill a myriad of productive ecosystems. Human activities that greatly interfere with either this diversity or productivity are counter to God's original intent.

6. God's providence and blessing continue to flow through creation. If we care for and coexist with the rest of creation in a loving fashion, we will receive the benefits of this blessing. If we deal with creation in an ungodly fashion (hatefully, greedily, or covetously) and plunder its resources, the blessing will fail.

7. Since humans do not have the power to create, they are subject to environmental limits of what God has already made. Despite their special relationship with God, humans are subject to the same natural laws as the animals.

In contemplating human conflicts with creation or among humans dependent on the resources present in the creation, we will find they originate in basic misunderstandings of the human relationship to God. First, a great deal of environmental destruction is due not only to a disrespect for nature but also to blatant disregard of the Golden Rule and of God's intent for our lives. In trying to capture resources before our neighbor has a chance to harvest them, we often leave an environmental wasteland behind. By not caring who drinks the water downstream, we pour pollutants in the river, and much environmental damage is done. Further, environmental abuse is fed by poverty. Our lack of care for one another burdens the entire earth.

Both reproduction and the bounty of creation are blessings to be enjoyed within the limits of divine will. Blessings cannot be wrenched away from others or demanded from God and remain blessings. Every act of procreation must be balanced by acts of stewardship and caring. When we find ourselves overdrafting providence, we should ask ourselves why the springs no longer flow. Our attitudes toward human population growth are reflections of our attitudes toward *both* other people and the community of creation. If we were completely within the will of God, there would be no conflict between caring for our human sisters and brothers and caring for the earth. Are we going to watch and preserve, and keep both the garden and our brother, or will we fertilize eroded fields with the blood of our kindred? Is dominion our execution of our responsibilities before God or our taking whatever we want whenever we want it? How can we best share the blessings and thereby make them grow beyond number?

QUESTIONS FOR REFLECTION

1. Can you think of any cases in your own region where human population expansion has caused serious environmental degradation? How could this have been prevented? Were human numbers the basic problem? Was the speed of population growth the problem? Was careless environmental stewardship the problem?
2. What ethical criteria should we utilize to determine what proportion of potentially arable land we should put into tillage?
3. A number of industrial nations have extensive forests and/or coal reserves, yet they use large volumes of petroleum for fuel. Considering the shortage of firewood in many regions of the developing world, how can this economic behavior be justified? How can energy resources best be shared internationally?
4. What responsibilities do Christians from the developed nations have to prevent phenomena, such as global warming or ozone depletion, that are primarily products of industrial culture? To what extent do you think these sorts of phenomena are related to population growth?
5. If rapid population growth is causing land abuse in a developing country, to what extent do you think displaced or landless farmers should take responsibility and try to modify population trends? To what extent do you think the government of the country ought to try to limit population? To what extent should land reform be the responsibility of the wealthy, professional, or educated social classes?

6

SHOVING CHILDREN
OUT OF LIFEBOATS

Environmental advocates and biologists have hardly been the first and only proponents of zero human population growth, but they have been among the most prolific writers on the topic and have proposed several ethical models of human population regulation (sometimes while denying their own ability to make social ethical statements). These models, particularly "lifeboat ethics" and "triage," are more than the opinions of single authors—they reflect a particular Western mindset. In completing a historic overview of population ethics, we will find that the best-known models of the post–World War II era represent a continuation of the Malthusian approach and have had widespread influence in the industrial nations. Even though these models may not be based on Christian values and may ultimately be unacceptable from a Christian standpoint, we need to carefully examine their suppositions in the light of a worldwide population explosion.

We must recognize first that contemporary environmental thought has been influenced not only by Malthusian but also by Darwinian concepts. Basic ecology texts often suggest that the potential for human population growth is exponential and that the human ability to exceed environmental carrying capacity is an imminent threat. Further, evolutionary theory holds that natural selection determines the characteristics of all species, including human beings. From a scientific perspective, real achievement in physical existence is only accomplished by passing one's genetic materials along to the next generation. In its most developed contemporary form—socio-biology—evolutionary philosophy proposes that altruism in humans and animals is selected if it increases the chances that offspring, siblings, and other near relatives will survive. Altruism directed toward distant relatives is only beneficial if, on the average, it provides some gain for the individual extending the help (in which case it is no longer altruism). The evolutionary models of life on earth are essentially reproductive account books, where the individual or genetically related group leaving the most offspring wins.[1]

The evolutionary model of "being" diverges from the Christian model of "being" primarily in its concept of the individual. In Christ's teachings on the kingdom, the individual has an eternal essence (the soul) and a relationship to God that transcend physical reality. The individual's earthly state is important, yet the individual's relationship to the divine supersedes it. New Testament Christianity, in fact, put much less emphasis on individual reproductive fitness than ancient Judaism did. One's willingness to adapt Christian values in population ethics will depend at least partially on whether one believes there is a resurrection and whether one believes our final state depends on our relationship to God rather than on the number of our progeny. New Testament teaching repeatedly proposes a divestment of personal resources in favor of propagating the kingdom. The New Testament is un-Darwinian when it holds that the disciple should "hate his own father and mother and wife and children and brothers and sisters, yea, and even his own life" (Luke 14:26) (meaning family concerns should be secondary to spiritual concerns) or when the disciple is commanded, "Sell all that you have and distribute to the poor, and you will have treasure in heaven" (Luke 18:22) (implying that giving to others increases otherworldly prosperity). Christianity's universality is, in fact, un-Darwinian in giving Christians obligations to those to whom they are not immediately related (the non-Christian on a remote shore) and to the reproductively unfit (such as the dying or the retarded). Western culture, in holding both Christian principles and modern science (with its this-world-only foundation) in high esteem, is automatically inviting conflict over personal and social reproductive values.

PROGENY VERSUS PROSPERITY

Environmental advocates have identified the "frontier ethic" (also known as the "cowboy ethic") of environmental exploitation and un-regulated human population growth as unacceptable in the industrialized twentieth century. The frontier ethic holds that resources are superabundant or available for the taking and that human beings should harvest what they need when they need it. Further, there is lots of room for humans to expand their populations into "undeveloped" or uncivilized lands (even if indigenous peoples are already residing on the territory), or to harvest the deep oceans. In a version of the frontier model based on human potential for problem solving rather than on the availability of unoccupied space, humans have "scientific supremacy" and thus can solve any problems caused by resource limitation.

Environmentalists, who are not necessarily pessimists by nature, do not believe science can overcome environmental problems as quickly as they are developing unless human societies assist in combatting environmental degradation by making the necessary social and economic adjustments. Biologist Garrett Hardin, in one of the best-known and most controversial of the environmental models for human population regulation, attacked not only human ignorance of resource limitations but also what Hardin saw as dangerous assistance to those who were careless enough to abuse their natural resources. Using metaphor, Hardin described world circumstances as a series of lifeboats, where

> each rich nation amounts to a lifeboat full of comparatively rich people. The poor of the world are in the other, much more crowded lifeboats. Continuously, so to speak, the poor fall out of their lifeboats and swim for a while in the water outside, hoping to be admitted to a rich lifeboat, or in some other way to benefit from the "goodies" on board. What should the passengers on a rich lifeboat do? This is the central problem of "the ethics of a lifeboat."[2]

Each poor lifeboat is assumed to be full or overloaded and sinking. The rich lifeboats are not full but have perhaps fifty passengers and a safe capacity of sixty. What happens if there are one hundred people swimming around a lifeboat carrying fifty?

Hardin rejected "the Christian ideal of being our brother's keeper"[3] out of hand on the grounds that complete justice will produce complete catastrophe. If the rich take all the swimmers into their boat, the boat will swamp and everyone will drown. Hardin also rejected just selecting ten of the needy swimmers, since it would be difficult to decide who to pull into the boat, and the rich boat would lose its safety factor. Further, Hardin assumed that the rich cannot let the poor nations "into the rich boats" because the poor nations are so greatly out-reproducing the rich that even if they don't sink the boat when first admitted, they will eventually. Hardin attempted to prove the danger with a simple example where the rich and poor in a boat start with equal numbers, but with the higher reproductive rate of the poor, eighty-seven years later they outnumber the rich eight to one. He also argued against a world food bank to assist with emergencies such as famines and crop failures on the grounds that such aid prevents the troubled population from dropping back to "normal levels." (Hardin did not attempt to calculate how much additional buoyancy might be provided in the rich lifeboats if armaments and automobiles were dropped overboard, nor did he attempt to calculate reproductive rates in the poor lifeboats if the condition of the poor improved.)

Before taking a critical look at Hardin's "lifeboat ethics," we have to investigate another of Hardin's models—"the tragedy of the commons"—whose suppositions are integral to lifeboat ethics. Hardin suggests that our physical environment, including shared land, air, and water resources, is like an old European or New England community pasture used for grazing sheep and cattle. If a herder is managing land properly, the herder will not put more livestock on the land than the land will bear. Too many sheep, for example, will consume all the grass, and the pasture will lose its productivity as erosion sets in. On common land, there is the temptation for each individual using the land to add one more head of stock than his or her share, thus maximizing production for themselves. If only one herder does this, it will probably make little difference, but if all participate in trying to get the most out of the land for themselves, it will soon be badly overgrazed if not permanently damaged. Hardin comments on Christian and Marxist responses to this dilemma:

> If a pasture is run as a commons open to all, the right of each to use it is not matched by an operational responsibility to take care of it. It is no use asking independent herdsmen in a commons to act responsibly, for they dare not. The considerate herdsman who refrains from overloading the commons suffers more than a selfish one who says his needs are greater. (As Leo Durocher says, "Nice guys finish last.") Christian [or] Marxist idealism is counterproductive. That it sounds nice is no excuse. With distribution systems, as with individual morality, good intentions are no substitute for good performance.
>
> A social system is stable only if it is insensitive to errors. To the Christian [or] Marxist idealist a selfish person is a sort of "error." Prosperity in the systems of the commons cannot survive errors. If *everyone* would only restrain himself then all would be well: but it takes *only one less than everyone* to ruin a system of voluntary restraint. In a crowded world of less than perfect human beings—and we will never know any other—mutual ruin is inevitable in the commons.[4]

From Hardin's perspective, human reproduction can easily overload the commons. Reproductive resources are rarely regulated; thus if one person wishes to have one more child than the next person (and take one more share of the food, water, educational resources, etc.), that is a step toward destroying the environmental resources on which human survival is dependent. Note that Hardin expects Christians to be idealistic in terms of sharing physical and economic necessities. He does not accuse Christendom, as he justifiably might, of ignoring the need to share reproductive resources (or of being just as greedy as their neighbors).

When Hardin's articles on lifeboat ethics were first published, they drew strong criticism that they were anti-people and that aid should not be summarily denied to those who needed it. Many environmentalists, in fact, disagreed with him. Population ecologist Paul Ehrlich proposed a more moderate strategy of "triage," based on a military field medical approach to the injured and dying. During the brutal fighting in the trenches during World War I, doctors were in short supply. The question became which of the injured would be treated first in situations where there were limited numbers of medical personnel or where it was difficult to evacuate the casualties. Reasoning that some of the injured would survive in any case and some would die regardless of what was done for them, the first treated were those who both could be saved and for whom medical treatment might make the difference between life and death. Those with more minor injuries could wait until the more seriously injured had been treated, and those with mortal wounds could forego treatment entirely. Ehrlich suggested that modern developing nations are similar to the injured in battle. Some could be helped by foreign aid or food aid, and some were going to continue on to population disaster regardless. Some, however, will survive without assistance and can probably solve their own environmental and population problems if left alone. Under triage, aid would not be provided to countries that were not taking appropriate steps to help themselves. At the time the concept of triage was first applied to food aid in the mid-1960s, India and China were thought to be beyond help.[5] Today, much of Africa might be considered to be on a fatal and irreversible course to population catastrophe and agricultural disaster.

In 1967 Ehrlich joined other antinatalists in suggesting that further public efforts encouraging birth control and limitation of family size were socially necessary. His book *The Population Bomb* accepted strategies that might be considered coercive, including the milder negative incentives such as taxing extra children or cribs and diapers, and the stronger limitations on individual choices, such as government regulations limiting procreation. (Ehrlich's more recent work expresses concern over the coercive aspects of the Chinese population management program.)[6] Ehrlich also favored abortion when he argued that exposure to culture was the most "humanizing element of the environment"; thus a child was not fully human until after birth. The loss of the fetus was, therefore, merely the loss of a potential human, not an actual human. Ehrlich thought "biologists must take the side of the hungry *living* billions today and tomorrow, not the side of *potential* human beings."[7] The unborn child should not be allowed to compete for resources with one that was already present.

CHRISTIAN IDEALISM?

In reviewing these models from a Christian perspective, rejecting frontier ethics should present few difficulties. Historically, frontier ethics has created numerous environmental and social problems and has generated case after case of wasteful natural resource use. Viewing the earth as a bountiful practice ground for human folly is hardly what the Psalmist meant when singing, "The earth is the Lord's and the fullness thereof." Frontier ethics is also tied to an optimistic form of humanism that assumes people can overcome any problem. This deviates from biblical concepts of human sin and dependence on the divine. Today, frontier ethics is generating more economic problems than it is temporarily relieving.

Lifeboat ethics and triage present more of a theological challenge. As environmental ethicist K. S. Shrader-Frechette points out, Hardin's and Ehrlich's versions of lifeboat ethics raise two key questions: Should the interests of the rich passengers be placed ahead of the interests of the poor passengers, and does "ultimate ecosystemic well-being" have "a higher value than equitable distribution of resources in the present."[8] Lifeboat ethics places the interests of the rich in opposition to those of the poor and the interests of humans against those of the environment. Both lifeboat ethics and triage sincerely believe in evil outcomes if individual people are left to their own devices without the intervention of more knowledgeable biologists and government officials.

In 1971 Richard J. Neuhaus published a Christian critique of the environmentalist views of the time, which accused Hardin and Ehrlich of being "anti-people." Neuhaus complained that "the literature of the movement is marked by a moving reverence for the 'seamless web of life,' accompanied by a shocking indifference to the weaker and less convenient forms of human life and by an almost cavalier readiness to disrupt the carefully woven web of civility and humane values."[9] Neuhaus asserts that lifeboat ethics places the needs of lower forms of life above those of the poor while it encourages society to care for nature rather than for people who are starving. Although Neuhaus was expressing a very common Christian sentiment, we must be careful to examine the key elements in the models before rejecting them completely. We must also determine if Neuhaus was too quickly dismissing very serious socioeconomic and environmental problems.

In the case of Ehrlich's triage model, Shrader-Frechette suggests, for example, that if one assumes aid cannot be made available to everyone, triage is merely a way of trying to save as many people as possible. One cannot, in a crisis, dismiss it as antilife. The real issue is whether the present state of the environment really has reached crisis proportions and whether famine due to excess population growth is unavoidable. If some countries really have passed the point of no return in terms of population overload, then triage could be humane because it directs resources toward those nations that still have an opportunity to avoid high mortality.[10] However, situations can change. For example, at the time Ehrlich proposed triage, China appeared to be on a hopeless course in terms of population growth. Whether or not we approve of how China altered her direction, there can be little doubt that she has. China's unexpected recovery should also remind us that the fate of a nation suffering famine or shortages is never so absolute as the death of an individual. People struggle through disasters, and children survive deprivation. Triage is a strategy aimed at dealing with absolute states—life or death. We cannot with any certainty declare a nation terminally ill. Even in worst-case scenarios, some individuals survive and can benefit from international assistance.

The example of Mother Teresa of Calcutta and her ministry to the dying presents an interesting lesson in our cultural perceptions of "terminal conditions." Mother Teresa initiated ministry specifically to people who were thought to be beyond medical help. Many of those whom she and her sisters have taken in from the street actually have died (in an atmosphere of peace and caring instead of despair), while many have recovered and have been released cured. Mother Teresa's ministry is effective because it is based on hope, is willing to cope with a poor prognosis, and considers the spiritual worth of the person rather than reproductive or economic productivity.

Among the real dangers of Ehrlich's model are its crisis orientation and its declaration that some nations are in a hopeless state and cannot be constructively aided. Ehrlich uses a prophecy of impending disaster to rationalize potentially coercive methods (more about this in chapter 10) and to declare that some "potential" humans should not be added to the "real" humans already tilling the fields and filling the cities. Shrader-Frechette notes that the crisis mentality "somehow justifies circumventing the time-consuming and sometimes-frustrating process of democracy and the inconvenient dictates of justice."[11] Neuhaus goes a step farther and compares the views of environmentalists who believe that the realities of natural processes must dominate human choices to those of National Socialism (i.e., the Nazis). Although the comparison is extreme and appears to be unjustified, Neuhaus correctly notes that Hitler thought humans were only on the correct course when they submitted to the laws of nature, a philosophical position that then allowed the dictator to sacrifice human lives and liberties to an immutable natural order.[12] Narrow Malthusian thinking does present the danger that we will become so convinced that natural laws hold sway that we will not attempt to wrestle with the basic spiritual issues or with the concerns of individual human beings. Or as was the case with the Irish potato famine, ceding to natural laws will become an excuse for not correcting economic or social injustice.

One of the central questions for Christians concerning the triage model is not whom we should help, but why we do not have enough "physicians." We also should ask ourselves (as we should in the case of warfare) why, considering the impacts of famine, poverty, and underdevelopment in nations with large Christian populations, so many Christians are among the casualties. We have to consider not only that our perception of those who are beyond hope may be incorrect but also that our perception of our ability or inability to aid them may be false. Further, Western Christians need to evaluate their nations' economic or military activities as factors that potentially maintain poverty and its associated unrelenting population growth in developing nations. We may theoretically reject Ehrlich's thinking as crisis oriented, but at least Ehrlich is attempting to do something to avert human suffering. Can Christians criticize his model without challenging his basic assumption that there will never be enough aid and enough resources for all? Can Christians constructively help those thought to be hopeless cases?

WHOSE CHILDREN SINK OR SWIM?

Hardin's lifeboat ethic portrays helping the poor lifeboats both as a potential threat to the rich and as detrimental to those who might survive in the poor lifeboats. The model is in many ways socially and economically unrealistic. First, the resources of the poor and rich lifeboats are not separate—many of them are shared. The rich lifeboats may actually be removing supplies from the poor ones. A developing country that raises coffee, tea, or cocoa (or cocaine plants) is producing luxury agricultural products for the international market, not food for its own people. Crops such as coffee may produce more monetary income per acre than upland rice, but the dollars acquired in trade are not necessarily reinvested in buying grain abroad (and much of the profit of these transactions goes to international financial interests). Further, the poor lifeboats have to compete with the rich ones for products useful in agriculture, like petroleum for making fertilizer and running machinery. Greater sharing of resources between the rich and poor nations might indeed lead to less comfort in the rich lifeboats, but the analogy of the poor piling into the rich lifeboats is inappropriate (and seems to reflect a deep fear of the "haves" of losing what they have to the "have nots")—it is more a question of how many rich lifeboats will sink without coffee.

Hardin's analogy also gives the impression the lifeboats are all the same size. Actually, some boats are much larger than others relative to the number of people they carry. The contemporary world situation is really more like an armada of destroyers and supertankers running down fleets of wooden fishing boats. Very few children from the poor vessels can actually enter the rich ones—the mere distance of the poor from the rich prevents the poor from swamping the rich craft.

A key issue in these models is the role of *distributive justice*, or the just sharing of resources among people. Hardin clearly rejects its importance, and Ehrlich diverts from the question by proposing that there are not enough physicians—or put in other terms, Ehrlich concludes that the needs of everyone cannot be met. As Shrader-Frechette points out, Hardin assumes "that since perfect justice is impossible . . . , we have no obligations to justice at all" and that "the rich nations have the right to decide who will live and who will die."[13] The Bible, in contrast, presents justice as resting in the hands of a righteous God, and the poor as God's special concern. Christ's teachings in the New Testament never set the complete disappearance of poverty and need as an earthly goal, yet they call for Christ's followers to forget themselves and give to others as best they can. The rich lifeboats of Hardin's metaphor thus seem, from a biblical perspective, much like the full barns of the rich man who found God calling for his soul before he was expecting it and discovering too late that his great piles of grain were going to do him no eternal good.

The Roman world was as stressed as ours is in terms of food resources, perhaps even more so. Famines with fatalities were frequent, and the Levant was probably overpopulated. Yet early Christian teaching emphasizes justice in distribution of material resources. Are Christian teachings too naive and outmoded to deal with a "modern problem," or are Christian teachings a very venerable and humane way of dealing with difficulties that are centuries old? As Christians, we might experiment with reversing Hardin's and Ehrlich's models, both of which center on whom we should abandon, and ask whom we should rescue. We can, for example, see ourselves as sailors on stormy seas who have no way of knowing which boats will make it safely through and which are likely to sink. (Christians from industrial nations should see themselves as possessing powerful cutters and launches.) Suppose we try to help whomever we can, be it those boats closest to us or those that have clearly been damaged. If we don't offer assistance, some boats may sink unnecessarily. Helping another boat entails a risk. Yet without the willingness to take risks, no one in trouble will ever be aided. (This is one of the points of the parable of the good Samaritan.) Hardin's model assumes that world problems with food resources and overpopulation cannot be solved without massive death and disaster. And perhaps Hardin is right, but if we don't try to dispense love and justice we will never know if the evil of the present situation can be overcome—we will passively succumb to it.

From a Christian perspective, if we reject Hardin's model as callous and economically inappropriate, we still have to ask whether his supposition that providing aid to the poor may actually harm them might sometimes be true. Hardin, however, rejects aid in general, rather than discriminating between useful and nonuseful aid. Hardin also assumes that if the rich lifeboats help the poor ones, the aid will probably be in terms of food. Actually, the aid can be in other forms such as educational assistance, industrial development, or medical technology, including the provision of contraceptives or the techniques for making them. Believing that aid is damaging might actually inhibit the developed countries from providing assistance specifically in the area of population control. (Aid in population regulation is often linked to other programs.) Just as we should not abandon justice because our actions may be inadequate to resolve a problem completely, we should not pursue inadequate solutions if we have an opportunity to do something more appropriate.

Unfortunately, providing emergency assistance, even very appropriate assistance, always falls a step short of true distributive justice. If a nation is really going to have food security, then it must have enough economic and technological control over its own resources to ensure a continuous flow of goods and services. Donating food may provide immediate relief from famine but rarely resolves the underlying social or economic difficulties that led to food shortage. Ultimately, justice results from equitable land tenure systems and sustainable agriculture. It also arises from chances to complete school, get a dependable job, or start a business. Hardin is probably right when he suggests that aid is not the answer, but he is right for the wrong reason. Hardin believes justice is not possible and that aid worsens population and land abuse problems. From a Christian perspective, aid is not the ultimate answer because God's justice is possible and is vastly superior to charity, especially to the one on the receiving end.

A last issue presented by Hardin and Ehrlich is, Dare we use resources to relieve current problems at the risk of damaging the interests of future generations? What about "ultimate ecosystemic well-being"? What if we allow the atmosphere and our agricultural lands to deteriorate? Hardin assumes we have already reached the point where many lifeboats will necessarily sink. Ehrlich assumes the unborn will steal the birthright from those already walking the earth. Neuhaus, in contrast, suggests that placing the needs of "lower forms of life" above those of poor humans is anti-people.

On one hand, we can ask ourselves, Is present accelerated population growth causing permanent natural resource damage? The answer is yes; even now some regions are producing less food and firewood than they were a generation ago. This damage, however, is probably not necessary, even at present population levels, and we could, *with proper resource management and equitable distribution of critical resources,* feed and care for the population we have, at least on a worldwide basis. (Some regions, particularly those with dry climates, would require substantial ecological restoration to support their present populations; thus population reduction may now be necessary for their indigenous residents to survive in the long run.) Further, there is no technological reason that the world population could not slowly decline or that the richer nations could not reduce their resource consumption. Only human will stands in the way. Without concern for land degradation and the condition of both agricultural and wild ecosystems (including those lower forms of life), we really may unnecessarily destroy resources that not only could be left for our grandchildren but that we also might need ourselves in the next ten years.

We need to recognize, however, that sharing and distributing resources will not cause future disaster nearly as fast as not sharing them will. (See chapter 8 for a discussion of the direct relationship between distributive justice and population reduction.) Further, we cannot throw the needs of people against those of creation. Perhaps we can't get very excited about protecting "lower organisms," but if the land dies, the people die with it. As discussed in chapter 5, God expects us to care for the earth and care for our neighbors.

Individual nations may already be in serious trouble, but the world community has the resources to assist them, and they may be able to slowly improve their own situations by confronting environmental and population problems. Rather than assume that a disastrous outcome cannot be averted and that the rich cannot afford to help the poor because it will make things worse, we might ask what responsibilities both the rich and the poor have to resolve the present situation and defuse future crisis. Hardin sees overreproduction as a problem of the poor but does not see overconsumption as a problem of the rich. His portrayal of the source of the crisis is one-sided and also assumes no positive action on the part of the poor lifeboats. What responsibilities do Christians from different nations and different social classes have in coping with present food shortages and in "protecting" the interests of potential humans, the unborn and the future generations?

CHRISTIAN MODELS?

Any analysis based on biblical teachings about the poor is likely to reject lifeboat ethics. We have to ask ourselves, however, whether Christians have anything to offer that is better. Faith and hope without a program are as likely as Hardin's dire forecasts to result in sunken vessels. Dare we reject triage until we have found a better, more humane strategy? At the moment Christians appear to be willing to provide food in cases of famine while they are unwilling to confront population issues or to consider what the future might hold for those already suffering. When famine repeatedly strikes the same area, do we follow Garrett Hardin and give up and go home? Is there a Christian alternative to shoving poor children out of lifeboats?

We will divert, in the next chapter, from the problem of population growth to that of population decline. Paul Ehrlich and other authors like him have convinced the middle class of the developed nations that reducing population growth is a noble pursuit. Social conviction in combination with economic pressures has, in fact, resulted in population stabilization or decline in some of the wealthier nations. Not everyone agrees that zero population growth is beneficial, however, and some Christians are voicing concerns about the demographic trends. The remainder of the volume will return to the issues raised by Malthus, Hardin, and Ehrlich and will attempt to apply biblical principles to problems Hardin holds will only be worsened by a Christian response.

QUESTIONS FOR REFLECTION

1. Can you name any nations in the world today that have exceeded their environmental carrying capacity? How do you know this?
2. Are there circumstances where Christians might consider triage as the appropriate strategy in Christian ministry to the poor? What are they? What do you think Teresa of Calcutta would have to say about triage?
3. To what extent do industrial nations "take" needed resources from less developed nations? Do you think the economic relationships between the developed and less developed nations are generally helpful or harmful to the less developed nations?
4. Do you think that caring for lower forms of life is necessary or unnecessary to long-term human survival on earth? Is Neuhaus's view realistic? Can you identify a point where neglecting the natural environment in favor of protecting people becomes self-defeating?

7

THE "DECLINING"
DEVELOPED NATIONS

Many Christians from the economically favored segments of world society are presently participating in the processes of population stabilization and decline. The trend toward lower fertility not only involves entire nations, such as Switzerland and Germany, but also has long affected relationships between different social classes and ethnic groups. In the United States, for example, both immigration and differential birthrates are slowly increasing the percentage of minorities, while the white middle class is proportionately decreasing. Through the next two decades, the percentage of black and Hispanic students will continue to increase in United States high schools, although the total number of students has been declining and will not show a major increase. Sometime before 2030, the United States may reach zero population growth. The major factor determining when and if this will occur is not the birthrate of United States citizens, which despite a baby boomlet is remaining relatively low, but the amount of legal and illegal immigration from surrounding nations. Relatively low birthrates for the white middle and upper classes can become a sensitive political issue in nations such as South Africa, where whites are already outnumbered by native Africans, coloreds, and Asian immigrants.

Although population decline has not received the public attention that population growth has, a number of social critics have chastised the West or Western Christians for their indifference to childbearing. Books such as *The Birth Dearth* by Ben Wattenberg[1] and *Age Wave* by

Ken Dychtwald[2] have brought some of these impending potential social changes to the attention of the reading public. Harold O. J. Brown in an editorial in *Christianity Today*[3] criticized denominations with declining birthrates and suggested Christians from industrial nations ought to meet biblical mandates to reproduce.

Authors such as Wattenberg and Brown pose a series of key ethical questions for Western Christians. One needs to decide, first, if their arguments for increasing the reproductive rate of white technologists are legitimate and, second, even if their arguments are rejected, if population decline should be encouraged or discouraged. We will begin by looking at Wattenberg's major concerns, which are primarily based on secular values but have important implications for Christian ethics.

The first of *The Birth Dearth*'s arguments is that population decline among those of European extraction will result in a loss of Western cultural values and influence worldwide, particularly the values of liberty and democracy.[4] Wattenberg sincerely believes the Third World, including the poorest nations, needs the industrial nations to improve their situation. Western culture provides much of what is good and new in the world, and population decline would restrict its innovation, its cultural dominance, and its transmission to nonindustrial and even Communist societies.

Second, Western democracies will be increasingly outnumbered by the populations of the nations of the former Communist bloc and the Third World. Wattenberg estimates that the "industrial democracies" constituted 22 percent of the world population in 1950 and 15 percent in 1985, and that they will constitute 9 percent in 2030 and 5 percent by 2100.[5] Wattenberg's book was written prior to the loosening of the Soviet grip in eastern Europe, but he rightly predicts that nonwhite cultures will become more prominent and play a greater role in international trade and international politics. They will also vastly outnumber the West in cases of armed conflict.

A third concern is that the United States and western Europe will lose international power and world leadership. There will be a shortage of younger men to serve in the armed forces. For Wattenberg, the torch of freedom is protected by the North Atlantic Treaty Organization, which is about to be severely understaffed.

In the fourth place, population decline will cause problems for the elderly, such as loss of social security support, and will require extensive reallocation of resources, such as the closing of schools and the opening of more nursing homes. As the ratio of the elderly to younger workers increases, a much greater proportion of the salary of younger workers will be needed to maintain the social security system. There will be less innovation and lower production per capita. This will have an economic impact that will influence the lifestyles of people of all ages.[6]

Finally, families will miss the emotional satisfaction of having children. An important life experience will be lost for many couples. Women who marry late or delay childbearing may eventually want a child and find themselves infertile. The only child will miss having brothers and sisters and will be spoiled rotten by four doting grandparents.[7]

CHRISTIANITY OR EURO-AMERICAN CULTURE

Wattenberg's arguments are, of course, ethnocentric. He assumes his own culture is better than any other. He also neglects the fact that Western Europeans had a tremendous increase in both total population and territory occupied worldwide during the colonial era and that much of this gain was at the expense of other ethnic and racial groups. One also needs to remember that some nations with high population growth rates may not belong to the "industrial democracies" but are still primarily European in terms of population origin and social organization. The developed Euro-American nations control much of the world's economy. The cultures originating somewhere between ancient Greece and Victorian Britain thus seem unlikely to disappear any time soon.

From a Christian perspective, we have to ask whether Western cultural values are the same as Christian values, and the answer is, of course, no. Christianity did not arise in western Europe, in industrial society, or in a democracy. Its roots are in a poor, politically oppressed, agricultural region of the Middle East. Although Christianity may have stimulated the rise of democracy and of Western technology—or at least encouraged a philosophical climate suitable for their development—the spread of Christianity is not dependent on the cultural prevalence of Western technology or of Western political systems. Many of the "industrial democracies" have declining church attendance and are moving into the so-called post-Christian era. Germany and Great Britain produce fine biblical scholars and very little religious fervor. Meanwhile, Christianity has been holding its own in Eastern Europe and the Soviet Union, where churches have grown despite political oppression and a lack of seminary-trained leadership. Western industry had made considerable inroads in oil-rich Arab nations, but Christianity has made almost no converts in some of the countries most willing to associate technology with the

West. At the same time, some poorer regions of Africa, caught between unstable governments and faltering economies, have experienced major church expansion. Pentecostalism and evangelicalism have greatly increased their influence in Latin America, in revitalization movements that appear to be independent of both economic improvement and the institution of truly democratic governments. Technological sophistication, wealth, and the presence of stable democratic governments are not correlated with the growth of the church. Biblical Christianity did not belong to any particular race or culture, nor will Christianity in the twenty-first century.

It is not within the realm of this book to determine whether declining populations in the industrial West will lead to the eventual reduction of military or social influence. It is fair to conclude, however, that Western-style elected governments do protect religious freedoms and often, although not invariably, help to prevent persecution of religious minorities. The progress of Christianity, however, has never been guaranteed by a favorable government, nor been completely stopped by an unfavorable one. Confusion of Christianity with other Western values, such as information technology or Euro-American economic dominance of non-Western cultures, has long been a problem on the mission field. Today, Christianity often finds itself competing with Western culture internationally. The "industrial democracies" are associated with video players, rock and roll, material prosperity, military interference, fossil fuel consumption, sexual license, economic exploitation, and nuclear arms development. Some of the values Wattenberg wishes to export are Christian, and many definitely are not.

Subtly buried in Wattenberg's arguments is an old problem, that of touting racial or cultural superiority. Should the white Anglo middle class in the United States, England, or South Africa reproduce with more vigor to prevent a proportionate increase in nonwhite populations? If one follows Wattenberg's reasoning on a domestic basis for the United States, we would conclude that the increase in black youth will lead to cultural decline and an increase in white offspring would be desirable to maintain "educational quality" in high schools and colleges, which would be better for blacks than their expanding in relative numbers. This reasoning, however, always leads to the conclusion that ethnic minorities (or majorities) should not have control of their own destinies, because these destinies are culturally inferior.

A key ethical issue that is often buried under other arguments is whether in cases where minority groups are increasing in numbers at a greater rate than the majority or the ruling class, the advantaged have an obligation to maintain levels of social services and to provide expanded advancement opportunities. In an urban United States school or state university system with increasing numbers of black, Native American, and Hispanic students, the white middle class may, for example, find itself increasingly personally disinterested in these publicly funded educational institutions. Does the white middle class have an ethical obligation to support taxation that in turn supports the schools? One should note that there is also a question of long-term community benefit here. If the schools are allowed to decline and very few minorities graduate with technical skills or strong educational backgrounds, is this productive or counterproductive for the welfare of the white middle class in the long run?

NATIONS TURNING GRAY

Wattenberg's concern for the care of the aged is a realistic one for nations with declining populations and certainly has implications for Christian ministries. Instability in population structure does lead to social stresses and changes in the distribution of social services. Despite this, the tremendous population growth of the early industrial era could not have continued indefinitely, and the question is now how to best accommodate the stabilizing trend. Western industrial economies developed in social environments with high rates of reproduction and human mortality. They were based on young labor and cheap labor—either from the urban poor, from immigrants, or from colonial peoples. Through the industrial era, however, scientists and social reformers have also set improved life-styles and longer lifespans as goals modern technology—a goal that has been achieved.

In the early industrial period in Britain, a child started work at twelve years of age or younger and worked until he or she died or was disabled by an accident or illness. By the beginning of the nineteenth century, child labor had been restricted, but there were still relatively few retirees. Today, a majority of the people in industrial nations reach retirement age and live for a least a few years when they are no longer working. Even if we correct for the fact that much of the increase in life expectancy over the last hundred years has been due to a decline in infant mortality, we still find a significant increase in life expectancy for the retirement years. In the United States in 1900, a person still alive at age 45 could expect to live to be 69.8 years old. In 1980 the 45-year-old could expect to live to 77.1 years. If we assume a typical retirement begins at age 65, the worker in 1900 could expect to be retired for 4.8 years. By 1980 the post-65 retirement period had extended two and a half times, to 12.1 years.[8]

The industrial democracies, needing literate and well-trained labor, have not only added the "retirement period," they have also increased the length of childhood dependence on either family or governmental support. The children of the middle class stay in college until they are about twenty-one or twenty-two, and those who go on for graduate degrees will probably not be working full time until they are between twenty-five and thirty years old (perhaps older). The residents of the industrial democracies therefore spend proportionately fewer years working for each year lived than did their early industrial ancestors.

At the beginning of the twentieth century, most elderly people in Western society either continued to work or were cared for by relatives, including not only children but also siblings, nephews, nieces, and cousins. Some elderly people were assisted by long-time neighbors who brought food and supplies. Both kinship and social bonds thus provided aid. Once incapacitated for work, the elderly would often be carried off by the various epidemic and contagious diseases, such as tuberculosis, that spread so readily in crowded Western communities. There were relatively few unemployed elderly per working adult. Today, the mobile nuclear family has become separated from other family members, requiring an increase in social services provided by the community (which are generally more expensive than care provided by the family). Costly long-term medical care for the aged was once rare because relatively few older people survived major illnesses, but today it is commonplace. The typical government-operated social security system is based on individuals and their spouses, not on the extended family. If you pay money into the social security system, only you and your spouse can benefit (and in some cases, dependent children). Your brother cannot withdraw the money, nor can your aunt or cousin, nor can your adult child.

Through the history of the Social Security system in the United States, the number of workers per retiree has declined. In 1989 there were 3.3 workers per retiree, a ratio expected to fall to a low of 1.9 workers per retiree by 2030.[9] This is not, however, solely due to a long-term fertility decline. The crude birthrate in 1936 was 18.4 children per thousand. This shot up to a peak of 25.3 in 1954, then fell below 15 by the mid-1970s and rose slightly to 16 by 1982.[10] When Social Security started, fertility was low, but there were also few eligible older workers in the system. The baby boomers, who are from a period of high fertility followed by a period of low fertility, will encounter a support deficit. This did not happen to workers born prior to the 1930s because fewer of them belonged to the system, and many of those who did retired after the baby boomers started working.

Wattenberg implies that increasing fertility will help to support retirees. But is this really true? Wattenberg does not compare the expense of raising children to the costs of retirement. Nor does Wattenberg look at other options for increasing the overall social security pool, such as more working wives and delayed retirement. In the real middle-class world, the costs of children are socially weighed against those of retirement. As many middle-class parents know, sending junior to the best liberal arts college may cost over $80,000. If the college costs for three children were placed in a retirement account instead, the account could produce over $30,000 a year for more than a decade. We should also note that although the Social Security system is supported by younger workers, many pension systems and savings-based retirement funds provide returns from individual contributions. The costs of raising children do, therefore, compete with the costs of retirement.

We should accept Wattenberg's concern that declining population may cause support difficulties for the elderly, but this does not rationalize promoting sudden population growth. A sudden increase in children might in fact be counterproductive, because they would need more social services and new facilities. The solution, instead, seems to lie in the overall Western attitude toward who should work and for how long. Wattenberg's concept of an ever-growing population, which assumes that a large pool of young workers will help pay for retirees (and their wives), also implies that each person should spend more in retirement than he or she contributed to retirement funds during his or her working life. This was actually a fair assumption back at the beginning of the century, when many workers did not live long enough to retire (so those that survived "won" the pension fund). Today, however, most people live to retirement age and plan to draw benefits. The industrial nations now have to cope with demographic phenomena that are actually the product of such social successes as expanded medical research and the growth of an educated middle class. Ultimately, the industrial world will have to balance the retirement accounts so that investments equal withdrawals.

Wattenberg suggests that a "gray" economy may lack innovation and initiative. Here we have to determine if Christian cultural values concerning aging are realistic. Western culture usually assumes that older people will be socially conservative and will tend to favor the status quo. The culture may also foist a "dependent" or "less productive" image on an older adult who has no wish to be either. As Ken

Dychtwald points out in *Age Wave,* Western culture, particularly American culture, "is deeply gerontophobic." Most of the cultural myths about aging are not true. Older workers, except in jobs requiring strenuous physical effort, are as productive as younger workers, and there is very little loss of mental capability for most people until they are very old, that is, in their middle to late eighties.[11] If we wish to extend life expectancy, then we need to make a healthy cultural adjustment to the changing age distributions. Redefining roles and expectations for different age groups is a more productive way of dealing with change than attempting to keep a low percentage of elderly in populations by producing as many children as possible.

Wattenberg's fifth point, that parents will miss the satisfaction of having children, certainly does apply in cases of severe population decline. If most families have one, two, and occasionally three children, however, populations can remain stable, and most couples will experience the joy of raising a child. Large families may indeed have emotional benefits. As the cultural mean, however, they assume high rates of population growth and, usually, high rates of child or adult mortality. As always, there are tradeoffs involved. The child of a large family may enjoy the company of brothers and sisters but may find other resources are more limited, such as funds for college or his or her parents' time. Late marriage in Western culture is no longer purposefully utilized for birth control but is most often dictated by educational, vocational, and economic circumstances. The question for the Christian community is, How can the resources to raise children best be shared?

A MULTITUDE OF BELIEVERS

Aside from approaching secular and Western industrial concerns about population decline, we also need to investigate some specifically Christian issues. These may be summarized as follows:

1. Population decline will mean a loss of Christian values and influence (a Christian version of the primary argument of Wattenberg, i.e., cultural values require large numbers of people to ensure their spread).
2. If Christian families have fewer children, there will be a lack of younger people to carry out Christian missions. Production of more Christians is a family calling. In addition, some denominations are now declining and may eventually disappear or merge with other groups due to lack of new members.

3. Traditional Christian values are best maintained by large families with several children to provide a variety of social relationships.
4. Population decline disobeys biblical commands to be fruitful and multiply and disregards biblical valuing of children.
5. Many middle-class couples have become self-centered and do not wish to have children because doing so interferes with their activities and interests. Having children would help to remove this self-centeredness.

In evaluating the first four arguments, we have to return to our analysis of biblical principles concerning children and families in chapter 3. The passage instructing us to be fruitful is a blessing rather than an unrelenting command. The early church emphasized evangelization and ministry to others for spreading the gospel and Christian values, rather than relying primarily on reproduction. Most people will only raise a few children to adulthood, while they can minister to dozens during the same interval. The family is, of course, important, and the Scriptures hold the nurturing of godly offspring in high regard (see, e.g., Paul's comments concerning Timothy's upbringing). Children are valued citizens of the kingdom. Whose children they are, however, is not the critical issue. We should also note that some biblical leaders, such as David, came from large families, while others, such as Isaac and John the Baptist, came from small ones.

Some individuals may choose not to reproduce so that the church can grow through their less distracted efforts. Others may wish to have children but are not able to. It should be remembered that any decline of Western Christianity is not due to declining population but to declining interest in belonging to and attending churches. Having more children does not attack this problem at its spiritual roots. The point has never been to produce biologically the most Christians, it has always been to bring the gospel and love of Christ to as large a proportion of the people as possible. The church is growing by leaps and bounds in some regions of the developing world. If Euro-American nations that are historic bastions of Christianity are stabilizing their populations, will it make any difference to overall Christian missions internationally? Perhaps if Christianity is declining in the industrial democracies, the highest priority for Christians from the developed nations should be to minister to their own home communities.

The central question for Christians is not whether we are raising children but whether we are reaching out to others. In this regard the fifth concern, that middle-class couples do not wish to have children because they do not wish to share, is by far the most serious charge. This deep spiritual problem can extend to Christian families with children as well. If the Western Christian family becomes an ingrown and self-serving institution largely pursuing its own interests and the interests of other similar families in its home church, it will have lost a key message of the New Testament. Is the couple who just don't have any time for children any worse off than a man who needs a son as an ego extension but doesn't spend any time with the boy, or a couple who become so preoccupied with their own offspring that they ignore the needs of the world at large? Can a couple who are justifiably busy at home with three young children feel free to judge a childless couple who are spending their weekends working with refugees, supervising a church youth group, or ministering to the homeless?

Changes in population age structure should be an important concern for Christian ministry. A population with a high percentage of older people obviously needs different distributions of ministries than a population with a high proportion of children. Further, an aging population does influence evangelization and Christian outreach. Currently, in the "industrial democracies" most Christian conversions are among the young, especially among adolescents (although many professionals with young families have returned to the fold in recent years). Again, cultural prejudices are important. We may see the young as being open to spiritual change and the most important recipients of educational efforts, but outreach ministries can also target older adults. The Western tendency to think of the church as already in the hands of the gray and aging may limit Christian perception of who can benefit from ministry in a nation with a stabilizing population.

Christians from the industrial nations need to recognize the degree to which economics and life-styles are controlling their social values. In societies with long periods of financial dependency and long life expectancies, large families offer numerous disadvantages. Christian communities need to adjust to these conditions (however tempting remaining in the bucolic agricultural past might be). On one hand, it is not the domain of Christian ethics to resolve the financial quandaries of the industrial middle class (actually the world's wealthy). On the other hand, the status of older people (particularly the socially marginalized, such as widows) is discussed in numerous biblical passages and should be a major concern of the Christian community. Books such as *Biblical Perspectives on Aging: God and the Elderly*[12] by J. Gordon Harris and *Affirmative Aging: A Resource for Ministry*,[13] edited by Lorraine D. Chaiventone and Julie A. Armstrong, provide theological foundations for Christian approaches to the increasing proportion of the elderly in Western society. The Christian community should not only reflect on and evaluate its own attitudes toward aging and the aged, it should also recognize that both population increases and declines stress societal resources.

By adding more children, Christians from the industrialized nations will do little to thwart societal changes initiated by Western economic systems, and they could accelerate consumption of limited world resources if they attempted to maintain current life-styles at greatly increased population levels (a problem covered in more detail in the last chapter). The solution for the developed world is not to encourage reproduction but rather to encourage appropriate social responses to a changing demographic profile, including an increasing percentage of older citizens and, in some countries, increased percentages of minority or immigrant youth. Christians who are "haves" need to consider the impact of population trends on the "have nots" and minister to those who suffer poverty, loss of critical resources, societal abandonment, or isolation because they are "too many"—be they infants, teenagers from the ghetto, or the aged and the infirm.

HOW MANY HAMBURGERS?

A last population issue concerning the industrial democracies is whether consumption rates should be considered in determining which nations are overpopulated. If we rated population problems not by total head count but by magnitude of environmental resource consumption and environmental damage, we would quickly come to the conclusion that some of the industrial democracies have the worst population problems in the world. Industrial nations and communities with extensive utilization of twentieth-century technologies are usually heavy consumers of energy, mineral, and food resources, not to mention forest products such as paper. A child in one of these communities therefore adds more waste to world systems, demands more mining and oil exploration, and uses more grain than a child in a developing nation. Many industrial nations, particularly in Europe, have much higher population densities per unit area than developing nations that are supposedly overpopulated. Even industrial nations that are important exporters of agricultural products also import products and may be heavy consumers of protein and luxury foodstuffs bought on the international market.

Arthur Simon in *Bread for the World*,[14] and Ron Sider in *Rich*

Christians in an Age of Hunger,[15] have already brought the vast disparities in consumption between the wealthy Christian nations and the rest of the world to the attention of the Christian community. These authors are hardly missionary alarmists. The scientific and economic literatures agree with their conclusion that the Western industrial nations are using a disproportionate percentage of the world's resources and are often wasteful in their consumption. A typical example from an environmental textbook estimates the average consumption per person in the United States as 900 kilograms of grain a year, 810 kilos of it transformed into animal products such as meat and milk, while estimating that of the average Indian as 180 kilograms of grain a year, or about 20 percent of what a United States citizen consumes.[16] Translated into reproductive terms, this means that a typical American family with two children consumes two to three times more of the world's agricultural production than an Indian family with five children.

The situation concerning energy use and the release of pollutants is even more disparate. Figures vary and so does the world economic situation, but a commonly cited statistic is that the United States alone burns about 30 percent of the world's fossil fuel production. American agriculture is a heavy consumer of petroleum products. The United States uses three times as much oil and gas energy per capita for agriculture as the developing countries utilize for all their energy needs.[17] A United States citizen might use one hundred times as many calories of energy per day as a hunter-gatherer or a warm-climate pastoralist depending on only a small fire for cooking. A United States citizen might expend ten times as many calories as a Third World agriculturist (and most of the calories used by the latter may be in muscle power produced by livestock, not in fossil fuels).[18] Even in the United States there are differences within the Christian community. An Amish farmer, depending primarily on energy from draft animals, wood, and perhaps wind or water, expands much less fossil fuel than his tractor-driving counterparts.

The question then becomes, With these vast differences in resource use per person, who is overpopulated? There is often some industrial nation hypocrisy in responding to this question. A simple answer might be, for example, that those nations or regions are overpopulated that cannot feed themselves and supply themselves with adequate fuel. A Christian from Canada might then point out that Canada is an important exporter of agricultural products and, therefore, underpopulated. There are many regions worldwide, however, where there is enough productive land in cultivation to feed the people with some excess, but production of cash crops or of animal products for an export market may actually be reducing the local agricultural products available to an underfed populace. Are these regions overpopulated or underpopulated? Further, some nations tend to use land inefficiently, while others farm very intensively and carefully, achieving very high productivity per acre. If a country inefficiently uses a great deal of energy or causes a great deal of soil erosion per unit of agricultural production and thus manages to obtain a surplus, does this means that nation is "underpopulated" and that further population growth is therefore justified?

The United States and Canada, after a very difficult economic transformation, could feed themselves if all foreign oil supplies failed. Both nations have lands in fallow that could support pasture and terraced farming. As of this writing, both nations have grain surpluses. But suppose we widen the economic network to include those regions or districts where the United States and Canada are buying oil (and where the local people are now depending on imports for food) and those regions or districts where interests in the United States and Canada largely control the cash crop economy or livestock economy, such as some parts of Central America. The North Americans are hardly giving food away. They are exchanging grain for other food items, for petroleum, or for other raw materials or manufactured goods. Should the people who are dependent on North American agricultural productivity be counted with the North American population? One could argue, even with this international network, that each nation should be able to feed itself. The counter argument is, of course, that each nation should also be self-sufficient in fuel. Without foreign oil, agriculture in the industrial nations will fall into crisis.

The evaluation can also be based not simply on which nations can feed themselves but also on which nations are doing the most environmental damage. What if nations that produce large volumes of pollutants per capita had to pay other nations for the damage they are doing to the world's atmosphere and its climate? Suppose there were an international carbon dioxide account to which nations had to contribute if they produced excess carbon dioxide either by burning fossil fuels or by destroying forests and removing plants that can absorb carbon dioxide? The nations that are cutting rain forests to provide land for displaced farmers would hardly be the worst offenders. A resident of the United States adds 5.4 tons of carbon equivalent to the atmosphere each year, while a resident of the United Kingdom adds 3.2 tons. A Nigerian, in contrast, adds 0.8, and a resident of India adds 0.4.[19] A newborn Californian therefore will potentially make a 14.5 times greater contribution than a newborn Indian to a major global environmental problem.

Even in biblical times, nations were interdependent in terms of natural resources. Joseph's brothers went to Egypt during a famine and sought to buy food. The early Christian church lived in a world where mighty Rome manipulated grain supplies throughout a captive empire. Agricultural produce from farms in Palestine fed Roman armies. Historically, Christians have had to face crises, such as the Irish potato famine, where the fates and food supplies of nations were dependent on the political whim and economies of other nations. The modern Western industrial societies must see themselves not only in terms of their self-sufficiencies but also in terms of their dependencies and their established relationships with the peoples of other states.

To consider per capita resource consumption without considering the total head count and to consider numbers without considering resource consumption are both equally inadequate ways of dealing with the ethics of human use of natural resources. If we consider just distribution of resources to be a Christian value, then we also can conclude that some resource distribution issues might be best evaluated on a per capita basis (something rich nations might prefer to avoid). Any evaluations of population impacts on world environmental resources, such as the ozone layer or the seas, can be legitimately reviewed in terms of either impact per existing person or probable future impact based on present population growth rates, and an "excess" of either is of ethical concern. High per capita rates of resource consumption and pollution production, rather than declining population, would thus seem to be the most critical "population" issue for the industrial democracies to address.

QUESTIONS FOR REFLECTION

1. The same medical advances that have given us longer lifespans have also given us longer working lifespans. How should we adapt our attitudes toward the appropriate social and working roles of older people to this development? Toward the role of older people in the Christian community?
2. How should Third World Christians view population decline in the developed nations? To what extent do Christians in developing nations need the continuing cultural assistance of the industrial democracies, as the arguments of Wattenberg suggest?
3. How should Christian ministries react to the graying of the industrial nations?
4. Some Christian denominations in the United States and Canada

still encourage large families (e.g., Amish farm families). What ethical justifications can you identify for this? How can we justify different average family sizes for different denominations and still have a "righteous" reproductive ethic?

5. If a white population is slowly being outnumbered by another racial group, how do you think its members should react? What are the ethical arguments for or against manipulating birthrates to achieve racial or ethnic "balance"?

6. Should nations that pollute the global environment have to pay for the damage they cause to other nations? Is there a just way to divide environmental responsibility among the nations? Does the size of a nation's population in any way influence its responsibility for environmental degradation? How?

8

THE EXPLODING THIRD WORLD

The population problems of the developing nations are linked through economic ties and technological exchanges to those of the developed nations, yet the population processes of many developing nations are diametrically opposed to those of the more industrialized states. While the wealthy Euro-American nations are stabilizing or even losing population, some of the poorest nations are experiencing dramatic increases. Since population growth has been implicated in recurring famine, high child mortality, educational shortages, and many of the other difficulties plaguing the developing countries, a careful analysis of the issues should precede both international Christian attempts at providing aid and Christian discussion of family and reproductive values within the nations with high growth rates.

A review of all possible situations is impossible within the limited scope of this book, so we will begin by looking at general trends in Africa, the continent with twenty-three of the thirty-five least-developed countries and also the highest reported population growth rates per nation. In 1986 the average population growth rate in Africa was 2.8 percent, or an annual increase of 16.3 million people added to a total estimated population of 583 million. Several countries, including Rwanda, Uganda, and Zambia, had birth rates above 3 percent, with Kenya having the highest at 4.2 percent.[1] Population increase by itself is not necessarily a problem if a nation's economy is keeping up with population expansion. In Africa many countries have both declining income per capita and, perhaps more critically, declining grain supplies. Between 1980 and 1986 income per person declined 28 percent in Nigeria and 8 percent in Kenya.[2] Between the early 1970s and 1985, grain production per person fell 7 percent for Nigeria, 11 percent for Ethiopia, 19 percent for Kenya, 25 percent for Zambia, and a worrisome 52 percent for Angola.[3]

Although these overall trends are the result of birthrates that have remained at traditionally high levels, in the face of declining death rates infant mortality is still high, averaging 100 infants per thousand born, or about one child in ten. In some rural areas 200 to 250 infants per thousand may perish, or one in four. Young children also have high rates of mortality, typically 25 to 30 per thousand.[4] Due to limited health care, many African women still die as a result of complications of childbirth.

A number of factors, not the least of which is contemporary medical technology, have encouraged accelerated population growth in Africa. Vaccination has eliminated diseases such as smallpox, and a mixture of prophylactic medicine, pesticides, environmental modification, and prompt treatment has been utilized to contain continuing threats such as malaria and yellow fever. Intertribal warfare still flares under the guise of ideological conflicts but has almost completely disappeared in the forms of repeated raiding and routine intergroup antagonism. Slave trading, important through the middle of the last century, is also fortunately gone. International aid and improved transportation and food storage systems have helped to mollify environmental crises such as droughts, floods, and famines.[5] On the darker side, AIDS is spreading widely in Africa, and diseases such as malaria are becoming increasingly resistant to modern chemistry, as are their vectors. An upsurge in contagious diseases is unlikely, however, to stem the general trend toward skyrocketing censuses.

Much of Africa's population is still rural, so accelerated population growth cannot be blamed on swift urbanization or industrialization. Africa's cities are expanding at a tremendous rate, but much of the increase is fed by immigration of people from poor rural areas seeking opportunities and a better life. Overall, Africa's population growth is both urban and rural, extending across diverse cultures and ecological regions.

WHY SO MANY, SO SUDDENLY?

Modern medicine may be a cause of accelerated population growth, but it does not explain why African cultures have not "adjusted" to their improved survivorship by reducing birthrates, nor does it explain the deeper socioeconomic roots of population growth. Some hypotheses about rapid population expansion in the developing world are academically controversial, but we can look at the most frequently suggested sources for an almost continent-wide population explosion.

A first source of high birthrates is the retention of traditional cultural values. Many native peoples of Africa and the other developing regions value children highly and favor large families. Among the Kipsigis of East Africa, for example, "one of the primary duties of a young warrior is to enrich the tribe by begetting many children."[6] Masculine or feminine self-esteem may be strongly linked to childbearing. In some cultures a wife may be rejected and returned to her parents if she does not bear offspring. The religions of agricultural cultures are often fertility oriented, and production in general is celebrated. Christian missionaries usually condone "family life" and "family values." A Christian from a developed nation may, in fact, admire the high value Africans place on their progeny and their extended families, since the ties of kinship have diminished so greatly in urban industrial culture. The family values of many Africans are closer to those of major biblical characters than are those of a typical western European.

A second source of accelerated population growth is in contrast to the first—the breakdown of traditional practices of birth control, child spacing, nursing, and/or infanticide. Some cultures, for example, have taboos against sexual intercourse for a set period following childbearing. This prevents the mother from conceiving another child while she is still caring for her new baby and helps to guarantee the survival of both. Taboos or traditions may also influence the length of time a mother nurses an infant. Some cultures essentially prescribe protracted nursing not only because it will inhibit conception but also because it provides an extended supply of protein for the infant,[7] which the infant will lose if another sibling is born too soon. Many cultures have taboos against premarital or extramarital intercourse, which may be abandoned when a culture loses its integrity or members of a culture enter new settings (such as urban environments). Some cultures (including the European) have traditionally abandoned young children they cannot feed or have sanctioned overt or covert infanticide. The !Kung, a hunting and gathering people of the Kalahari desert, for example, hold children in high regard. Their strong interest in adequately feeding the children they have is, in fact, their rationale for disposing of a baby born too close to its siblings.[8]

Here Christianity and industrial culture may have an unintentional, undesirable impact. Often when religions are displaced, their taboos go with them, and childbearing and childrearing practices may change. Breastfeeding may even be subtly discouraged because it seems primitive or indecent. Further, a well-meaning attempt to curtail infanticide may not consider why people who value children highly have practiced it for centuries. A hunter-gatherer may not be able to feed the extra baby without stressing the available resources and perhaps limiting food for other children. In the first few years abandoning infanticide may not make much difference in a small family band, but it eventually will cause environmental and social stress and probably more fatalities unless another means of limiting population and ensuring proper birth spacing is found.

As notable a theological figure as John Wesley, on fleeing from the English colony of Georgia, soundly condemned the natives for disposing of their offspring. Writing on Friday, December 2, 1737, Wesley complained, "They [the Georgia coastal Indians] are implacable, unmerciful; murderers of fathers, murderers of mothers, murderers of their own children; it being a common thing for a son to shoot his father or mother, because they are old and past labour; and for a woman either to procure an abortion, or to throw her child into the next river, because she will go with her husband to war."[9] At the time, Wesley did not reflect on whether similar practices might ever have been the norm in European culture or to what extent they were due to disruption of native culture by the Europeans. He did, however, in deep encounter with his own spiritual state three weeks later, pen his well-known confession: "I went to America to convert the Indians; but oh! who shall convert me! Who, what is he that will deliver me from this evil heart of unbelief?"[10] Christians of European stock have been less than objective about the historic population regulation methods of their own culture and often naively assume that practices such as infanticide are due either to a lack of civilization (was ancient Rome uncivilized?) or to the "darkened souls" of peoples native to other parts of the world. They incorrectly conclude that simply Westernizing the culture will eliminate such evils, and that the people in question will automatically be the better for it with no further social adjustments.

A third source of accelerated population growth is lack of education. Literacy rates in Africa are still low, with less than 30 percent of the adults in a number of countries able to read. Millions of school-age children can find no place in a classroom, and some rural areas still have few schools. "Only about 5 to 20 percent of children who complete the primary grades gain admission to secondary schools and only a tiny fraction of these find places in universities or advanced training institutes."[11] The educational problem both feeds population growth and is fed by it. The poor and illiterate are less likely to use birth control or to try to limit family size. An illiterate person cannot read instructions on a contraceptives prescription. Meanwhile, the more children there are, the more teachers and classrooms the children will need, and the more likely a poor child is to be left without a place in school. African governments, incidentally, value education and place substantial portions of their economic resources into instructional programs. A typical African nation invests 25 to 35 percent of its annual budget in education, a figure it would be difficult to increase.[12]

Related to the lack of schools is the lack of health care facilities, particularly in rural areas. Many women of childbearing age receive no medical care, even during pregnancy and childbirth. Needless to say, where there are no health clinics, some types of contraceptives will not be available, and families will have limited access to health care professionals familiar with family planning. Again, the lack of clinics both encourages population growth and is exacerbated by it. Children in districts without adequate facilities will not be treated for common childhood diseases and parasites. The more children there are, the more difficult it becomes to provide adequate care for all. The more children who are threatened by disease, the less the reproductive security of the parents. If the chances of a child's dying are high, a married couple may opt to have several so that at least one or two will survive to adulthood.

Inadequate food resources are also tied to health problems. Where there are food shortages, children are likely to suffer from vitamin, mineral, and protein deficiencies and malnutrition. Pregnant and nursing women are more susceptible than other adults to nutritional deficiencies. Protein-calorie malnutrition is more prevalent among children when births are closely spaced. A year-old infant displaced from breastfeeding by the birth of a new sibling frequently suffers protein-calorie malnutrition and may die as a result.[13] The malnourished child needs medical care and runs a high risk of contracting infectious diseases or of sustaining permanent damage from dietary deficiencies. The more children there are, the more difficult it is to feed all of them adequately.

Another very important element in Africa's population growth is the status of women. Particularly in rural areas, African women are tied to family food production and to childbearing roles. Far fewer female children than male children attend school, and girls are much less likely than boys to go on for secondary education. Under subsistence agriculture, African women have been the primary calorie producers, since they usually have responsibility for family garden plots. With conversion to cash crops or to machine-driven agriculture, women are often left out of the picture, and their social needs are not considered. Traditionally, African women marry young and begin to raise a family immediately. Childbearing continues until a woman is no longer able to conceive, so a typical African woman, even with proper child spacing, will produce four to eight children or more.[14] Where health care or food shortages prevail, women often are neglected. A number of cultures worldwide feed males, including young boys, before women and girls are fed. Thus in some geographic locations, girls are more likely to be malnourished than boys.[15] (The opposite is rarely the case.) The youngest and the oldest females are, in fact, the most likely to suffer in times of shortage.[16]

Both the infant mortality rates and the use of contraception and family planning are linked to the educational levels of women. A number of studies have shown that illiterate women lose more infants than those with a primary education. In some countries, a woman with no schooling is two to three times more likely to have her baby die than a woman with seven to nine years of school.[17] Traditional large families have higher infant mortality than small ones, and the lower a child is in the birth order, the higher the probability it will die. In Rwanda, for example, a fifth-born infant has one chance in five of dying before its first birthday, and an infant with eight or more older siblings has two chances in five of dying before reaching age one.[18] Women in developing nations die far more frequently from pregnancy-related causes than do women in the developed world. In 1987, for example, Ethiopia had 3,500 maternal deaths per 100,000 live births, while Norway had 2 maternal deaths per 100,000. The total Third World maternal fatalities are at least 500,000 women and may be as high as 1 million women per year. Many of these could be prevented by better birth spacing or avoidance of pregnancy when the mother is in poor health.[19]

Women who are literate, and particularly those who have secondary educations, are more likely to use family planning. In countries such as Sri Lanka where women have been given opportunities for advanced education and professional or technical employment, birthrates tend to fall, even if the country as a whole is still poor. In Africa, women who Westernize are also more likely to limit family size, perhaps due to both better access to family planning and a change in personal values. Western ideals include the small nuclear family, possession of consumer goods, a high-status job, and advanced education, all of which discourage starting families at a young age or having large numbers of children.[20] Westernization, of course, presents other difficulties, including loss of cultural identity, and is, by itself, hardly the solution for entire nations now undergoing greatly accelerated population growth.

Christian missions have been active in providing both educational opportunities and health care in developing countries. Although activities and strategies vary among denominations, Christian schools and child support programs usually are open to both girls and boys. Over the years, many Christians serving the people of Africa have been women, and women started many of the first mission schools. Christianity, however, has lacked a conscious strategy for dealing with questions concerning traditional gender roles in changing socioeconomic environments. Perhaps due to ongoing conflicts in the industrial nations over the status of women in the church, Christians either shy away from confronting gender issues or favor traditional roles for women without grappling with their potential implications in contemporary social and economic settings. Christians wishing rightly to confirm the value of children and childbearing have neglected to find socially viable alternatives to the "more is better" system of affirming women in maternal roles.

Christians in the industrial nations have also been in philosophical crisis over whether they should be evangelizing in the developing nations or providing various forms of aid. The argument unfortunately makes Euro-American churchgoers skeptical about contributing to missions favoring health care and ignores the fact that education and improving literacy can be effective means of evangelization. In addition, eighteenth- and nineteenth-century attitudes portraying the residents of colonial nations as less able have inhibited transfer of skills to native practitioners. The recent trend toward missionary support of indigenous ministers and evangelists is likely to continue and should incorporate the training and support of indigenous educational and health care professionals with a Christian orientation.

POVERTY BREEDS MORE POVERTY?

Lurking in the background of the contemporary population dilemma is the issue of the deep economic and political roots for the existing trends. From an economic perspective, there may in fact be three conflicting sets of forces: the traditional resources management of tribal and agrarian peoples, the patterns established by colonialism, and the pressures created by contemporary Euro-American and East Asian control of world markets despite the disintegration of the empires and the rise of nationalism among former subject nations. We also need to determine if economic success is necessary to demographic transition, or vice versa.

Traditional rural economies lack social security systems. Children are not only an important component of the work force, they are also the only dependable source of support in old age. Where child mortality is high, people will tend to have more children to ensure the survival of a son to take care of aging parents. In some areas without adequate health care facilities, a family may need to produce six or seven children to be certain one son survives to adulthood. Unlike the developed nations, where each child is very expensive to raise and must be supported through early adulthood, children in traditional agricultural societies may begin to work and add to family income before they reach adolescence. In "modern" economies, however, this practice may be against the best interests of the children because it keeps them out of school. Further, if a farmer raises a large number of sons to maturity, there may not be enough land to support all of them when they are ready to start farms of their own. A culture's openness to family planning is strongly influenced by the relationship between family structure and flow of income. In many cultures with extended family structure, cash and necessities move from children to parents to grandparents. In the nuclear families common in the Euro-American nations, income usually flows from the older generations to the younger.[21]

Colonialism may have encouraged the production of children for the workforce and certainly disrupted indigenous landholding patterns and social organization throughout the tropics and subtropics. In Africa the best land was taken by European interlopers, a pattern still found in many countries where the middle and upper classes, either white or black, retain control of a large portion of the most fertile properties. Industries in the colonies were discouraged by tariffs and in some cases by open political (and military) interference, while production of raw materials for export by white planters was encouraged. The conversion from relatively stable indigenous village economies that also supported local manufacture of goods such as cloth and iron products to plantations that shipped chocolate and bananas back to England and France left the African farmer landless and lost in an economic system that paid low wages, provided few personal benefits, encouraged purchase of manufactured goods from abroad, and extracted more taxes every time Europeans chose to argue among themselves by going to war. In addition, nomads were moved from their original territories, either because the pastoralists were considered a threat to complete government control of a re-

gion, European settlers wanted their lands, or the colonial governments wished to create game preserves for European hunters. The
so-called civilization process actually discouraged skills and trades
that had been fostered by indigenous agriculture and cottage industry, disrupted local food production, and left most of the native residents of the colonies an illiterate lower class.[22] Europe, not satisfied
to keep tragedies like the Irish potato famine in the northern climes,
took the methods the English had utilized in ruling their Celtic
neighbors to the economic advantage of Britain and spread them
worldwide.

Christians from the developed nations often assume that African
management is just behind the times, and that African problems are
rooted in the inability of traditional cultures to adapt to modern
economies and technologies. Traditional African agriculture has already been severely disrupted. The liberation of African nations
from European political control did not provide liberation from international economic forces. There is still strong dependence on
plantation-style agriculture for cash flow and little self-sufficiency in
trade goods. International tariffs and multinational development
strategies still favor Third World production of raw materials, be
they jute, mahogany, ivory, peanuts, or crude oil. Some tribes no
longer occupy their original homelands, and some have been forced
to change from pastoralism to settled agriculture or from hunting and
gathering to hired labor. Civil wars and political conflicts within nations have inhibited economic development.

Fueling population and economic crisis is Africa's growing refugee
dilemma. Christians from the developed world tend to think of Africa's refugee problem as primarily the result of drought, famine, and
poor agricultural management, which are indeed part of the picture.
The colonial legacy, however, has played a major role in precipitat-
ing intergroup strife and political instability. The colonial powers,
for example, often made arbitrary decisions concerning national
boundaries, and these have been little modified as African nations
have sought independence. As a result, tribal and religious groups
have been trapped or split by international frontiers. Africans suffering under apartheid have fled their homes, as have those brutalized
by dictatorial regimes or terrorized by warring factions. International economic interests have sometimes displaced workers, and
economic inequality between regions or between urban and rural
areas induces the landless and unemployed to migrate. Displaced
people are always at an economic disadvantage, and most of Africa's
refugees are fleeing from intolerable conditions or being forced to
move rather than voluntarily heading toward better financial oppor-

tunities. Farmers leaving the countryside to find protection and supplies in town do nothing to improve agricultural productivity, although they still need to be fed. Depopulating the countryside without improving industry and trade encourages famine rather than discourages it.[23]

Unemployment and underemployment continue to keep Africans from finding an adequate settled livelihood. Many work as seasonal laborers and have no income for part of the year. Others complete a few years of primary education and discover it does no good in obtaining a steady job. Unemployment and unstable employment conditions encourage one-parent families and bearing children without being able to adequately support them. Large families in turn pour more undertrained people into a workforce with few good jobs. All this keeps African labor cheap and inhibits economic development that will benefit Africans in the long run.[24]

Through the 1970s, many African leaders did not worry about population as an element in Africa's economic difficulties, on the grounds that Africa has much undeveloped land and many undeveloped resources. Opening new lands can, however, be very problematic. Often tropical soils are poor and need special management. Many of Africa's uncultivated acres are already utilized by pastoralists or will require irrigation to raise crops. Translocating the peoples already living in a region or requiring them to abandon traditional economies causes social distress, while establishing sophisticated irrigation systems requires both capital and well-trained agriculturalists to be certain soils are not ruined by salinization. Widespread short-rotation slash and burn agriculture wastes forest resources, keeps poor farmers on the move, and results in degraded soils. The tsetse fly still rules vast areas, and although it may ultimately be controlled, it continues to inhibit agricultural development. Disease problems actually make about 45 percent of Africa's potentially arable lands uninhabitable for humans and their livestock.[25]

The strain accelerated population growth places on Africa's educational programs also undermines further agricultural development. Opening new lands and farming tropical soils requires well thought out strategies, executed by farmers who know how to care for land and water resources. A flood of people abandoning depleted old fields and haphazardly invading virgin territories provides temporary relief from food shortage at best, and at worst results in millions of damaged acres and a long-term decline in agricultural productivity. The green revolution has developed higher-yield crop plants and, with adequate inputs of fertilizer, will increase production per acre. Farmers need to make cash outlays to use the techniques, however, and both men *and women* need to be educated in new methods. Africa can open more acreage for tillage. The question is when and how. Ironically, failure of present agricultural economies drives people away from the countryside into city slums and refugee camps and does nothing to improve food production per capita. It also encourages importation of food, which in turn drains the capital needed to improve agriculture, expand educational opportunities, and develop new industries.

ECONOMIC OR SOCIAL TRANSITION

Through the late 1970s and the 1980s, African leaders began to modify their opinions on the importance of family planning. Some began to accept contraception for birth spacing, with the concomitant health benefits for mother and child, while still considering overall population growth an unimportant issue. Today, some, but not all, African leaders are beginning to incorporate population regulation into development efforts. The International Planned Parenthood Federation has taken a leadership role in establishing family planning programs in a majority of African nations. (It should be noted, however, that Christians often oppose the activities of Planned Parenthood in the developed countries and have also attacked their international programs, primarily because of concerns over "un-Christian" sex education or improved population regulation fostering abortion.)

A key issue in the integration of family planning in development programs is the possibility of initiating a population transition without first initiating an economic transition. Three combinations of economic and social change in Asian nations appear to have been effective in reducing population growth. The first of these is strong economic improvement, with the development of industry and international markets. This places more men and women in salaried jobs and improves economic and educational opportunities for everyone. It also discourages large families because of the constraints of both technical/industrial employment and the advantage of delaying marriage and childbearing in order to utilize improved educational opportunities. Although no one would accuse Japan of falling short of the Western nations in population regulation, experts have argued over whether or not nations such as Taiwan and Hong Kong have undergone a true demographic transition when annual rates of population growth have fallen below 2 percent. In these "new industrial nations" working women purposefully limit family size and stop reproducing after they have the desired number of surviving children. It is not known, however, if present reductions in birthrates represent a long-term trend or whether they will continue to decline to zero population growth. The fact remains, however, that improved economies help to lower birthrates. Women who attend school and then enter the workforce tend to both marry later and purposefully limit family size. We should recognize, though, there are situations where mild economic improvement or provision of external economic or food aid could encourage population growth. In displaced or heavily stressed populations, low levels of economic improvement may stimulate resumption of childbearing or greatly improve child survivorship without establishing a resource base adequate to support the children when they reach maturity.

The second type of social change resulting in decreased birth rates is the improvement of education and social services and an increase in the equality of their distribution. In this case, national income may remain low, but everyone has access to health care, secondary education, and other social support such as food subsidies. Some experts would argue that this type of change is more effective than an improved national income in discouraging rapid population expansion because it spreads needed resources and food security, as well as access to family planning, to the greatest number of people possible. Nations such as South Africa and Mexico with relatively high per capita incomes and relatively great income inequality have higher birthrates than many nations with much lower per capita finances. Conversely, nations with low income inequality, such as Sri Lanka and Taiwan, have dramatically reduced birthrates. Both the relative inequality of income and the per capita income of the poorest 40 percent are strongly correlated to national reproductive rates. Population ecologist William Murdoch suggests, "Unevenness of income distribution in poor countries causes the poor to be absolutely poorer than they would be if the same national income were evenly distributed. This is what causes their higher fertility. . . . To the degree that income measures economic welfare, most of the variability in fertility among developing nations can be explained by the level of economic welfare of the poorer majority of families in each nation."[26] From a Christian perspective, this suggests that *distributive justice* is one of the keys to dealing with accelerated population growth. Further, it supports the concept that economics may be more crucial than sexual behavior or family values in determining population trends.

China, which has had the most effective population reduction programs of anywhere in the developing world, exemplifies the third type of social change. Aside from making family planning assistance widely available, the Chinese have regulated family size through social incentives and disincentives. In the early 1970s, after long avoidance of the problem during the Mao Zedong era, China developed a national population regulation strategy encouraging "delayed marriage, longer birth intervals, and smaller families."[27] This program did not slow population growth sufficiently, so the Chinese government instituted a one child per family policy. The one-child families benefit from "substantial pay increases, better housing, longer maternity leaves, and priority access to education" while those having more children are subject to "heavy fines and social criticism."[28] Although city dwellers are expected to adhere strictly to the single progeny policy, rural residents and members of ethnic minorities may have two or more children.[29]

The Chinese ability to gain social consensus and some concerted enforcement efforts have resulted in smaller families but have not completely changed Chinese values concerning childbearing. Most Chinese would still consider larger families of two or more children to be the ideal, and most desire at least one male child. Although this ideal is not the same as the large families with many sons of the previous generations, traditional childbearing goals have not been completely suppressed.

Christians have criticized the Chinese for prescribing abortion for pregnant women who already have children. There has also been international controversy over the possibility of forced abortions and of female infanticide or selective abortion of female fetuses by families desiring male offspring. Determining exactly how coercive Chinese abortion practices are is beyond the scope of this volume. There can be no doubt, however, the Chinese are utilizing abortion to assist in population regulation, and Chinese citizens are sharing reproductive resources, whether they as individuals wish to or not. Further, selection against female infants is a widespread social phenomenon in a wide range of cultures that favor sons and are resource limited. It would not, therefore, be surprising to encounter it as a practice in a nation pursuing a one child per family policy, even if it was not the government's intent to encourage lethal prejudice against females.

The Euro-American reader needs to realize that although the Chinese policies of population regulation appear to be a major intrusion on individual rights, the Chinese perception of their disadvantages may not be the same as the Euro-American perception. The Chinese are more concerned about societal affiliation than are Euro-Americans. Chinese also prefer to pursue self-actualization in serving their society, whereas the typical United States citizen will pursue self-actualization in individual development.[30] The major conflict for the Chinese is to see the nation rather than the extended family as the prime recipient of individual effort and sacrifice. From a Christian ethical viewpoint, therefore, it is important to distinguish the rather variable cultural perceptions of how individuals and families fit into their societies from basic violations of human integrity. Euro-Americans also need to remember that the Chinese were under serious stress from population growth when they initiated their restrictive policies. With a billion people and over a fifth of the world's population living on a mere 7 percent of the world's tillable acres, they could not look to new lands or expansive industrialization to avert food shortages.[31]

In summary, there are three basic models of social or economic change that could potentially initiate declines in birthrates in developing nations.

First, the economic growth model holds that transition to a healthy industrial economy will discourage population growth. This model assumes that increased wealth and development precede declining birthrates. Unfortunately, most developing nations may have little chance, in the immediate future, to greatly improve national income.

Second, the resource distribution model holds that relatively equal availability of adequate social and educational services will discourage accelerated population growth. If people do not need their children to support them, have educational opportunities that encourage late marriage, have job opportunities, and have access to affordable health care and family planning, birthrates will fall. This model assumes that adequate educational and health care facilities can be provided (some very poor countries have managed this) and also assumes that the upper and middle classes cannot maintain a stranglehold on a majority of a nation's resources (obviously not a popular policy among the "haves"). The major disadvantage of this model is that it cannot completely counteract cultural traditions. In societies that value sons, for example, one-child families remain unlikely for those who have daughters first.

Third, the social control model assumes that the government must regulate reproduction in order to overcome individual unwillingness to share reproductive resources and cultural traditions that encourage large families. This model also assumes that existing population trends will ultimately cause disaster and that the right of the individual to decide his or her own reproductive future must be overridden by the need of the society at large to reduce population growth. This model usually results in equitable sharing of reproductive resources (for example, all families must have only one child, but all families may have a child), but greatly restricts the reproductive choices of the individual.

From a Christian ethical perspective, deciding to initiate social change concerning population growth and choosing the most righteous means for doing this requires us to consider several different types of values. The above models, all of which have been to some extent successful in reducing birthrates in real-world situations, are based on distribution of economic and reproductive resources rather than on regulation of sexual behavior itself. The differences between them rest, first, in what a society thinks it can realistically achieve economically (rather than in moral terms) and, second, in how much the society (or its leadership) believes it is necessary to restrict the behavior of the individual or to sacrifice some of the reproductive resources of the individual for the common good.

For Christians it is imperative to recognize that population is a distributive justice issue. It concerns who has access to what sorts of resources as well as who behaves in a socially acceptable way. In Africa, old economic and political injustices and unresolved development problems are critical underpinnings to present population dilemmas. The three types of change that actually appear to be effective in reducing population growth argue strongly against Garrett Hardin's conclusion that perfect justice will bring perfect disaster. In the Sri Lankan case, for example, reduction of population growth rates required neither monstrous sums of foreign aid nor an invasion of rich lifeboats. Relatively equitable distribution of resources within the society, accompanied by broad-based public education and health programs, have helped to curtail population expansion. All the successful models either increase resource availability or encourage (or enforce) equitable sharing of resources. Hardin, ironically, is attempting to protect the natural environment. Yet if we maintain the economic gulf between the rich and the poor, as he suggests, the populations of many developing nations will continue their unrelenting growth, and the wastage of forests, field, and range will be tremendous.

Christians need to also recognize that accelerated population growth is related to how cultures deal with change. Christian missionary activities by their very nature initiate change and may either worsen or ease transitions. The blind application of Euro-American values will not help, nor will clinging tenaciously to old traditions, if a culture is already in flux. Christianity needs to weigh what is good and valuable in the old and the new, in the indigenous and the exogenous, and provide guidance in a world desperate for sustenance, peace, and justice.

QUESTIONS FOR REFLECTION

1. In your society or culture, in what ways do women who work at home and women who work away from home have different attitudes and problems concerning childrearing? What about women from different social classes and backgrounds?

2. In your culture, to what extent is male or female self-esteem linked to childbearing? How do perceptions of masculine or feminine activities or sexual roles influence cultural ideals of family size?

3. Suppose you were a missionary to a tribe of hunter-gatherers who still live in a desert area and move their camps frequently. The tribe exposes an infant if it is born too close to a sibling or if the mother is unable to nurse it properly or is ill. The tribe does not have continuing access to government health care facilities. What attitude would you take toward the practice of exposing children?

4. If you were teaching at a school in a poor rural area and many of the parents did not send their daughters, would you try to encourage them to send them? If so, what rationale would you use to encourage this? If you think girls should be encouraged, what if there were a limited number of spaces and more girls would either displace the boys or overfill the classrooms?

5. What types of social roles should Christianity affirm for women in traditional rural cultures? In poorer urban areas? In middle-class suburbs? Should Christian affirmation of women be the same from social setting to social setting, or should it differ?

6. Do you think Christian missions have worsened population and land degradation problems by providing vaccines and nutritional supplements for African children? If you think Christian missions have contributed to the problems, is there anything that can be done to counteract this?

9

POPULATION REGULATION
AND JUSTICE

Perhaps the most serious mistake made by Christians attempting to resolve issues in population ethics is to cling to the preconception that Christianity must be pronatalist because it is prochildren. Assuming that "more children" is better is too simplistic an approach. The social context of "more children" needs to be determined, and the "right" answer may not be the same for all Christian individuals or cultures. We all have an unfortunate preference for averages (the neat middle-class family with two toddlers, a boy and a girl) or for trends (larger families, smaller families, families with sons). We also possess a stubborn unwillingness to accommodate diversions from the norm or the ideal, or to believe that right action might differ in different cultural settings.

For the Christian, the social context of population questions arises from the sum of many individual actions. A concern for population growth at the world, national, or regional level should not, however, cause us to lose our concern for the individual. Christian population ethics must begin with the basics—the needs of the mother, the needs of the child, and the responsibilities of a married couple. Population ethics must also operate at the level of the Christian congregation or denomination, since the local Christian community usually provides social and educational support for its members (and its neighbors, one hopes) and their children. The local Christian community may also consciously or unconsciously establish "acceptable" patterns of childbearing or may rationalize and legitimize the reproductive standards of a social or economic class (such as the American professional middle class).

Governments the world over establish policies that influence childbearing, the health of children and their mothers, the education of children and the potential opportunities for a child when he or she grows up. Christian communities may not dominate the politics of the nations in which they reside, yet Christians, at the very least, set an example to others in a national context by their actions concerning childbearing and childrearing. Politically and socially active Christians can potentially be very influential in national child care and population regulation policies. Christianity is a major world religion, and Christians are very active internationally in disseminating "Christian values" through missionary work. The values of Christians in one national setting may thus influence the values of both Christians and non-Christians in another. If reproductive values are not openly discussed, they may still be transferred by example. World population growth, as it influences food supply, international exchange, environmental degradation, the plight of refugees, and the ability of families to make adequate livings for themselves, affects all international Christian efforts to help our neighbors.

THE INDIVIDUAL, THE FAMILY, THE TRIBE, THE STATE

The ethical quandaries that face nations with high rates of population growth pose a series of questions. First, should the government or other social organizations (tribes, towns, churches, educational institutions) intervene in population processes, and if intervention is justified, when is it justified? Second, how should the government or social organizations intervene? Are coercive methods ever appropriate? What sorts of "coercion" or positive and negative social reinforcement are ethically justified?

Let's begin constructing an ethical response to the first question by establishing some standards for human welfare that both Christians and non-Christians are likely to accept:

1. A mother should be able to safely bear and raise a child to maturity. High child and maternal mortality is undesirable.
2. Everyone should have access to the basic necessities of life including food, water, clothing, housing, and health care. Lack of the physical resources to support individual children and adults is undesirable.
3. Couples should be able to have children if they so desire.

4. Children should grow up having the opportunity for an education, a job or other socially productive role, marriage, and a family.

Societal response to population processes is necessary when individual couples, desiring to attain the above conditions, behave in ways that prevent the above conditions from being met in the society at large. This could happen if the couples are only considering their own self-interest, if they have family goals that are not appropriate to current economic conditions, or if they do not have the societal support or the physical resources necessary to change their behavior. If large numbers of people are competing for limited commodities and services, some degree of community organization is needed to distribute those resources fairly. We can argue further that the actions of one person regarding reproduction do influence resource availability for the entire community. Thus in terms of shared resources, the community may move to influence the behavior of its members. The Bible, in numerous passages, sets social standards for childbearing and childrearing. Dealing with family values at the level of the entire community or nation has been a historic necessity.

Societal response should begin as soon as there is a deviation from these four standards for human welfare, or when there is a significant risk of such a deviation. Attempting to redirect population processes is only appropriate, however, when population is actually the source of the difficulties and when the social group is also dealing with other factors that may limit the availability of critical resources. High reproductive rates were related to high mortality in early industrial England, but physical conditions in the factories and factory towns and financial exploitation of the workforce were also key problems. To have reduced reproduction without protecting child laborers and improving sanitation would not have relieved the major health threats. It is hypocritical for the rich to condemn the poor for large family size if a surviving son is the only social security a poor family has and a poor family does not have adequate educational opportunities and health care.

We should further recognize that there are tensions and conflicts in beginning social action to regulate population. First, many of us hesitate to intervene in the personal lives of other people. Euro-American culture, for instance, has always held privacy in high regard and treats sexuality as a matter of individual choice. Within a community, however, much can be done to encourage responsible childbearing *without forcing* others to change their behaviors. The industrial nations, for example, have voluntarily undergone demographic transition. Second, many people might hesitate to encourage family planning because they feel they are potentially taking something away from someone else—that is, the joy and benefits of having lots of children. The distributive justice model of population change described in the previous chapter, however, suggests that couples in some of the developing nations will gladly reduce family size if they can be certain most of their children will survive and their youngsters will be able to attend school and obtain adequate nutrition. Some of the best methods for encouraging smaller families do not restrict individual reproductive rights; they provide better social, economic, and reproductive security for the individual. Although a number of governmental family planning efforts have removed rights and freedoms and thus were based on "taking from," others have provided better public services and thus were based on "giving to." We will look specifically at the ethics of restricting individual options in the last chapter of this book, but for the present we should note that coercion is not always necessary to change.

Another source of doubt is the prediction of the future, be it demographic, economic, or agricultural. How can we know there will not be enough jobs for all the children in Kenya? How can we know the Sahel will have further problems with famine and drought? Can we be certain Africa will not need a huge unskilled labor force? Actually, we cannot know the future, and the economics of any region may change radically. What nineteenth-century European colonial administrator would have predicted that there would someday be a major world power clash over the natural resources of Kuwait? Our economic and demographic predictions have to be based on current knowledge and current possibilities. In the realm of human demography, there are extreme optimists and extreme pessimists, and only time will prove the case.

A possible ethical strategy is to place priority on current and well-documented problems. If there are not enough classrooms and clinics for today's children, then this should become the first target for social action. Predictions of the future should then be carefully weighed and discussed by those who may find themselves and their offspring affected. Environmental ethicists acknowledge the legitimacy of concern for future generations. The Bible repeatedly discusses human responsibility to leave a godly spiritual heritage for those, both related and unrelated, who follow. Our concern for future generations, therefore, should extend at least to those whom we are personally likely to know. We can, at a minimum, show reasonable care for the natural resources, industries, agricultural lands, and environments we will leave for our grandchildren. Each of us has some ability to provide "an inheritance" for the next two or three generations and to assist them as they grow to adulthood. What the year 2050 will be like is a difficult question; what can be done to improve the lives of our children and grandchildren, based on the way things are now, is a reasonable one. There isn't much use in worrying about the year 2050 if I leave my daughter eroded fields or my son a cardboard shack at the edge of a city slum.

Although contemporary extended families expect financial resources to flow from children to parents, the biblical model of inheritance assumes that godly behaviors and righteousness flow from parents to children, and that the unrighteous action or selfishness of any family member may have dire consequences for the remainder of the group. Our management of our families should therefore consider the spiritual and physical needs and responsibilities of all generations. It should be clear from the very restrictive Chinese population regulation program that delaying social response to population growth may worsen the associated economic stress, resource deterioration, and health problems. Appropriate sharing of resources in this generation will help to prevent radical redistribution in the next. Christians must also recognize that rapid population growth often increases the economic distance between the "haves" and the "have nots." Modifying population trends can be integral to resolving long-term resource shortages and can help to reverse economic declines in regions with limited agricultural land or industry.

OUR CULTURE, OUR CHURCH, OUR LIVES

When exposed to problems that cause child mortality, Christians from the developed nations usually chastize themselves for not providing enough aid to sisters and brothers elsewhere in the world. The response of Western technologists is, of course, very important in confronting population issues. The ethical strategies chosen by the Christians of the developing nations themselves must, however, come first. A Christian in Sweden cannot tell Christians in Kenya that birth control and family planning are ethical imperatives. The Christians in Kenya must weigh the theological, cultural, and economic variables and must frame their own response to the issues raised by accelerated population growth and adapt their response both to their Christian beliefs and to their own social setting.

Many Christians in the developing world will find themselves caught between conflicting values. Westernization may be intruding in traditional regional culture. Christian missionaries may have confirmed some traditional values and disregarded others. Or the culture may have been Christian for centuries, but the information age, urbanization, economic pressures, drought, agricultural failures, and other factors have disrupted established life-styles. Changes in sexual mores may be separating younger people from the church and posing a threat to basic Christian beliefs. But through all the possible social changes and cultural threats to Christian integrity, shying away from the issues produced by rapid population growth is a mistake because it permits economics, national governments, and the social values of our neighbors to make decisions for us.

Even in our complex postindustrial milieu, simplicity remains a virtue. A Christian ethic of human reproduction and population regulation should be based on few simple tenets of faith. Let us begin by adding just seven biblical principles of concern for our neighbor, for creation, and for the growth of Christ's kingdom, to the four principles of human welfare listed above:

1. Christ taught that each child, regardless of parentage, was welcome in the kingdom.
2. The spiritual worth of an individual is not determined by reproductive fitness or by marital status. Faith is the key, not an individual household filled with offspring. In Christian community, we are all part of the family of Christ.
3. We should love our neighbors as ourselves. Our childbearing and childrearing should accommodate the needs of others, including those outside our immediate family, and should socially affirm women and children.
4. We should care for the widow, the orphan, and the sojourner and obtain justice for the poor and the downtrodden.
5. The New Testament directs Christians to raise godly children *and* to carry the gospel to others and to all nations.
6. The earth and all the creatures dwelling in it are the Lord's and have been blessed by God. We should share the blessing of reproduction with them.
7. We have a responsibility to care *both* for our human brothers and sisters *and* for the earth.

Note that none of these principles address desirable numbers of children or family size (or even particular male or female roles). They concern Christ's call and our basic relationships to other people, regardless of social or marital circumstances.

SOCIAL ROLES, REPRODUCTIVE RESPONSIBILITIES

Population growth is tied, often subtly, to numerous societal conditions of concern to Christians. Rapidly expanding populations challenge Christian views of the future and ask what kind of present and future Christians desired for their children and for all the children whom Christ welcomed into the kingdom. An African woman once could expect to lose one or more of her infants, and frequent death of the very young, though a source of great sorrow, had to be accepted. Today, infant mortality is much reduced, yet could certainly be reduced still further. If children from large families are more likely to be malnourished or per capita food availability is falling, is it ethically correct to attempt to reduce family size to provide better resources for the individual child? Should the youngest child have a chance of survival equal to that of the oldest child?

Within the Christian community, then, the first question to address is, What is best for the children? And not just our children, but the children of the neighbors as well. A possible rule of thumb is that a Christian congregation ought to be able to provide Christian education for all of "its own" and provide for any children in the congregation who are underfed or lack adequate health care. In addition, the congregation should be able to share some resources with children outside their own social sphere. Every child in the Christian community should have the opportunity to learn to read the Scriptures and to study Christian history. Every child should be well nourished, both physically and spiritually. In addition, the love of Christ should be carried to those who are not Christians or not members of the home congregation. A poor congregation may have some difficulty doing this, but perhaps if funds are short, then some time can be set aside to aid a child whose mother is ill, or to help a child learn to read. Our population ethic should welcome children into the kingdom and should allow us the resources to care for the widow, the orphan, and the dispossessed. Often we think of ethical decisions concerning the number of offspring people should have as primarily dependent on the Christian concept of the family. Such decisions, though, also concern how we share resources, both within the Christian community and between Christians and non-Christians.

We need to recognize that one of the resources we share both within and between generations is the ability to have and raise children. Will we leave our children an adequate acreage of productive agricultural lands so that they can feed their families? Will the next generation have to reduce family size because there were so many children in this generation? If the next three generations all have the same size families, how big could those families be and still have adequate natural resources to support themselves fully? We can easily conceive of ourselves as giving life to our children. Yet children should also be a joy for their parents and received as a great gift from God. In an increasingly crowded world, this joy may suddenly be restricted by shortages, resource competition and, ultimately, societal regulation. Will our children's children be able to have families without having to meet strict government limits on how large those families can be?

Also central to the Christian response to population growth are the changing roles of women. While the self-esteem of women in traditional agricultural cultures is often tied to childbearing, the New Testament does not require reproductive fitness for a place in the kingdom. In a cultural setting where barren women have traditionally been socially rejected, do Christians have an ethical responsibility to socially accept contemporary Sarahs and Hannahs? What of Rachel, bearing only Joseph and Benjamin? How is the Christian community going to respond to changes in family structure caused by shifts from rural to urban environments? The financial pressures wrought by development often move women from home-oriented labor to jobs in the industrial or service sectors of an economy. Can the Christian community assist in these transitions? If resources are strained and it would improve conditions for individual women and children to reduce family size, can the Christian community offer women other means of finding self-esteem than raising large families?

Within the Christian community, therefore, the second question to address is, What is the role of women in serving Christ? Although this question concerns all Christian women, it is a major issue for women from the developing nations and those in changing socioeconomic environments. Mothers, including single mothers, need social support, as do childless women, be they single or married. If social and economic conditions are such that having large families strains available resources, the Christian community should be able to affirm women with small families. This can be accomplished by removing social stigmas, such as treating working mothers as if they are somehow less worthy than women who can afford to stay home or hinting that the woman with one child is not doing her part in filling the Sunday school. Affirmation can also be accomplished by expanding both educational and ministry opportunities for laywomen (and laymen) in the church. For example, in a cultural setting where women have traditionally raised large families and worked at home, a transition to smaller families may leave women without youngsters around

the house while they are still relatively young and interested in raising children. Women whose own progeny are all in school or are
grown can be organized into a ministry group to aid mothers who
have new infants, are ill, or are forced to work away from the house.
Women can also lead educational and health care ministries. If young
mothers find themselves, out of financial necessity, taking factory or
service sector jobs away from their children, women of the Christian
community can place a high priority on developing safe, psychologically healthy child care. The Christian community can thus serve as
an extended family, offering women meaningful roles and self-
esteem in cultures in transition and assisting them with their most
pressing problems.

Christians need to recognize, however, when initiating ministries
by and for women, that the relationship of women to childbearing
and children is usually quite socially complex, even in a traditional
rural society (perhaps more so in traditional societies). When women
from a maize storage cooperative in Nigeria were asked about the
advantages of having children, for example, they most frequently
mentioned not only financial security in old age but also "assurance
of conjugal status in the husband's house."[1] A childless widow did
not have the right to live in her husband's house, nor would she receive any inheritance from her husband's property. If she had children, however, she could receive part of his wealth and status in his
household through them. These Nigerian women also found that
having children raised their social status and that the barren woman
"was seen as a person apart, different from the rest, a mere onlooker.
. . . Life [was] not viewed as worthwhile without children."[2] The
women, in turn, saw feeding and clothing their children as the major
benefit of the profits they gained from working in the cooperative;
thus children were very central to their identities as workers. It is
clear, in a situation such as this, that mere Christian affirmation of a
barren woman's worth in Christ does not solve her potential economic problems. Further, if child mortality is high, reducing family
size increases the risk that a woman will eventually end up without
adequate family ties and economic support. The first step in attempting to reduce birthrates, therefore, would be to improve child survivorship, so that a woman with a small number of children can be
certain two or three will survive and ensure an inheritance. The second step would be to reduce the association between high fertility
and female self-esteem by providing other means of social affirmation. (Changing the inheritance system is also a possibility, but inheritance is very central to a culture and probably difficult to modify
without restructuring almost all social relationships.)

If the roles of women are changing, then the social roles of men are likely to be changing as well. In cultures where male social status is acquired through virility, men may resist family planning or place their desire to increase the size of their own family above the needs of the community. The reasons may extend past a need for support in old age to matters of social integration, such as the desire of Indian men "to continue the family line and perform ritual obligations."[3] A preference for sons is also tied to cultural emphasis on "maleness." Christian teaching can help men weigh the social value of various family planning strategies, while Christian emphasis on faith can help to free men from the need to prove themselves through fathering large numbers of offspring. Family planning programs are often oriented toward women, yet in many cultures men greatly influence or control the use of contraceptives. In urban areas in Indonesia, for example, the husband's approval is one of the key determinants in a woman's participation in family planning.[4] In Khartoum, Sudan, a study found that the decision not to practice family planning is "male-dominated, and husbands are responsible for providing contraceptives when family planning is practiced."[5] A women in Zaire not only worries that her husband will disapprove of surgical sterilization but fears that his family, who desire large numbers of children, will be an additional source of social pressure. She faces the very real possibility that her marriage will be dissolved and she will be abandoned if it becomes common knowledge she is no longer fertile.[6]

Women usually bear the brunt of the socioeconomic and medical burdens generated by accelerated population growth. Men need to recognize the difficulties rapid population expansion may create for their families and become equal partners in reproductive planning. If the men in the community do not accept responsibility for establishing patterns of childbearing and childrearing consistent with Christian values and the needs of the community as a whole, all Christian family planning efforts will be undermined from the start. From a biblical perspective, fatherhood is as important as motherhood, and fathers have both economic and spiritual responsibilities in caring for their wives and children.

An important strategy for limiting family size is delaying marriage or childbearing for a few years. In contemporary industrial culture, putting off having a family until a couple are at least in their early twenties reduces health risks for both mother and child and allows younger people to finish their education and become established in the labor force before assuming the responsibilities children bring. Again, the Christian community can provide social settings that help to reduce social pressures to enter into immature sexual relationships (married or otherwise) and can provide an environment that nurtures new marriages, with or without children. Younger people can be encouraged to participate in Christian ministries and perhaps offer a year or two of service before entering into wedlock or beginning family life. In some cultures, the man or woman without children is not a full adult member of the family group. In Christianity, only faith is necessary to mature membership in the community. As Paul repeatedly taught, reducing the pressure to marry (and reducing reproductive insecurity) will leave Christians freer to serve Christ, the kingdom, and their neighbors. A Christian population ethic should affirm all faithful believers, regardless of marital or reproductive status, and encourage everyone to minister to others according to the gifts God has provided.

Early Christianity offered women meaningful spiritual roles in societies where they all too frequently found themselves treated as less than fully human. Further, the New Testament offers an inheritance not subject to military conquest, financial failure, or resource competition. In a time of great political stress (for Palestine) and of great social change (for the cultures conquered by Greece and Rome), Christianity was able to produce the New Testament and loving communities, while at the same time accommodating both genders and a variety of cultures and social classes. A renewal of this steadfastness of purpose, as far as justice and care for our sisters and brothers is concerned, combined with an ability to adapt to new social circumstances and economic pressures, would be a powerful means of helping societies to adapt to changing demography.

CONTRACEPTION AND COMMUNITY DISCIPLINE

Some Christians view family planning as a threat because they believe it may encourage sexually irresponsible behavior and fornication. If contraceptives are easily available, there is always some increased risk that teenagers and young adults will become involved in uncommitted and immature relationships and that the married will be tempted into adultery. Lack of family planning, however, does not necessarily keep fathers at home with their progeny, and it certainly does not prevent teenage pregnancies and abortions. Christian communities, caught between traditional values, biblical values, and the sexual revolution, far too frequently stick their heads in the sand and let each age group and social class decide what it wants to do about the apparent conflicts.

Thus the third question for the local Christian community is, What is our approach to family planning and contraception? Pastors, deacons, elders, and mature Christian adults may need to meet and determine a congregational or denominational policy. To avoid doing this, in fact, defaults social control to the government and to popular culture. In wealthier congregations, where everyone has access to a private physician, married couples may need little medical advice on birth control or child nutrition. Teenagers, however, will almost certainly need guidance and may be under substantial peer pressure to become sexually active. A Christian education program may, therefore, discuss basics of sexual morality with teens while discussing world population dilemmas and deeper ethical issues such as adultery and divorce with adults.

There are some congregations, in contrast, that may need special guidance or medical-technical assistance concerning family planning and child health. These congregations include those

1. where individuals do not have adequate or easily available medical care,
2. where people are in transition from rural to urban environments or from traditional to industrial societies,
3. where families are under economic stress or suffering shortages of basic necessities,
4. where child or maternal mortality is high,
5. where single parents or teenage pregnancies are prevalent,
6. where AIDS (including AIDS transmitted by heterosexual contact) and other sexually transmitted diseases are major health problems, and
7. where the national government or the surrounding culture do not support or condone Christian family and sexual values.

In such congregations, family planning might become a key topic in adult Christian education. Some subjects, such as the importance of commitment in marriage, can be preached from the pulpit, while others, such as changing family values and structures, can be discussed in adult Sunday school classes and Bible study groups. Pastors may wish to take the lead in dealing with questions concerning sexual morality. Lay people, including health care workers, teachers, and mature women who have raised families, may be better prepared to advise on birth spacing and infant nutrition. The Christian community can thus supplement inadequate public health programs by providing information on contraception within a Christian ethical framework and by providing training and social support for young mothers. As with every other element of the Christian life, good example is one of the best teachers, and affirmation of the community can encourage individuals to find Christian pathways through the ethical tangles presented by a socially indifferent industrotechnical culture.

Christians from communities with limited health services or problems with child mortality may find that the available Christian literature on family issues is not appropriate to their problems. There are numerous Christian volumes available on sex education, for example, but since most have been produced for use in nations with adequate medical services, these books are usually intended for parents to use with children and teenagers and are not necessarily appropriate for other audiences.[7] Further, they reflect the social pressures of Western culture and ignore many issues of interest elsewhere in the world. In other words, they concentrate on fornication and sexually transmitted diseases and have nothing to say about child spacing or early marriage in a society with strong parental control.

Further, cultures in transition may find themselves with special communication problems. In recent years in Nigeria, for example, younger unmarried women have become increasingly involved in premarital sexual activity, resulting in many unwanted pregnancies. Nigerian society has "undergone marked social change," and researchers have found "that premarital sexual behavior appears to be more common among women who come from nontraditional backgrounds."[8] As the influence of traditional family support systems and parental control have declined, the number of teenage pregnancies has increased. Although the problems here are similar to those surrounding teenage pregnancy in the United States, the shift in values is in a different cultural context, with the both the girls and their parents caught in major social transition. Pastors and church leaders working outside Euro-American and techno-industrial settings will need to carefully analyze the concerns of their own community, discuss them in a biblical framework, and develop approaches appropriate to their own socioeconomic and cultural environments.

GOD'S LAND, OUR LIVELIHOOD

The questions raised by increasing population incorporate a series of environmental and resource harvest concerns. Christians in both the industrial and the developing world need to examine carefully their stewardship of the resources God has provided for them. Are we spoiling the land? Is increasing human reproduction resulting in decreasing fertility of the land? Are we poisoning ourselves and our children? Are we producing so many progeny that in rushing to provide for them, we are destroying the land? Will our children find that we have wasted their inheritance while we were trying to make a better world? How are we treating God's creatures? Are we stealing their blessing? Are we robbing our human sisters and brothers of God's providence, and ruining their lands through air pollution and other environmental abuses?

The fourth question, therefore, for the local Christian community is, Are we caring for our land and for the earth in general? Again, it is foolish to wrestle with population if population is not the primary problem. If we are mistreating resources, dumping toxic waste into rivers and the air, allowing soils to erode, and logging forests without encouraging regeneration of more trees, slowing population growth will make little difference. If, however, we are taking good care of our fields, but there are simply more people than the land can support, trying to balance the population ledger makes sense. Some regions of the earth could still accommodate more human activity. Many more are already overcrowded in terms of contemporary agricultural production. The Christian community, knowing of God's love for creation, should set an example to others concerning our care for the earth and our willingness to share its resources with our neighbors.

A last question for the local Christian community is, Are our family ethics harming anyone or excluding anyone? If the emphasis is on small families, how do we treat childless people and those with large families? What is our attitude toward single mothers? Are we so interested in young children that we are neglecting older people (or vice versa)? It may be impossible to establish an organized ministry for every family and demographic need, but it is not impossible to treat everyone as a full citizen of the kingdom and as a brother or sister in Christ.

In countries where population growth is related to ethnic, religious, or racial tensions, the local Christian community's attitudes toward procreation may reflect deep societal insecurities or attitudes of antagonism toward other neighboring groups. Christians should trust God for their future and express love toward their neighbors. Trying to out reproduce the opposition is an act of fear rather than love and will accomplish little in the long run other than increasing competition for land and other resources. Denominations that think that their own virility forwards Christianity often produce ethnic barriers rather than social bonds and may actually be ignoring Christ's call to bring the kingdom to others.

CARING AND ACTION

Christians from nations with high population growth rates will find that they have several alternatives for operating in the social sphere, including

1. thinking about and studying reproductive, economic, and population ethics from a Christian perspective,
2. ministering and teaching in the arena of reproductive and family values within the Christian community,
3. opening a discussion with non-Christians concerning family values,
4. setting an example for others in terms of childbearing and childrearing, and
5. participating in national decision-making processes and speaking for or against government and international family planning programs (speaking against is covered in detail in the next chapter).

As mentioned in chapter 8, one of the keys to resolving population dilemmas is the pursuit of justice and the equitable sharing of economic and reproductive resources both with and between communities. Christians from all economic backgrounds may pursue ministries that help to alleviate the problems caused by rapid population growth, or, conversely, they may attempt to alleviate the adverse economic conditions that stimulate population increase. Christians may assist by "giving to" or "providing for" rather than by taking from. There are many possibilities for action:

First, Christians may work with other Christians who believe that human population growth is causing serious socioeconomic problems and environmental damage. Organizations such as Ministry for Population Concerns[9] lobby for greater availability of contraceptives and family planning assistance and help provide communication among interested Christians.

Second, Christians may campaign for or actually provide equitable opportunities for education within their home community, state, or nation. Christians may also provide educational assistance to others, particularly those too poor to pay school fees. A variety of established international Christian ministries provide literacy training, free or inexpensive schools, or free meals for children in school. Even purely religious educational activities such as distributing Bibles and giving away "beginning reader" Scripture portions help populations to learn to read. Of special importance is encouraging girls to go to school and obtain a secondary or higher-level education.

Despite the criticism that the "sponsor a child" programs are more expensive to run than some other types of ministries to children, they fill several of the criteria for desirable assistance programs. First, they provide support for both girls and boys. Second, the child receives care over several years, and the programs stimulate sponsor commitment. Third, the programs provide basic health care and help the children remain in school through secondary education. These programs thus forward the equitable resource distribution and social stability that underlie the distributive justice model of human population regulation. Their real weakness is that they are not reaching enough children in need.

Christians have long been active in education, but Christians from the developed nations have become so accustomed to well-supported public school systems that they may not recognize the limitations of educational systems in the developing world. Further investment, particularly in rural schools, education for women, and institutions of higher learning, can only help resolve the growing population problems of the developing nations.

A third means whereby Christians may assist in ameliorating population problems is in working toward food *security,* rather than just providing food, for those subject to famine and food shortages. As most of the relief agencies recognize, emergency aid is only a short-term solution. Unless families find a continuing source of income and sustenance, they will need help again and again. As mentioned previously, repeated provision of emergency supplies without moving the people of a region toward self-sufficiency may worsen both population support and resource damage problems.

Relief and development agencies complain that Christians will contribute to emergency programs but will not support long-term development efforts. In other words, a picture of a starving child draws a response, but a picture of a family looking longingly across land they cannot afford to farm does not. Christian participation in programs aimed at *sustained agricultural and regional development* will provide the best long-term defense against hunger. Whenever Christians provide emergency aid, they should ask themselves, What is needed after the emergency is over?

A fourth means is helping to provide or working toward good quality health care for mothers and their children and for families in general. Improving child survivorship increases reproductive security. Where health care services are generally available, family planning is much facilitated. Again, the question is not whether Christians should be providing medical assistance but whether such assistance is reaching everyone who needs it.

169

Christians from the developed world may avoid discussing the role of family planning in medical missions. They may consider it too controversial to mention or may leave the matter to the discretion of medical personnel in the field. Instead of ignoring the issue, denominations should establish clear guidelines for including family planning in medical missions programs and should work with medical, sociological, and anthropological professionals to establish *family values ministries* appropriate to different cultural settings. Since AIDS has become a major source of mortality in parts of the developing world (particularly in Africa), Christian health education should encompass the full span of issues concerning personal reproductive behavior and potential contraceptive techniques. Helping others to understand the risks and consequences of unrestrained sexual activity, as well as the potential benefits of a responsibly conducted family life, is as important as vaccines and antibiotics in saving lives.

Fifth, Christians may provide educational assistance to young mothers and nutritional assistance to their offspring. New mothers from a variety of socioeconomic backgrounds may not know the basics of child care and nutrition, nor will they necessarily understand the relationship of family planning to child survival. Losing one infant after another produces nothing but suffering for both the children and the mother. Christian ministries can, in conjunction with other activities, specifically assist women in starting families. They can also emphasize childrearing methods, such as breastfeeding, that provide the best nutrition for the child and help to prevent conception.

Working for effective social security systems is a sixth method. This includes participating in political, union, corporate, and charitable activities that deal with pensions and retirement funds, as well as helping the elderly with their needs. It also means working to ensure that the jobless and the poor have enough to eat and a roof over their heads. One of the primary motives for having a large family is fear of an unsupported old age. Caring for widows and others who cannot provide all the necessities of life for themselves has deep roots in Old Testament law and was a major concern of the early church. Both increasing and declining populations may be influenced by social security or the lack of it.

A seventh method is for Christians to seek social and economic justice. This, of course, is a tall order, and there are wide differences among Christians as to how the justice God desires for the poor and dispossessed can be achieved. On the activist fringe are the liberation theologians who see establishing social justice as a key Christian calling and hold political involvement as a necessity. Toward the center are Christians called to fight poverty who run missionary organizations specializing in education, health care, or agricultural development. Whatever our political leanings, the past successes of Christian social reformers provide a lesson. Christians fighting the injustices and health hazards created by eighteenth- and nineteenth-century industrial cities fed and clothed malnourished children. They also campaigned for legislation to protect those children and their parents from labor abuses, hazardous working environments, and unsanitary conditions. A program that really attacks the sources of food or medical shortages or of child mortality must honestly analyze the roots of the problems and work for long-term solutions, be they through legislation, reorganization of social institutions, or economic reform, and for immediate relief for those in need.

One of the keys to population justice is justice for women. The social status of women, the economic and educational opportunities available to women, and the degree to which women's health care needs are realized are all key factors in pursuing population stabilization in areas with accelerated growth. If the environmental problems of the developing world seem awesome, and if economic change seems interminably slow, bettering the lives and opportunities for women from all strata of society is a goal that can be forwarded by something as simple as modifying attitudes concerning female social roles. Other attainable possibilities include legislation to protect economic and educational rights, public health programs directed toward women's needs, child mortality reduction efforts, agricultural and cottage industry development efforts, and programs to provide social security for widows and childless women. Christian organizations can be either a great help or a great hindrance in assisting women struggling with contemporary social pressures and cultural change.

When pursuing distributive justice, Christians interested in missions should recognize that international aid, especially emergency aid, is an insecure source of food and health care. Outsiders may leave, or their home organizations may withdraw program funding. Outsiders are likely to discontinue activities in the face of political upheavals. Further, aid programs sponsored by foreign governments may invite external interference in domestic politics or may become sources of political blackmail (e.g., the foreign government threatens to terminate aid if the country in question does something the foreign government does not approve of). Government-sponsored foreign aid programs often have heavy military components and may favor the interests of economically or politically powerful social classes (which may worsen population problems by creating political instability, spawning refugee populations, or by increasing the social distance between the rich and the poor). The most viable long-term aid strategies should include the establishment of locally managed programs that provide secure food supplies, medical services, and educational facilities within a nation or region. Therefore, Christians should assist with educational programs aimed at technology transfer and producing indigenous educators, as well as in establishing self-supporting farms and businesses that provide social stability and are local sources of food and trade goods.

Christians must also realize that raising income in a developing region may not, by itself, be effective in stemming population growth. A small income increase, especially where there is still great social inequality or resource insecurity, may stimulate fertility. (There is still controversy in the economics literature about the relationship of income to fertility.) It should also be recognized that some of the other relationships between fertility and socioeconomic status may not hold for the poorest strata of society. There is evidence, for example, that increasing education levels in rural areas may increase fertility up to a certain point, after which it begins to decrease.[10] Improving income will do little good if child mortality remains high. Elevated child mortality among the economically disadvantaged, in fact, "provides a powerful incentive for overinvestment in children, especially in view of the importance of children for long term family security."[11] A program attempting to both reduce poverty and slow population expansion must thus consider several variables simultaneously in order to be effective. In pursuing justice, particularly economic justice for the Third World, we have to grapple with the fact that rapid population increase impedes development, while lack of development stimulates population growth.[12]

BACK TO TRIAGE?

In concluding this chapter, we should note that only one of the actions suggested above, providing better health care, directly concerns contraception. All of the others improve the lives of individuals and ease the effects of poverty and food shortages. We should recognize, however, that we have not completely escaped Ehrlich's and Hardin's arguments. Hardin suggests that providing emergency food to people who have overgrown their agricultural carrying capacity worsens overpopulation and just leads to a bigger population crash, with more death and misery farther down the line. This could indeed be the case if people repeatedly experience famine and food production per capita continues to decline. In Africa, as of this writing, the action of individual African governments and international aid efforts have not curtailed population growth, nor have they put most of the continent back on the road to food security and surplus agricultural production. There is plenty of evidence that present population trends can be reversed and agricultural productivity can be improved in Third World nations. The longer action is delayed, however, the more difficult it will be to alter direction without further mortality and suffering. Can Christians from both the developing and the developed nations work together to reduce land degradation, food shortages, poverty, and the impact of cultural changes in ways that are, at the same time, loving and economically, environmentally and politically effective?

We can theoretically reject Ehrlich's triage strategy as unbiblical, but our true rejection of the model lies not in our words but in our actions. Triage remains a viable alternative as long as the necessities of survival remain in critically short supply and there is not enough assistance to go around. Can Christians, at the very least, reduce their own contributions both to population growth and to economic inequalities? Can Christians reach out to non-Christians and, free of fear, show them why faith is so important?

QUESTIONS FOR REFLECTION

1. What policies would be appropriate for your denomination concerning family planning? Your home congregation? Any of your denomination's missions efforts?
2. How can Christian relief strategies be organized to discourage future food crises?
3. Christians in developed nations can lobby for or against the foreign aid policies of their governments. If you are from a developed nation, what sorts of foreign aid policies do you think your government should have relative to food production in developing nations? Relative to population regulation and health care? Is there any type of foreign aid your government is providing developing nations that is worsening population, economic, or environmental problems? If you are from a developing nation, what sorts of foreign aid would be the most helpful to your nation? What sorts might cause social, economic, or environmental damage? Do you think it might be better to stop foreign aid completely?
4. If you could take one action or make one contribution yourself to

assist a developing nation or region, what would that be? If you could take an action in reducing either the social or environmental impacts of accelerated population growth, what would that be?

5. If your denomination is active in cross-cultural ministries or missions, what policies or attitudes do they have concerning the role of women in traditional or changing cultures? What, if any, policies do they have concerning the degree of Westernization they encourage? What do you think the best policies for your denomination would be concerning family values in a non-Western culture?

10

COERCION AND ABORTION
IN POPULATION MANAGEMENT

In this last chapter we will approach two of the more difficult ethical quandaries presented by human population growth. These issues concern the relationship between the reproductive rights of an individual and the needs of a group to reduce overall population increase. We will first investigate two questions left unanswered in the last chapter: Are coercive methods ever appropriate? And what sorts of coercion or positive and negative social reinforcements are ethically justified? We will then look at the role of abortion politics in terms of encouraging or discouraging family planning internationally.

COERCION: WHEN AND WHOM?

Through history, various forms of social sanctions and positive and negative incentives have been implemented in attempts to suppress or to stimulate population growth. Although professional ethicists most often concern themselves with legislation and the actions of governments, cultures may also limit population growth through social conventions, such as ostracism of unwed mothers or late marriage. Historically, population limitation techniques have varied from making disparaging remarks about couples with large families to state-enforced infanticide. Government-mandated destruction of infants is at least as ancient as Pharaoh's attempt to limit the numbers of his Hebrew slaves by killing all the newborn males. Almost any technique that attempts to influence reproductive rates through reward or punishment will be at least mildly controversial and will raise questions concerning the rights of the couple, the rights of the child, and possible injustice to a specific gender or social class. We have to ask ourselves, How far dare a government or a community go? And what justifies government interference?

Positive Incentives

In terms of free services, positive rewards, and incentives, governments can offer the following:

1. free sex education
2. free family planning services, such as hormone implants or birth control pills
3. free health services, with added attractions such as check-ups and other health care
4. free sterilization
5. social acknowledgment or achievement awards for participation in family planning
6. cash incentives or other rewards for individuals or couples participating in a family planning program employing contraceptives
7. cash incentives or other material rewards for sterilization
8. cash incentives or tax breaks for small families
9. better housing or jobs for people with small families
10. scholarships and other educational support for children from small families
11. special professional opportunities for people who delay marriage or raising children
12. group incentives, such as offering a village a new water system, a school, or a fish pond if it reduces its overall birth rates.[1]

The previous chapters lauded distributive justice, particularly providing education and health services to everyone who needs them. This is not the same, however, as providing a reward for a specific type of behavior. Distributing rewards means distributing something differentially. Thus someone may not have access to a resource or may be left out. We should discriminate between the first four items listed above, which are social services made available to all, and the last eight, which are contingent on behavior and social response and may result in differential resource availability.

There is also the question of who receives the reward or punishment. In the case of giving educational opportunities to small families, it is the children of the large family or the youngest child of several who will not have a place in a school, not the parents making reproductive choices. Further, if an additional child causes the family as a whole to lose access to a resource, the child may be blamed for the loss and may suffer psychologically and socially as a consequence. Some systems of reward may be prejudiced against the poor, who out of greater need are more likely to participate in government-sponsored programs. This has been a major criticism of "sterilization for cash" (or for a transistor radio).

Christendom has historically been more concerned with preventing fornication or sexual immorality than it has been concerned with protecting the economic or marriage rights of younger children. For long centuries, inheritance in rural Europe was determined by birth order. No attempt was made to distribute the rewards in the system equally to all siblings, much less, in communities strongly stratified by social class and land tenure, to all the children in the neighborhood. (In the Bible, ironically, birth orders and spiritual inheritance are often reversed. Jacob, the second son, took Esau's birthright, for example, and David, the youngest son of Jesse, was God's choice for king.) Dominated by economics, European traditions actually countered one of the principles of just distribution of reproductive resources presented in the previous chapter because they did not give everyone an opportunity to marry and have children. Residents of the industrial democracies have now become so used to thinking all children should have an opportunity to get an education that they forget that this type of equal resource access is a relatively recent ideal.

We can, in dealing with rewards, identify some potential ethical concerns. First, a reward system that denies children from large families access to resources or makes lower birth order children responsible for a loss of resources may harm individuals who did not choose their own social circumstances. Thus special educational benefits for small families can be undesirable alternatives because they leave some children out. If possible, reward systems should instead directly influence adult behavior concerning contraception and should not target specific social classes or ethnic groups. In countries where access to contraceptives has been limited by poor health facilities, the first step is not to establish an incentive system but to make contraceptives available to all couples who wish to use them. After adequate family planning services have been established, initiation of a reward system may be ethically justified where there are competing social values. When India, for example, first made family planning services widely available to the rural populace in the mid-1960s, they found that birthrates did not fall because family values had not changed.[2] In a community where a large number of sons has traditionally carried high social status or been considered economically advantageous, a reward system may supply other symbols of status or other means of income to the family and thus merely replace one means of support or status with another.

One cannot consider "benefits" to be true incentives if they are forced (e.g., the only way to receive a food allotment is to be sterilized). Using rewards or incentives under false pretenses is, of course, ethically questionable because it is dishonest. India, for example, was criticized for implementing a sterilization program where the participants were not always properly informed about the effects of the procedures on their future reproductive abilities. Users of incentive programs may also "cheat," so programs based on short-term and nonpermanent methods (i.e., birth control pills) are better avoided unless there is an easy means of monitoring compliance, such as having a local health official verify that the family has had no births in a given year.

Although a perfectly equitable incentive system is probably impossible, some emphases are better than others. India has been able to increase participation in sterilization programs through cash payments. During the early 1970s when India increased emphasis on this approach, rates varied from state to state, but they were typically less than $20 for a vasectomy and about $2 for a tubectomy.[3] One problem with a program of this sort is that the participants will wait until they have as many children as they want (it could be seven or eight) and then will go in for surgery and the money. India has therefore experimented with paying more to participants with smaller families. Another problem, and perhaps an inescapable one, is that such programs are more attractive to the poor. One means of reducing injustice, however, is to try to reduce child mortality so that if a poor man or a poor woman is sterilized after having a small number of children, these children are likely to survive. If incentives help to equalize surviving family size between social classes, they are probably relatively justly distributed. If they lead to unequal sharing of reproductive resources, especially if they encourage larger surviving family sizes for the wealthy, incentives should be considered ethically suspect.

A possibility for a reward system that is more flexible may be found in the new hormonal implants, which last for several years.[4] A woman could enroll in a family planning program and allow medical personnel to insert an implant. She would then receive an incentive appropriate to the cultural environment. To stay in the program she must return on a regular schedule for a physical check-up and to have the implant replaced, if needed. Each time she returned, she would receive another incentive. In some cases, increasing the level of incentive relative to the length of continuous tenure in the program might be valuable because it would discourage dropping out of the program for a year, having another child, and then reentering. Providing large incentives for women with three children (or some other small number of children) might also be helpful. Incentives need not be cash. They can be things that help the woman's family, such as bags of rice, powdered milk, or coupons that can be used to buy clothes or school supplies.[5] The implant has an advantage because the woman cannot forget or suddenly stop using it. If the woman wishes to have another child, she can have the implant removed and then reenter the program at a later date (perhaps losing her "seniority" in the process). This type of program might work well in nations where traditional values still favor large families and a reduction of two or more children per household would be helpful. This system does not penalize children, although it would be well to gain the consent or cooperation of a woman's husband before enrolling her. It does have the disadvantage of being relatively more attractive to poorer women, although since entry and exit is potentially flexible, a woman whose financial circumstances had improved would not be locked into participation.

Negative Incentives

If positive incentives do not work, or if a community or government thinks it cannot afford them, negative incentives or some other form of social coercion may be suggested, including these:

1. social ostracism for large families
2. extra taxes or fees for extra children (above a certain number) and the services they use, including school fees
3. legislating family size and fining (or jailing) people who exceed the limits (or removing jobs, salary, vacations, or other family benefits)
4. forced use of contraceptives, particularly long-term contraceptives such as intrauterine devices (IUDs)[6] and hormone implants
5. forced sterilization after a given family size is reached
6. forced abortion after a given family size is reached
7. killing or abandoning, according to law or custom, unwanted in-

fants, those born too soon after a sibling, those born to large families, or those born inopportunely during times of community stress

In Western culture marriage rather than fertility as such has often been manipulated, primarily by utilizing social sanctions rather than by legislation. Modern nations, such as India, have tried legally raising the age of marriage specifically to reduce fertility. There are therefore several ways to delay childbearing:

1. Families and communities condemn or ostracize those who marry at an early age.
2. Families and communities condemn or ostracize those who marry without owning land or some other form of wealth such as cattle. (This system, as you will remember from chapter 4, not only delayed marriage for older European siblings, since they had to wait for their parents to leave them the farm, but also tended to leave younger siblings permanently unmarried because land was inherited by the eldest son, and the younger siblings did not have adequate financial resources to marry.)
3. The age at marriage, the size of a dowry, or the extent of financial assets is legislated, and offenders are fined or unable to legally marry.

Hard Choices

Negative incentives present some of the same difficulties that positive reward systems present—the impact of the social controls may fall on the innocent. Even if the parent is fined for having too many progeny, for example, the wrath of adults and their frustrations over the punishment may fall on the "extra" child or children. If larger families pay greater taxes, younger children, who are likely to be shortchanged in terms of access to family resources anyway, may suffer loss of financial support and even shortage of food resources. If some type of population regulation is legislated, it is preferable that it directly affect the childbearing capabilities of adults rather than undermine the opportunities for their children.

All coercive methods restrict the rights or choices of the individual and thereby conflict with basic values in Euro-American culture, where privacy and the sexual choices of the individual are held in high regard. Civil libertarians, who have fought hard to prevent governmental interference in sexual acts between consenting adults, would be hard pressed to condone such an overt invasion of privacy as forced sterilization. Sterilization of women on welfare, ethnic minorities, and the institutionalized, including the mentally retarded and psychiatric patients, has been a legal and individual rights issue even when tacit consent has been obtained.[7] Patients have sometimes been ill informed of the procedures, and there is evidence that in the past, operations such as hysterectomies were performed on minorities when not medically necessary.

Coercive methods of population regulation potentially represent a collision between two competing sets of values: the integrity of the individual and the safety of the community. Following contemporary ideals that consider the rights of the individual inalienable, we could only consider violating the right of privacy when, as in the case of war, the community is really under a life-or-death threat. This is a "lesser of two evils" argument which requires that several criteria be met before coercive means of regulating population can be considered: First, coercive methods should only be employed where famine is a serious threat or mortality due to *widespread* malnutrition is occurring, and the crisis is directly related to population levels and not to some other factor such as lack of land for peasant farming. In other words, some restriction of individual reproductive options is appropriate where mortality or great suffering will result if populations continue to expand. The threat must be proven—the projections of environmental alarmists are not by themselves adequate to justify coercion. Second, food, health care, educational opportunities, and other resources are relatively equitably distributed within the society. Coercion is not appropriate where malnutrition is strongly related to social class, where a majority of the populace is well fed, or where socioeconomic problems independent of population growth are causing shortages. In the latter case, just distribution of resources would be the first step in relieving famine. Third, an attempt has already been made to make family planning services widely available, and people have not been willing to use them or have been unwilling to reduce family size. Fourth and last, other methods of encouraging reduced birthrates have already been seriously attempted and have failed. These methods might include honest persuasion, such as advertising campaigns that tout the benefits of adequate birth spacing.

Very few societies worldwide presently meet these criteria. Many developing nations, for example, have not coped with land tenure problems. Throughout much of the Third World, rural populations still do not have easy access to family planning. Further, although almost all traditional societies successfully manipulate individual choices like age of marriage through social sanctions and economic control, democratic governments have found that the populace will reject direct government interference in their reproductive lives. Customs concerning marriage and childbearing often have long cultural histories and are supported by most of the adults and leaders within a specific cultural group. A majority of people will follow these customs because they are what they have always been taught was right and they expect community affirmation for their compliance. When a government initiates coercive methods, they may be no worse than the social sanctions or punishments imposed by the community for violation of traditional mores. Government coercion, however, may represent quick and unwanted change, may be viewed as external interference without community consent, and may create deep values conflicts. A Moslem, for example, may have the government tell him large families are bad and unpatriotic, while his upbringing and religious culture have taught him that large families are good. The Moslem will probably respond by placing the values of a centuries-old religion and of his cultural heritage above those of a changeable and politically suspect contemporary bureaucracy.

When Paul Ehrlich, in *The Population Bomb*, suggests that use of coercive methods is ethically justified at present population growth rates, he is very much the biological and social expert taking a parental attitude toward those who do not understand the dangers of accelerated population growth. As Shrader-Frechette commented, he is unwilling to wait for democracy to operate. Coercive methods pose the dangers of racism, sexism, classism, and culturism. Social sanctions have always been most effective when a majority of the populace agree to their use and willingly participate in both obeying the rules and in enforcing them. Although China, where central governmental control is exceptionally strong, has been successful in using negative incentives in controlling fertility,[8] India has found population politics can influence elections. In 1975 Prime Minister Indira Gandhi used powers of emergency rule to upgrade a fertility reduction campaign. Some Indian states used strong negative incentives such as withholding food rations from those with more than three children or threatening salary loss to those who did not participate in a sterilization program. Actual cases of coercion, in concert with rumors of further planned coercive actions, helped to defeat Mrs. Gandhi's government in an election in 1977.[9] In order to preserve democratic processes and protect human rights, we can add a further criterion to the implementation of coercive methods and negative incentives: The implementation of coercive methods should not depart from democratic processes. The populace should favor and support any social sanctions or negative incentives used (just as one would hope the citizens of a nation would all vote in favor of legislation aimed at controlling drunk driving). Legislation should be instituted by vote, and public programs should be approved by elected bodies or other appropriate governmental units, such as village elders.

With advances in birth control technology producing more long-term contraceptive strategies that are reversible, the options for temporary restrictions on reproduction are increased. Not all possible strategies are equally desirable, however. In actually establishing a program utilizing mildly coercive methods or negative incentives (assuming famine or similar crisis), the following are possible ethical criteria for selecting techniques:

First, methods of birth control or fertility regulation causing possible death or injury of either parents or children should be avoided. The foundling hospital, for example, is not an appropriate method of population regulation. From a Christian perspective, practicing infanticide to avoid mortality of older children or adults is trading one life for another. Prevention of conception should be emphasized as the appropriate means for reducing total population size. Historically many cultures have abandoned certain types of individuals during periods of resource limitation or social stress. Those left without support have included female infants, infants in general, younger children, older women, or the aged in general. The modern trend has been to consider all individuals of equal worth—an idea that Christianity has forwarded.

Second, use of reversible contraceptives (particularly long-term contraceptives) is to be favored over other methods of reducing family size. This preserves the greatest number of options for the individual couple, should family or economic circumstances change. (Voluntary sterilization might be encouraged as an alternative for couples who *know* they have as many children as they want.)

Third, if legislation establishes family size criteria for participation in certain programs (including the receipt of rewards), these should ultimately be based on number of children surviving the high-risk early childhood period rather than on the number of births. Family limitations based solely on number of infants delivered are usually prejudiced against the poor, who are more likely to lose a young child. Allowing a woman who has lost a child to bear another will help couples to achieve the goal of having progeny available to assist them in their old age.

Fourth, application of family size criteria should be equal for all social strata in a society. If large families are discouraged, the rich, well-educated, and fully employed should be under the same sanctions as the poor, uneducated, and underemployed.

Fifth, programs should avoid strategies that result in discrimination against female children, especially de facto infanticide of girls. In societies that have traditionally favored sons, trying to achieve very small family sizes or extensively utilizing abortion to limit family size is likely to result in gender bias.

Sixth, negative incentives should not directly or indirectly harm children—for example, subjecting them to parental rejection or denying them places in school.

Seventh, forced sterilization and abortion are invasions of the individual person (or, put in Western terms, violations of individual rights and of privacy) and are not acceptable. (There is a potential counter argument here: that sterilization after producing several offspring has not prevented the individual from reproducing and does little personal damage [there is less risk for men than for women], whereas in time of severe food shortages, bearing more children will result in further resource stress and further mortalities. Protecting privacy and reproductive potential does not take precedence over preventing further deaths. For many Christians who believe the fetus is a human person, however, this argument cannot apply to forced abortion. Since abortion results in the death of a fetus, we can only trade the life of fetus for the life of a "postnatal" person, if we believe the fetus is of lower status or is not a person at all.)

Eighth, legislating the age of marriage or requiring a certain economic status prior to marriage is acceptable for delaying the onset of childbearing providing restrictions do not force women to bear children outside of legally sanctioned matrimony and do not discriminate against the poor or against particular ethnic groups. That is, delaying marriage is acceptable if the delay is equally shared among all individuals of reproductive age and if it does not force unmarried pregnant women into a marginal social status.

Ninth, since most contraceptive techniques are not completely dependable and fertility varies from person to person, establishing patterns of childbearing based on absolutes is highly undesirable. A woman who has no intention of conceiving another child may become pregnant despite her best efforts. It might be appropriate to require a woman who has had three children to utilize a hormonal implant in order to receive an extra food allotment. It would not be appropriate to take the food allotment away permanently if contraception failed and she delivered a fourth child. Restrictions based on absolutes generate social cruelty and force women into very specific childbearing roles they may or may not be willing or able to fulfill.

Tenth and last, eliciting individually responsible behavior and giving couples an opportunity to regulate their own fertility is always superior to government-enforced efforts to maintain a specific reproductive standard.

In summary, we can conclude that negative incentives and coercion in general are ethically problematic and should be employed only as a last resort. Even in crisis, however, some methods preserve the rights and options of the individual better than others, and programs must be carefully planned to avoid doing more harm than good. Very few, if any, nations presently meet the criteria for utilizing coercion. The Chinese program, on one hand, is just because it (1) originated in response to famine and to genuine resource shortages, (2) was preceded by an attempt to make family planning assistance widely available, (3) is based in a society that is attempting to share resources relatively equitably, and (4) pursues family size restrictions that are free of social class distinctions. As successful as the program has been in terms of stabilizing population growth, however, the program violates several of the ethical criteria listed above. It has (1) been established without consideration of democratic processes, (2) greatly restricted individual reproductive options, (3) violated individual privacy, and (4) forwarded gender discrimination. If one considers abortion to be killing a person or violating the rights of a child, then the Chinese program trades one life for another. Further, even though the government does not sanction it, the program may have encouraged the killing of newborns. The Chinese have done very well in making the program socially equitable and poorly in preserving the integrity of the individual. We have to ask ourselves if this is the necessary result of letting population growth get out of hand, and if widespread mortality from famine can only be resolved with the sacrifice of individual rights. The weaknesses of the Chinese program make a timely attempt at a distributive justice approach even more attractive and suggest that the nations of the developing world should take population issues very seriously as they struggle to obtain better lives and greater freedoms for their peoples.

Male or Female Contraception?

Even when couples volunteer for family planning, who actually utilizes the contraceptive may be an issue. A number of methods available cause permanent sterility. Further, some methods have potential side effects. The new hormonal implants, for example, can cause abnormal bleeding and disruption of a woman's menstrual cycle. Although possible long-term side effects of birth control pills are still controversial, women may worry about increased cancer risk. Birth control hormones can cause circulatory disorders, may be problematic if used during pregnancy, may affect a woman's need for vitamins and minerals, and can reduce breast milk production during lactation.[10] Many women abandon the pill, the IUD, injectables, or implants because of undesirable side effects.[11] Men may be concerned that sterilization implies a reduction in sexual performance. In Sudan, for example, misconceptions about vasectomy make it unacceptable to most men.[12] A study conducted in Kenya found that men favored tubal ligation for their wives and were willing "to endure criticism" from their elders when their wives submitted to it. These same men, however, were "uniformly negative" toward vasectomy.[13]

Some of these potential problems, such as increase in cancer risk, may be more acute for Third World women who have poor access to medical services and examinations. Implants and hormone injections may cause medical difficulties if employed under unsterile conditions or without appropriate follow-up. Since extraction of implants is more difficult than insertion, women may find it difficult to have them removed when they wish.[14] Surgical sterilization presents more risks for women than for men, even when performed in adequate medical facilities. Tubal ligation has a mortality rate of 25 to 30 per 100,000, while vasectomy causes almost no mortality. In Third World settings, proper sterile procedures may be neglected, and women may not be given adequate postoperative care, raising the risk of mortality or permanent disability.[15] A woman from a traditional rural culture who is unable to work in the fields due to pain from a botched surgical procedure may find herself abandoned by her husband.

Since the most successful medically approved temporary contraceptive methods are primarily for women, women have assumed most of the risk and discomfort associated with various contraceptive alternatives. Women of course also assume the risks of ill-timed pregnancies and may suffer greatly from a pregnancy when their own nutritional status or health is poor. A general ethical goal of any population regulation effort (be it increasing or decreasing birthrates) should be to relieve physical, psychological, and social stresses on women and to forward equal responsibility (and to some extent shared personal contribution) between the sexes.

ABORTION AND POPULATION REGULATION

The preceding chapter suggested a series of positive Christian responses to accelerated population growth. Thus far we have used the term "family planning" in a general sense and have not considered what specific means of limiting births might be acceptable or unacceptable to Christians.(Most Protestant ethicists deem medical technologies that inhibit contact between ova and sperm as morally acceptable. These include birth control pills and other methods that inhibit ovulation and condoms and similar devices or compounds that prevent sperm from entering the female reproductive tract or kill sperm once they enter.)Surgical sterilization of either the male or the female is also usually considered ethically acceptable if a mature decision has been made and both partners in a marriage agree that permanent prevention of fertility is desirable. Differences of opinion appear, however, over medical technologies that prevent implantation of a fertilized egg[16] (which might be considered a potential person), techniques that cause a woman to reject the implanted fertilized egg, and methods that remove a developing fetus (abortion). In addition, Protestants differ over the morality of sexual practices that prematurely terminate or displace vaginal intercourse (e.g., coitus interruptus and oral and anal intercourse).

The ethics of individual contraceptive techniques and of terminating pregnancies have been well argued in the medical and sexual ethics literature, and the reader is referred to these discussions concerning specific strategies for inhibiting conception and preventing birth. We should recognize, however, that if adequate health services are available, couples can select medically effective and relatively safe contraceptive techniques that neither discourage vaginal intercourse nor damage a fertilized egg or a fetus in any way. If we accept such contraceptive strategies as ethically correct for Christians, many people will then ask whether other methods, such as abortion, are necessary to population regulation. This question, however, should be rephrased to read, Do population levels (or resource shortages) in any way change the rights or the status of the fetus? This may appear to be a contemporary issue, but it is actually centuries old, and different cultures have resolved it in a number of different ways.

Most ethical discussions over the status of the fetus begin by trying to decide if the fetus is a person or not. There are three possibilities:

1. The fetus is not a person, or the fetus prior to some point in development is not a person.
2. The fetus is a person, but its right to existence or to resources is relative to the availability of those resources. Or, the fetus is a person, but it has lower status than its mother or than an older sibling, or other classes of persons.

3. The fetus is a person and has the same rights to resources and to life as anyone else.

Through history, many cultures have actually placed the fetus and newborn infants in the second category rather than in the first or third. This follows one genre of cultural strategies for dealing with resource limitations. If food is in short supply, cultures will feed those whom they most wish to survive or those who are high-status persons, rather than those who are low-status persons. In communities where the male line inherits, the well nourished are often men and boys. In societies where fertility is held in high regard, reproductive-age women may be differentially protected. Cultures have tended to abandon those who are at highest risk (young children) or have low reproductive fitness (the aged). Through history, the fetus has been at very high risk (it may be miscarried, die at birth, or not survive the first year of childhood). It also represents the least investment of energy and resources and is probably the easiest "person" to replace. (Notice how Darwinian this all sounds.) In crisis, the extra child may still be valued, but the community will place her interests below those of her mother or of her five-year-old brother. During famine, the fetus or the newborn may threaten her mother's health and may take critical resources from her siblings. We should recognize that these types of solutions to cultural stress generally do not just give lower priority to the unborn or newborn, they often select against children (females, lower birth order), certain social classes, and some adults as well.

One of the major developments in Christian ethics, particularly since the time of the Reformation, has been the trend toward viewing all "persons" as having equal value before God (and equal rights before the law). This position has a strong New Testament foundation. Early Christianity was very egalitarian, accepting both genders, all ages, all ethnic backgrounds, and all social strata. Paul spoke to the issue when he wrote in Galatians 3:28, "There is neither Jew nor Greek, there is neither slave nor free, there is neither male nor female; for you are all one in Christ Jesus." Christians have been leaders in abolishing slavery in Euro-American culture, in securing women's suffrage, and in protecting the rights of minorities. Christ acknowledged the spiritual importance of children and gave them full status in the coming kingdom, while in Roman society they were lower-status persons or, if born into slavery, barely persons at all. Many contemporary Christian missions are oriented toward children, and their funding campaigns emphasize "saving the children" or "child rescue." As previously mentioned, nineteenth-century

Christian reformers did much to protect the interests and status of children growing up in industrial slums.

Christian ethics has thus moved steadily away from the idea that someone might be more or less a person, or someone might be a person but have lower status or less right to community support than someone else. This tends to undermine the idea that in times of resource stress, someone, be it the upper class, men, whites, reproductive-age adults, or the oldest child, should be fed while other people (the poor, blacks, baby girls, aged women) are left to starve. Christians no longer have stratified categories of personhood—you are either a person or you are not, and if you are a person, you are loved by God and should be loved by Christians as well. One of the reasons for the violent debate over the personhood of the fetus in Christian ethical circles is that Christianity has, probably fortunately, been abolishing all intermediate or second-class categories (infant, slave, woman, widow) and now feels uncomfortable leaving the fetus in limbo in an intermediate status.

When Ehrlich proposes that the fetus is a "potential person," he is moving the fetus back into an intermediate category of personhood and making the fetus's survival dependent on available room on an already crowded planet. The fetus thus has less status than living humans. This is compatible with triage, which ceases to assist those at greatest risk. The fetus carried by an African woman with limited food resources may have less than a 50 percent chance of surviving to three years of age, for instance. Suppose we look at infants and children in this light, however. Are infants in Kenya any less people than those in relatively unpopulated Montana? Holland is a densely populated country; does that affect the personhood of the Dutch? Is a malnourished year-old infant in the Sahel less a person than a chubby Swiss baby, not because the young Schweisser has a much greater chance of becoming a banker but simply because he has a much greater chance of living to adulthood?

We can then ask the question, Is the value or the status of the fetus contingent on food supply or on the chances of survival? The question of risk, in fact, has changed during the modern era. Today, in well-fed, well-doctored northern Europe, infant mortality is extremely low. Although the fetus is still at higher risk than a newborn, and a newborn is still at higher risk than an older child, very few infants and late-stage fetuses are lost (other than to medically induced abortion). The distribution of risk to young children worldwide is not primarily by age but by social class and geographic location. Birth order is an important risk factor among the poor, not among the rich. To make the value or status of the fetus contingent on either its chances of survival or the availability of resources is to return to the concept that certain social strata or ethnic groups are not fully people, a position that conflicts with much recent and historic Christian thought.

This suggests that accelerated population growth should not serve as a basic justification for abortion and that Christians should determine whether the fetus is a person or not without considering population issues. Since the resources necessary to human life are not equitably distributed, rationalizing abortion because resources are not available to everyone actually conflicts with the principles of distributive justice. It also makes personhood contingent on economics. One might argue that poor women need abortion to protect their health. This position, however, implies that the lack of health services and food resources encountered by poor women somehow justifies abortion. A better solution is to provide adequate medical care, contraceptive access, and nutrition.

The question of the legitimacy of terminating a pregnancy at any stage, therefore, *does* belong in the realm of medical and legal ethics, including ethical determination of the rights of both the mother and the child, and must be addressed prior to suggesting that a specific medical technique be utilized for reducing the birthrate.[17] If we delete lower-status personhood, based on chances of survival or resource availability, we have two basic options. One is that termination of pregnancy at some stage is legitimate and may be utilized for population regulation (or for any other purpose). The other is that abortion is unethical and should not be utilized to reduce birthrates. In most of the industrial democracies, the fetus is presently not considered a person under the law, and abortion is legal or is allowed up to some given point in the fetus's development. In countries such as the United States, the fetus may have some rights and some degree of legal protection, but so do corpses, ships, and corporations. Legal ethicist Leonard Glantz has noted that under United States law, "It is . . . possible to give fetuses rights within the limitation that these rights do not abridge the rights of persons now existing."[18] The lawyers and the courts, of course, are not necessarily ethically right.[19]

If Christians take the position that the fetus, up to some point in development, is not a person, then they have few conflicts with Planned Parenthood and Paul Ehrlich (although their reasons for accepting abortion may be different). If Christians reject abortion, and many do, are they not making population regulation more problematic, if not impossible? The answer is that reducing birthrates is, of course, more difficult if abortion is not used. The elimination of any

190

option for preventing conception, pregnancy, and birth makes managing fertility more of a challenge. There is no reason, however, why an anti-abortion stance should be in unrelenting conflict with family planning.

Lobbies, Protest, and Death Against Death

As was mentioned in chapter 1, Christians in the United States who are against abortion as a means of terminating a pregnancy to protect the social and economic (as opposed to the life-threatening medical) interests of the mother or as a method of family size limitation or population regulation have also blocked family planning and contraceptive aid to international programs that they believe provide or promote abortion. Christian lobbies have fought against public health services that provide contraceptives (and in some cases, abortions) to those unable to pay for private medical care and have attacked sex education programs in state-run schools. Although many of the Christians who disapprove of government-sponsored family planning programs use contraception and family planning themselves, they are afraid public programs will make contraceptives available to teenagers and other unmarried persons who will then enter into promiscuous sexual relationships and perhaps conceive out of wedlock despite the use of contraceptives. Christians fear that government intervention in such a personal matter as family planning will infuse non-biblical values into their own adolescent offspring and into the world in general.

Christians who are strong opponents of abortion have taken a number of positions relative to population regulation issues. One of the most common is to consider population an unimportant problem. For example, a recent book proposing to answer the "tough questions about abortion" stated that the population explosion was "myth." The authors went on to mistakenly claim that world population had grown a mere 1.8 percent between 1975 and 1989. (They were probably misquoting a source reporting that world population had grown 1.8 percent *per year* between 1975 and 1989.) They finished their short paragraph on the subject by suggesting, rightly, that resource distribution was actually the difficulty, but they neglected to relate this to accelerated population growth.[20] The authors thereby avoided one of the tough questions by misunderstanding the problem.

In the United States, most of the Christian anti-abortion literature does not really answer the arguments of antinatalists concerned about population trends in the developing world. The discussions in pro-life volumes are centered on the court case *Roe v. Wade*, on women's rights, on federal and state legislation, and on strategies for political action. R. C. Sproul, a prolific popular writer and capable Calvinist theologian, devoted several chapters in a recent book on abortion ethics to such topics as the role of the government in abortion and "the problem of unwanted pregnancies" but put all his arguments in a United States context.[21] This approach, although it thoroughly reviews the situation in the United States, neglects the concerns of the larger Christian community.

As much as they might avoid international population issues, one of the things anti-abortion activists do tackle is the International Planned Parenthood Federation's role in promoting abortion and the flow of tax dollars and foreign aid monies to Planned Parenthood and similar organizations. One exposé of Planned Parenthood comments that "internationally, various Planned Parenthood agencies have been able to skim the cream off of virtually every United States foreign aid package. This includes a lion's share of the more than two hundred million dollars in International Population Assistance funds, and the more than one hundred million dollars in contraceptive and abortifacient research appropriations."[22] This writer also observes that Planned Parenthood is funded by the United Nations, the World Bank, and the Agency for International Development.[23] Another anti-abortion volume claims, "What is truly alarming is not just the vast amounts of money flowing with minimal accountability into a single multi-national collective, but the end product of it all: the highly organized, carefully planned deaths of millions of unborn children. . . . Far from promoting joyful motherhood, Planned Parenthood promotes worldwide genocide."[24] Anti-abortion lobbyists in the United States have worked hard to try to cut off public funds to Planned Parenthood, including their international operations.

These political battles have had far-reaching impacts in the field of population regulation and contraceptive technology. Funding for contraceptives and family planning, and even other types of medical aid, has disappeared along with funds that might have been used for abortions. The irony of inhibiting funding for contraception or public health in order to halt abortions is that it is, again, trading one source of mortality for another. Stopping abortion funding saves fetuses, and that is all. It does not protect the newborn infants or their mothers and siblings from food shortages and disease outbreaks. Further, limiting the availability of family planning puts new mothers and young children at risk from the stresses of a baby born too soon (and a child born immediately after another is at high risk of mortality itself). Blocking contraceptive access for ten Third World women saves no one and may result in one or more deaths—a fetal death, the death of a two-year-old, the death of a newborn, and/or the death of a woman in poor health before she conceived.

In addition to limiting international funding for family planning programs, Christian sensitivity over both abortion and publicly funded family planning has had negative impacts on the development of safer, longer lasting, and less expensive contraceptive techniques. Pharmaceutical firms, for instance, are reticent to sponsor and market products they think might be controversial. New methods of birth control also require expensive testing and present the risk of lawsuits if there are any unexpected side effects once a new contraceptive is made available to the public. In addition, government agencies that might sponsor research will avoid topics that are likely to stimulate political antagonism and cannot, in any case, begin a major program without congressionally approved federal funding. Elected officials may steer away from foreign aid that includes controversial family planning provisions and may be unwilling to support public health packages that provide family planning assistance to all those requesting it if they think there will be a backlash among their constituency.

If one were to criticize from an ethical perspective the political strategies of anti-abortion activists from the developed nations, relative to population regulation, the major defects would be these:

1. Many anti-abortion activists assume world population problems are unimportant or are greatly overstated. They aren't.
2. Many anti-abortion activists from the developed world expect child survivorship patterns in the developing world to be similar to those in their own environments and assume that if a fetus is saved, a child is also saved. This is not the case.
3. Many anti-abortion activists from the developed world assume that lack of contraception does not cause extensive child or maternal mortality. This is also not the case.
4. Many anti-abortion activists assume women in the developing nations will have other options for limiting family size if there is no government funding available. In poorer and rural regions, this is rarely the case.
5. Many anti-abortion activists from the developed nations see other people in other settings as having the social options of the financially secure. They do not.

Economics and Justice Again

Aside from the abortion controversy, some basic Christian social attitudes are causing an inconsistent approach to both population regulation issues and family planning in general. Most married middle-class Christians from the developed nations are now using some form of contraception or family planning. National figures on family sizes indicate this, and attendance at a typical middle-class church, be it mainline, evangelical, or charismatic, provides easy evidence that Christian families have about the same number of children as non-Christian families from the same socioeconomic backgrounds (and this is not because they marry any later). Middle-class Christians often equate marriage with stability and assume it is the couple's business to seek medical assistance and to pay a practitioner to provide contraceptive assistance. They therefore also assume that if you cannot pay for this, then you are either very young or not financially established and should not be engaging in sexual intercourse or thinking about getting married. Christian concerns about fornication thus become entangled with the family planning needs of the poor. Further, Christians feel ambivalent about contraception. They need to use family planning to regulate their own reproduction so they will produce the number of children they want, when they are best able to take care of them. Yet many believe publicly funded sex education and contraception encourage sexual immorality and quickly become public evils. Christians, particularly Christian parents, fear that easy availability of contraceptives will encourage initiation of sexual relationships—relationships that are not only immature and in conflict with biblical injunctions against fornication but also very likely to result in an unwanted pregnancy. All contraceptive methods occasionally fail, and younger users are both more likely to make mistakes and more likely to conceive if contraception is inadequate.

Josh McDowell, in a book criticizing sex education trends and methods in the United States, makes the argument that despite the fact that the number of teenage clients at birth control clinics in the United States increased dramatically between 1971 and 1981, the number of teenage pregnancies per year had not only increased but also increased per thousand women, from 95 to 113.[25] The number of teenage abortions more than doubled during the same time period. A decline in the birth rate among teens was therefore not due to better availability of contraceptives or better sex education but was due to greater use of abortion to terminate pregnancies.[26] McDowell cites figures (found in a journal published by Planned Parenthood) indicating that a single woman under age eighteen who is trying to prevent pregnancy by using birth control pills has an 11 percent chance of becoming pregnant in her first year of such use. This is over five times the conception rate of a single woman over thirty utilizing the same method.[27] The vulnerability of teenagers to an unwanted pregnancy is presumably due to a mixture of inexperience, lack of self-discipline, and the naturally higher fertility of younger women. Interestingly, married women under twenty have only 1.6 percent chance of pregnancy during their first year of using the pill. The failure rates for other methods are substantially higher, exceeding 30 percent for girls under eighteen who try to prevent pregnancy by using a diaphragm or spermicides.[28] Further, 48.8 percent of all eighteen- to nineteen-year-olds obtaining an abortion in a United States study conducted in 1987 were using a contraceptive method during the month when they conceived.[29] In recent years, about one third of sexually active teenagers in the United States have had a premarital pregnancy some time before they reached their twentieth birthdays.[30] McDowell argues that contraceptive use among teenagers does not absolutely protect them from pregnancy and certainly does not completely protect them from sexually transmitted diseases, and McDowell is right.

Teenage pregnancy is a problem elsewhere in the world, including developing nations such as Nigeria.[31] The parental concern over teenage use or abuse of contraceptives should not, however, become completely confused with international concerns over accelerated population growth. Christians should certainly avoid assuming that if contraceptives and sex education are not solving the teenage pregnancy problem in the United States, they will not help women elsewhere in the world regulate family size. If one unmarried teenager in ten becomes pregnant each year, it creates difficulties for the girl, her family, and her community. Giving a married woman in a developing country the opportunity to safely reduce her family from eight children to three is a different issue. Some risk of pregnancy in this circumstance is acceptable, and even an occasional contraceptive failure may not create a major difficulty. A reduction of fertility to 10 percent of present levels for married women who already had two or three children would cause a major reduction in birth rate in regions with greatly expanding populations. Older married women are more likely to use contraceptives properly than are unmarried teenagers, and ironically, since married women are expecting to engage in sexual intercourse on a regular basis, they may be more likely to use contraceptives consistently.

Assuming that distributive justice is desirable, we should be cautious when we mix questions of sexual morality with economics. If financially well off Christians declare themselves unwilling to provide a major medical technology to those who are less well off on the grounds that the technology may encourage immorality, this is not only the developed world casting judgment on the Third World or on the poor, it is also a culturally uneducated position. Many societies in the developing world are highly moral by any Christian sexual standard, and very family oriented. If denying contraceptives to someone really prevents immorality, it might be justified. If, however, one denies contraceptives or family planning to someone because she or he is poor, it is merely the "haves" keeping a technological blessing to themselves and making certain old social barriers stay in place.

It is easy to be forgiving about the double standards that surround contraception because middle-class Christians are as much in transition concerning sexual and family values as anyone else. It is critical, however, to distinguish the demographic problems generated by poverty and high child mortality from those involving personal sexual ethics. We can treat modern contraceptive techniques like a legion of demons that has to be kept in a tight middle- and upper-class box, or we can treat them as one of the greatest blessings of modern medicine—a blessing that needs to be carefully distributed and managed, but a blessing all the same. Family planning, contraception, and proper child spacing are integral parts of the miracle of reduced infant and child mortality that has benefited mothers worldwide.

Cutting the Gordian Knot

Now, as an exercise, let us adopt the ethical position, among currently available Christian alternatives, that has the broadest definition of the sanctity of human life—the completely pro-life position. Proponents of completely pro-life ethics believe that all life is valued, all children (including the unborn) are to be protected and nurtured, and no one is to be considered less worthy before God because he or she is weak, poor, unfit, or dispossessed. In addition, the completely pro-life position requires that all activities that threaten human life, such as the development of nuclear weapons and the international arms race, be replaced by peaceful alternatives and that all sources of structural violence, such as land tenure systems that force hunger people onto poor land, be replaced by just social systems.[32] In the completely pro-life model, protecting the unborn becomes more than stopping medical termination of pregnancies. It also requires being certain the mother is well-nourished and the child can expect adequate food and care after delivery. The completely pro-life position, in fact, grew out of a concern that the so-called pro-lifers were only trying to stop abortion and were either taking no stance on other life-threatening issues or were actually condoning such potential killers as nuclear weapons.

Not everyone reading this book will agree with all the tenets of a completely pro-life position; some may be in favor of further development of high-tech arsenals, for example. The completely pro-life model, however, is a useful tool for examining possible approaches in population ethics because it allows no trading of mortalities. One cannot save fetuses to lose infants or save mothers to lose toddlers and stay within the constraints of the completely pro-life model.

So, under the completely pro-life model, are family planning and population regulation pro- or anti-life? Since family planning (which may utilize abstention as a potential method of preventing or delaying childbirth) allows life to start at the best time, under the best possible circumstances, it is not only pro-life but in many regions with limited natural resources also necessary to an over all pro-life ethic. A mother does not want to have a child while she is nursing, or while it is a drought year and food is in short supply. In a completely pro-life ethic, the child is as valued as any other human being, and waiting for better conditions gives the child a much better chance of survival. Family planning protects the little boy who was just vaccinated and the girl who comes to the mission for a hot lunch. It also protects the mother who already has three young children or who is in ill health and trying to care for a new baby.

This suggests some possible ethical directions for Christians from developed nations in regard to aid for developing nations:

First, international funding for family planning should not be stopped or reduced because of the abortion issue. If one believes abortion is killing a human being, blocking funding for health services is merely trading one source of mortality for another, which is unacceptable and unnecessary. A completely pro-life stance suggests that international family planning aid should be increased, not decreased. If for some reason pro-life lobbyists wish to block family planning funding to a specific agency, alternative sources of family planning services should be found and the funding distributed. Further, pro-life activities should not cause the poor to suffer from a loss of medical resources that are not related to abortion. If Christians do not care for the personal sexual mores encouraged by international family planning organizations, they should start their own programs in this area.

Second, Christians should encourage the development of contraceptive technologies that are safer for women in ill health, are less expensive, and are easier to use in areas with inadequate health services. This provides better health care options for those with the least access to and greatest need for medical services. The development of safe, dependable, relatively long-term contraceptive methods that do not require repeated visits to a health care center or expensive prescription drugs could, for example, greatly facilitate family planning in less developed rural areas and urban slums with few clinics. Political activities that discourage better family planning methodologies indirectly result in mortalities of women and children and should be avoided.

Many Christians would be embarrassed to tell the members of their congregation they were trying to design a better condom with a lower failure rate. Yet the better condom could be very helpful to women who cannot use hormonal contraceptives or have just had a baby and temporarily wish to avoid using hormones. It is a deep irony of Western culture that so many Christians are "called" to build new fighter bombers and nuclear submarines and so few are "called" to work on barrier contraceptives.

Third, Garrett Hardin aside, family planning is a legitimate component of international medical ministry. Christians should be open to supporting medical missions that are willing to say they provide family planning assistance. Moral judgments are difficult to make over thousands of miles and between cultures. Christians from developed nations (who may not be setting the best example themselves) should try to avoid judging the morality of Christians in the developing nations and should encourage indigenous churches to show leadership within their own cultural context both in personal sexual ethics and in family planning and population ethics.

A Contraceptive Ethos

Christian sexual ethics have long emphasized reproductive responsibility. These ethics should be expanded to include a "contraceptive ethos,"[33] with clear principles concerning not only who may engage in sexual intercourse but also who should be using contraception. Christians should be affirmative of properly implemented family planning and should rid themselves of their ambivalent stance by better defining how and when prevention of conception should take place. A contraceptive ethos should be developed with appropriate denominational and cultural frameworks while considering the needs of the greater Christian community. The contraceptive ethos should recognize the health and failure risks posed by the available contraceptive techniques, relative to gender, age, marital status, and medical history. The ethos should consider the needs of both sexes and should not unduly place greater risk or responsibility on one or the other. The ethos needs to recognize that younger contraceptive users may be less responsible and that teenage pregnancy will not be halted by mere contraceptive availability. The ethos must understand that birth timing and spacing are never under perfect human control, except for the absence of pregnancy maintained by abstention from sexual activity, so the ethic must always be able to answer the question, What if another child is born?

Christian sexual ethics often treats avoidance of fornication and adultery as a behavioral absolute, or nearly so. Contraceptive ethics must be somewhat more relative because they are partially dependent on the types of medical facilities available, the socioeconomic environment, the demography of the region, the health of the individual, and the properties of the contraceptives themselves. However, the ethics of both sexual activity and contraception deal with tensions between the rights of the individual and the responsibilities of the individual—to God, to other people, and to themselves.

We should note here that Christian traditions that oppose "artificial" contraception and prescribe abstention instead have fallen short in terms of dealing with contemporary cultural conditions. For abstention from sexual activity within marriage alone to adequately meet completely pro-life criteria concerning the sanctity of human life, additional cultural taboos are necessary. A married couple should, for example, abstain from intercourse for a long period after childbirth, during times of resource shortage, and while the wife is in ill health. The Roman Catholic Church has abandoned most of its medieval taboos discouraging intercourse at certain times or under certain conditions but has not replaced them with sanctions adequate to protect the lives of Third World women and children. If "sexual purity" is to be considered as important as "the sanctity of human life," "care of the poor," and "care of the earth," then it needs a revised social context that does not displace or ignore these other key Christian values.

The reduction of population growth rates can be attained through community acceptance of personal restraint in sexual activities, thoughtful approaches to managing family life, and mature, well-disciplined application of contraceptive technologies. Abortion is usually employed as a substitute for one or more of these behavioral strategies. An anti-abortion ethic does not necessarily imply a rabid pronatalist stance. Do we, as Christians, value sexual prowess, reproductive fitness, or children for their own sakes? Accelerated population growth is a critical ethical issue for all Christians, and demographic processes are something Christians can influence without devaluing other people or desanctifying human life.

A FINAL WORD

The purpose of this book is not to convince the reader that everything proposed here is the last word on population ethics. This volume is intended to bring the major issues to the attention of the Christian community and to precipitate thoughtful discussion. The sections on distributive justice, coercion, abortion, and consumption are basic, at best, and do not cover every important issue or every major argument. The reader is encouraged to take issue with this presentation, and to seek other references. Most important, however, the reader is encouraged to deal with the issues as they relate to his or her own community or denomination and to bring other Christians into active discourse concerning just Christian responses to the problems created by changes in human demography.

QUESTIONS FOR REFLECTION

1. Can you identify any nations that can presently justify use of rewards or positive incentives to regulate population growth? Can you identify any nations that can presently justify use of negative incentives or legislated restrictions to regulate population growth? What ethical criteria do you think justify the use of positive and negative incentives?
2. Under what circumstances, if any, can forced sterilization be ethically justified?
3. Describe some cases where a government might ethically abandon democratic processes in order to speed population regulation, or argue against the existence of such situations.
4. If your home congregation or denomination has taken a position on the ethics of abortion, how does it relate to population regulation? Do you think your denomination has dealt adequately with the relationship between abortion politics and international needs for family planning? Why or why not?
5. If teenage pregnancy is a concern in a developing nation, will increasing the availability of contraceptives to the population in general reduce or worsen this problem? What are some realistic ways to provide family planning services without encouraging teenagers to enter into immature sexual relationships?
6. Should the developed nations support international population regulation and family planning organizations? Should they support those that offer abortions? Should they provide funding directly to the governments of developing nations for family

planning programs? Should the developed nations restrict how these funds are spent? If so, what sorts of restrictions should they impose? How can restrictions be placed without inhibiting funding for basic health services and family planning programs?

NOTES

CHAPTER 1

1. Ralph Hamil, "The Arrival of the 5-Billionth Human," *The Futurist* (July–Aug. 1987): 36–37.

2. "Day of the Five Billion, Triumph or Threat," *UN Chronicle* 24 (November 1987): 40.

3. "State of the World Population 1988: Safeguarding the Future," *UN Population Fund Report* (New York: United National Population Fund, 1988), p. 7.

4. Edward Stockwell and H. T. Groat, *World Population: An Introduction to Demography* (New York: Franklin Watts, 1984), pp. 26–27.

5. Ibid., p. 31.

6. Ibid., pp. 27–32.

7. Jodi L. Jacobson, *Planning the Global Family*, Worldwatch Paper no. 80 (Washington D.C.: Worldwatch Institute), p. 5.

8. Five articles on population in *Journal of the American Scientific Affiliation* 26, no. 1 (March 1974): Larry Ward, "A Six-Letter Obscenity," pp. 1–3; Everett R. Irish, "Research on Complex Societal Problems," pp. 3–6; C. Richard Terman, "Sociobiology and Population Problems: Perspectives," pp. 6–13; Elizabeth Canfield, "Negative Population Growth: A Proposal for Action," pp. 13–15, reprinted from Emko Newsletter (February 1973); and Jerry P. Albert et al., "Consulting Editors Respond," pp. 15–21. 18th General Assembly of the Presbyterian Church (U.S.A.), "The Global Population Crisis." *Church and Society* 64, no. 2 (Nov.–Dec. 1973): 31–35.

9. In 1967 historian Lynn White, Jr., published a controversial essay, "The Historical Roots of Our Ecological Crisis," *Science* 155 (1967): 1203–7. The essay suggested that the transcendent God of Judaism and Christianity allowed the followers of these religions to see themselves as divorced

from nature. White also noted that passages such as those in the beginning of Genesis that "command" taking dominion over the earth lead to abuse.

10. In twentieth-century American Christianity, conservative Christians often champion personal ethics and liberal Christians often champion social ethics. This split was not evident in the revivalist (and abolitionist) atmosphere of the early 1800s. The split between conservatives and liberals and the turning away of evangelicals from social ethics if often referred to as the "great reversal." See the account by David Moberg, *The Great Reversal: Evangelism Versus Social Concern* (Philadelphia: J. B. Lippincott Co., 1972). A very readable account of American Christian social ethics in the nineteenth century can be found in Donald Dayton, *Discovering an Evangelical Heritage* (New York: Harper & Row, 1976).

11. Paul Ehrlich, *The Population Bomb* (New York: Ballantine Books, 1968).

12. Lord P. T. Bauer, quoted in Ben Wattenberg and Karl Zinsmeister, eds., *Are World Population Trends a Problem?* (Washington, D.C.: American Enterprise Institute for Public Policy Research, 1985), pp. 19–25.

13. Ibid.

14. Kathleen Newland, *Infant Mortality and the Health of Societies*, Worldwatch Paper no. 47 (Washington, D.C.: Worldwatch Institute, 1981).

15. Thomas J. Goliber, "Sub-Saharan Africa: Population Pressures on Development," *Population Bulletin* 40 (Feb. 1985): p. 47.

16. Lester R. Brown and Jodi L. Jacobson, *Our Demographically Divided World*, Worldwatch Paper no. 74 (Washington, D.C.: Worldwatch Institute, 1987), p. 9.

17. Ibid, p. 10.

18. Dirk J. van de Kaa, "Europe's Second Demographic Transition," *Population Bulletin* 42 (Mar. 1987): 59.

19. Brown and Jacobson, "Our Demographically Divided World," pp. 6–9.

20. Ibid., pp. 9–11.

21. Jane Menken, "Introduction and Overview," in Jane Menken, ed., *World Population and U.S. Policy: The Choices Ahead* (New York: W. W. Norton & Co., 1986), p. 8.

22. Statement from *Population and Development Review*, White House Office of Policy Development, United States Government Statement prepared for the United Nations International Conference on Population, Mexico City, 1984, quoted in Menken, *World Population and U.S. Policy*, p. 9.

23. Ibid., p. 11.

24. Ibid., pp. 12–13.

25. Private communication of Joseph Speidel, Population Crisis Committee, cited in Jacobson, *Planning the Global Family*, p. 46.

26. Ibid.

27. Ibid., p. 34.

28. Brown and Jacobson, *Our Demographically Divided World*, p. 48.

29. Bauer, quoted in Wattenberg and Zinsmeister, *Are World Population Trends a Problem?* p. 24.

CHAPTER 2

1. Edward Stockwell and H. T. Groat, *World Population: An Introduction to Demography* (New York: Franklin Watts, 1984), pp. 59, 79.

2. W. L. Langer, "American Foods and Europe's Population Growth, 1750–1850," *Journal of Social History* (Winter 1975): 51.

3. Richard G. Wilkerson, "The English Industrial Revolution," in Donald Worster, ed., *The Ends of the Earth: Perspectives on Modern Environmental History* (Cambridge: Cambridge University Press, 1988), p. 91.

4. Marvin Harris and Eric B. Ross, *Death, Sex and Fertility: Population Regulation in Preindustrial and Developing Societies* (New York: Columbia University Press, 1987), pp. 106–13.

5. Stockwell and Groat, *World Population: An Introduction to Demography*, pp. 68–72.

6. Harris and Ross, *Death, Sex and Fertility*, p. 113.

7. Ibid., p. 111.

8. Ibid., pp. 113–25.

9. Ibid., pp. 115–16.

10. Ibid., pp. 116–22.

11. Stockwell and Groat, *World Population: An Introduction to Demography*, pp. 155–59.

12. Ibid., p. 154, and Lester Brown and Jodi Jacobson, *Our Demographically Divided World*, Worldwatch Paper no. 74 (Washington, D.C., Worldwatch Institute, 1982), p. 9.

13. William W. Murdoch, *The Poverty of Nations: The Political Economy of Hunger and Population* (Baltimore: Johns Hopkins University Press, 1980), p. 69.

14. Ibid., p.70.

15. Ibid., p. 69–73.

16. Ibid., pp. 73–75.

17. Stockwell and Groat, *World Population: An Introduction to Demography*, pp. 260–61.

18. U.S. Census Bureau statistics cited in Ken Dychtwald and Joe Flower, *Age Wave: The Challenges and Opportunities of Aging America* (Los Angeles: Jeremy P. Tarcher, 1989), pp. 8–9.

CHAPTER 3

1. Biblical quotations marked "W" are from Claus Westermann, *Genesis 1–11, A Commentary*, trans. John J. Scullion (Minneapolis: Augsburg Publishing House, 1984) or Claus Westermann, *Genesis 12–36*, trans. John J. Scullion (Minneapolis: Augsburg Publishing House, 1985).

2. Walter Brueggemann, *Genesis: Interpretation, A Biblical Commentary for Teaching and Preaching* (Atlanta: John Knox Press, 1982), p. 28.

3. Quotes and the inspiration for this discussion from ibid., pp. 36–37.

4. Roland de Vaux, *Ancient Israel*, vol. 1: *Social Institutions* (New York: McGraw-Hill Book Co., 1965), p. 41.

5. Ibid.

6. Ibid.

7. Brueggemann, *Genesis*, p. 125.

8. Westermann, *Genesis 12–36*, p. 149.

9. Ibid., p. 150.

10. Brueggemann, *Genesis*, p. 131.

11. See Brueggemann, *Genesis*, pp. 140–48, for a stimulating discussion of Genesis 15.

12. Westermann, *Genesis 12–36*, p. 248.

13. Biblical quotations marked "H" are from Hans Hertzberg, *I & II Samuel* (Philadelphia: Westminster Press, 1964), pp. 21 and 24.

14. de Vaux, *Social Institutions*, p 24.

15. Ibid.

16. Ibid., p. 25.

17. Walter Kaiser, *Old Testament Ethics* (Grand Rapids: Zondervan Publishing House, 1983), pp. 182–90.

18. See ibid., pp. 185–86, for a discussion of this passage.

19. Hertzberger, *I & II Samuel*, p. 272.

20. Walter Brueggemann, *I Kings* (Atlanta: John Knox Press, 1982), p. 52.

21. See also Matthew 19:13–15 and Luke 18:15–17.

22. George Eldon Ladd, *A Theology of the New Testament* (Grand Rapids: Wm. B. Eerdmans, 1974), p. 65.

23. William L. Lane, *The International Commentary on the New Testament: The Gospel of Mark* (Grand Rapids: Wm. B. Eerdmans, 1974), p. 361.

24. Gerd Theissen, *Sociology of Early Palestinian Christianity* (Philadelphia: Fortress Press, 1978), p. 33.

25. Ibid., pp. 37–39.

26. Peter Garnsey, *Famine and Food Supply in the Graeco-Roman World: Responses to Risk and Crisis* (Cambridge: Cambridge University Press, 1988), p. 25.

27. Ibid., p. 34.

28. Ibid., p. 218–27.

29. Ibid., p. 21.

30. Theissen, *Sociology of Early Palestinian Christianity*, p. 40.

31. Flavius Josephus, "Wars of the Jews," book III, chapter 3, passage 2, in *The Works of Flavius Josephus*, trans. William Wiston (New York: Leavitt & Allen, 1853), p. 651.

32. Josephus, "Life," passage 45, in ibid., p. 15.

33. Josephus, "Wars of the Jews," book III, chapter 3, passage 2, in ibid., p. 651.

34. Michael Avi-Yonah, *The Holy Land from the Persian to the Arab Conquest (536 B.C.–A.D. 640)* (Grand Rapids: Baker Book House, 1977), pp. 219–21.

35. Ibid., p. 221.

36. Theissen, *Sociology of Early Palestinian Christianity*, p. 41.

37. Victor Paul Furnish, *The Moral Teaching of Paul: Selected Issues* (Nashville: Abingdon Press, 1985), pp. 36–37.

38. Leonard Swidler, *Biblical Affirmations of Women* (Philadelphia: Westminster Press, 1979), p. 336.

39. Ibid., p. 337.

40. Evelyn and Frank Stagg, *Women in the World of Jesus* (Philadelphia: Westminster Press, 1978). p. 201.

41. Luke T. Johnson, *First and Second Timothy and Titus* (Atlanta: John Knox Press, 1987), p. 71.

42. Don Williams, *The Apostle Paul & Women in the Church* (Ventura, Calif.: Regal Books, 1977), p. 113.

43. Paul Jewett, *Man as Male and Female* (Grand Rapids: Wm. B. Eerdmans, 1975), p. 60.

44. See any commentary on Leviticus, such as Gordon J. Wenham, *The Book of Leviticus* (Grand Rapids: Wm. B. Eerdmans, 1979), pp. 214–25.

45. See ibid., pp. 185–89, and Lloyd Bailey, *Leviticus* (Atlanta: John Knox Press, 1987), pp. 63–65.

46. F. F. Bruce, *The Book of Acts* (Grand Rapids: Wm. B. Eerdmans, 1988), pp. 174–75, and Ernst Haenchen, *The Acts of the Apostles* (Philadelphia: Westminster Press, 1971), pp. 310–11.

47. Marvin Harris and Eric B. Ross suggest that the New Testament is anti-natalist in *Death, Sex and Fertility: Population Regulation in Preindustrial and Developing Societies* (New York: Columbia University Press, 1987), pp. 84–85.

CHAPTER 4

1. Josiah Cox Russell, *The Control of Late Ancient and Medieval Population*, vol. 160 of Proceedings of the American Philosophical Society (Philadelphia: American Philosophical Society, 1985), p. 36.

2. Ibid., p. xiv.

3. John Boswell, *The Kindness of Strangers: The Abandonment of Children in Western Europe from Late Antiquity to the Renaissance* (New York: Pantheon Books, 1988), p. 269.

4. Russell, *The Control of Late Ancient and Medieval Population*, p. 36.

5. Lewis W. Spitz, *The Renaissance and Reformation Movements*, vol. 1: *The Renaissance* (St. Louis: Concordia, 1971), p. 10–12.

6. Russell, *The Control of Late Ancient and Medieval Population*, p. 196.

7. Ibid., pp. 203–10, and E. A. Wrigley, *Population and History* (New York: McGraw-Hill Book Co., 1969), p. 78.

8. Gustaf Utterstorm, "Climate Fluctuations and Population Problems in Early Modern History," in Donald Worster, ed., *The End of the Earth: Perspectives on Modern Environmental History* (Cambridge: Cambridge University Press, 1988), pp. 39–79.

9. Ibid., p.73.

10. Wrigley, *Population and History*, p. 69.

11. Spitz, *The Renaissance and Reformation Movements*, vol.1, p. 10.

12. George Huppert, *After the Black Death: A Social History of Early Modern Europe* (Bloomington, Ind.: Indiana University Press, 1986), pp. 1–13.

13. Boswell, *The Kindness of Strangers*, p. 257.

14. Wrigley, *Population and History*, p. 66.

15. Peter Brown, *The Body and Society: Men, Women and Sexual Renunciation in Early Christianity* (New York: Columbia University Press, 1988).

16. Russell, *Control of Late Ancient and Medieval Population*, p. xii.

17. Boswell, *The Kindness of Strangers*, pp. 318–21.

18. Ibid., pp. 270–363. John Boswell's discussion of these issues is excellent and highly recommended reading for anyone interested in the historic record.

19. Wrigley, *Population and History*, pp. 86–89.

20. David Herlihy, *Medieval Households* (Cambridge: Harvard University Press, 1985), pp. 74–75.

21. Ibid., pp. 98–99.

22. Josiah Russell, *Control of Late Ancient and Medieval Population*, p. 207.

23. Huppert, *After the Black Death*, pp. 1–12.

24. Steven Ozment, *When Fathers Ruled: Family Life in Reformation Europe* (Cambridge: Harvard University Press, 1983), p. 38.

25. Wrigley, *Population and History*, p. 119.

26. H. J. Habakkuk, *Population Growth and Economic Development Since 1750* (Leicester: Leicester University Press, 1981), p. 72.

27. Marvin Harris and Eric B. Ross, *Death, Sex and Fertility: Population Regulation in Preindustrial and Developing Societies* (New York: Columbia University Press, 1987), p. 85.

28. John Bossey, *Christianity in the West: 1400–1700* (Oxford: Oxford University Press, 1987), p. 19.

29. Ibid., p. 20.

30. From "Apology for Christians," quoted in John T. Noonan, *Contraception: A History of Its Treatment by the Catholic Theologians and Canonists* (Cambridge: Harvard University Press, 1986), p. 76.

31. From *Stromata*, quoted in ibid., p.76.

32. From *Opera II: Opera monastica*, quoted in David Herlihy, *Medieval Households*, p. 24.

33. John T. Noonan, *Contraception*, pp. 82–83.

34. Herlihy, *Medieval Households*, pp. 24–25.

35. Ibid., p. 25. The quote from Augustine is from Sermo 250 in *Opera omnia* 1837, vol. 5, p. 1506. Herlihy's translation.

36. Noonan, *Contraception*, p. 245.

37. Harris and Ross, *Death, Sex and Fertility*, pp. 86–87.

38. Noonan, *Contraception*, p. 76.

39. Ibid., pp. 77–101.

40. From *Marriage and Concupisence*, quoted in ibid., p. 136.

41. Ibid., pp. 119–39.

42. Russell, *Control of Late Ancient and Medieval Population*, p. 204.

43. Wrigley, *Population and History*, pp. 87–89 and 123–26.

44. Russell, *Control of Late Ancient and Medieval Population*, pp. 153–60.

45. See Wrigley, *Population and History*, pp. 123–26; Harris and Ross, *Death, Sex and Fertility*, pp. 88–94; Richard C. Trexler, "Infanticide in Florence: New Sources and First Results," *History of Childhood Quarterly* 1, no. 2 (1973): 98–116; Barbara A. Kellum, "Infanticide in England in the Later Middle Ages," *History of Childhood Quarterly* 1, no. 3 (1974): 367–88.

46. William L. Langer, "Infanticide: A Historical Survey," *History of Childhood Quarterly* 1, no. 3 (1974): 361.

47. Ibid., pp. 360–62.

48. Boswell, *The Kindness of Strangers*.

49. See Boswell and the references in notes 45 and 46 for this chapter for details. This discussion and that in the next paragraph trust Boswell's summary of the available literature.

50. Boswell, *The Kindness of Strangers*, summarizes some of the available historic data on pp. 14–17.

51. Langer, "Infanticide: A Historic Survey," p. 361.

52. Carl Braaten, *The Ethics of Conception and Contraception*, (quoted in Stephen E. Lammers and Allen Verhey, *On Moral Medicine: Theological Perspectives in Medical Ethics* (Grand Rapids: Wm. B. Eerdmans, 1987), p. 330.

53. Ibid.

54. E. R. R. Green, "The Great Famine (1845–1850)," in T. W. Moody and F. X. Martin, eds., *The Course of Irish History* (Cork, Ireland: Mercer Press, 1967), pp. 263–74.

55. Phelim Boyle and Cormac O'Grada, "Fertility Trends, Excess Mortality and the Great Irish Famine," *Demography* 23, no. 4 (1986): 543–58.

56. Ibid.

57. Mary Daly, *The Famine in Ireland* (Dublin: Dundalgan Press, 1986), pp. 56–60.

58. Thomas Gallagher, *Paddy's Lament: Ireland 1846–1847, Prelude to Hatred* (New York: Harcourt Brace Jovanovich, 1982).

59. *The Times*, Mar. 31, 1947, quoted in ibid., p. 70.

60. *The Times*, Mar. 26, 1847, quoted in ibid., p.68.

61. Green, "The Great Famine," p. 261.

62. Gallagher, *Paddy's Lament*, pp. 171–258.

63. Ibid., p. 85.

64. Ibid., pp. 82–86.

65. Daly, *The Famine in Ireland*, pp. 89–92.

66. Ibid., p. 68.

67. Green, "The Great Famine." See also Harris and Ross, *Death, Sex and Fertility*, pp. 125–36.

68. Thomas Robert Malthus, *Population: The First Essay* (reprint; Ann Arbor, Mich.: University of Michigan Press, 1964).

69. M. A. MacDowell, "Malthus and George on the Irish Question," in John Cunningham Wood, ed., *Thomas Robert Malthus: Critical Assessments,*

vol. 4 (London: Croom Helm, 1986), pp. 206–20; William Petersen, *Malthus* (Cambridge: Harvard University Press, 1979), pp. 103–11.

70. Anne Digby, "Malthus and Reform of the Poor Law," in J. Dupaquier, A. Fauve-Chamoux, and E. Grebnik, eds., *Malthus Past and Present* (New York: Academic Press, 1983), pp. 97–109; Thomas Robert Malthus, *An Essay on the Principle of Population: Text Sources and Background Criticism* (New York: W. W. Norton & Co., 1976), pp. 36–44, 132–37.

71. T. H. Hollingsworth, "The Influence of Malthus on British Thought," in Dupaquier, Fauve-Chamoux, and Grebnik, *Malthus Past and Present*, pp. 213–21.

72. Malthus, "An Essay on the Principle of Population, 1803," in Malthus, *An Essay on the Principle of Population: Text Sources and Background Criticism*, p. 132.

73. J. M. Pullen, "Malthus' Theological Ideas and Their Influence on His Principle of Population," in Wood, *Thomas Robert Malthus: Critical Assessments*, vol. 2, pp. 203–16.

74. For an overview see Alfred Crosby, *Ecological Imperialism: The Biological Expansion of Europe: 900–1900.* (Cambridge: Cambridge University Press, 1986), particularly the chapter titled "Ills," pp. 195–216.

75. James Axtell, *The Invasion Within: The Conquest of Cultures in Colonial North America* (New York: Oxford University Press, 1985), p. 97.

76. Ibid.

77. Ibid., p. 98.

78. John Winthrop, *Winthrop Papers, 1631–1637*, vol. 3 (Boston: Massachusetts Historical Society, 1943), p. 167, cited in Crosby, *Ecological Imperialism*, p. 208.

79. Axtell, *The Invasion Within*, p. 147.

80. William Cronon, *Changes in the Land: Indians, Colonists, and the Ecology of New England* (New York: Hill & Wang, 1983), P. 90.

81. Ibid., p. 160.

CHAPTER 5

1. Susan Bratton, "Oaks, Wolves and Love: Celtic Monks and Northern Forests," *Journal of Forest History* 33, no. 1 (1989): 4–20.

2. Norman Myers, *The Primary Source: Tropical Forests and Our Future* (New York: W. W. Norton & Co., 1984), pp. 116–17.

3. Judith Gradwohl and Russell Greenberg, *Saving the Tropical Forests* (Washington, D.C.: Island Press, 1988), p. 50.

4. Myers, *The Primary Source*, pp. 143–51.

5. Gradwohl and Greenberg, *Saving the Tropical Forests*, p. 39.

6. Aerial E. Lugo, "The Future of the Forest,"*Environment* 30, no. 7 (1988): 17–20, 41–45.

7. Myers, *The Primary Source*, p. 150.

8. Ibid., pp. 150–51.

9. Food for the Hungry, *World Hunger: A Brief Summary about Hunger*

and Poverty in Our World (Scottsdale, Ariz.: Food for the Hungry, 1989), p. 14.

10. Loren Wilkenson, ed., *Earthkeeping: Christian Stewardship of Natural Resources* (Grand Rapids: Wm. B. Eerdmans, 1980), p. 16.

11. Sandra Postel, "Halting Land Degradation," in *State of the World 1989*, ed. Lester Brown et al. (New York: W. W. Norton & Co., 1989), pp. 21–90.

12. Ibid.

13. Lester R. Brown, "Reexamining the World Food Prospect," in *State of the World 1989*, ed. Lester Brown et al., pp. 41–58.

14. Walter Eichrodt, *Theology of the Old Testament*, vol. 2 (Philadelphia: Westminister Press, 1967), p. 48.

15. Claus Westermann, *Elements of Old Testament Theology* (Atlanta: John Knox Press, 1982), p. 93.

16. Gerhard von Rad, *Genesis* (Philadelphia: Westminister Press, 1972), p. 59.

17. James Barr, "Man and Nature: The Ecological Controversy over the Old Testament," in David and Ellen Spring, eds., *Ecology and Religion in History* (New York: Harper & Row, 1974), pp. 63–64.

18. Wilkinson, *Earthkeeping*, p. 209.

19. See Walter Brueggemann, *The Land: Place as Gift, Promise and Challenge in Biblical Faith* (Philadelphia: Fortress Press, 1977), and Leviticus 25 and Deuteronomy 14, 15, and 26.

CHAPTER 6

1. For a very readable explanation of sociobiology by one of its founders see Robert Trivers, *Social Evolution* (Menlo Park, Calif.: Benjamin/Cummings Publishing Co., 1985).

2. Garrett Hardin, "Living on a Lifeboat," originally published in *Bioscience* 24, no. 10 (1974) and also available in several anthologies, including Garrett Hardin and John Baden, eds., *Managing the Commons* (San Francisco: W. H. Freeman & Co., 1977), pp. 261–79.

3. Hardin and Baden, *Managing the Commons*, p. 263.

4. Ibid., p.265.

5. Paul Ehrlich, *The Population Bomb* (New York: Ballantine Books, 1968), pp. 158–73. Although Ehrlich usually is credited for bringing the idea of triage into the population arena, it was originally transferred from the medical to the food relief context by William and Paul Paddock in their book *Famine–1975!* (Boston: Little, Brown & Co., 1967).

6. Ehrlich, *The Population Bomb*, pp. 132–57. In a more recent volume Paul and Anne Ehrlich comment, "Despite its success, there are two sad things about the Chinese [population control] program. The first is that the nation waited so long that, when a serious attempt was made to bring down birthrates, the program had many elements of coercion that are offensive to those of us who believe reproductive behavior should basically remain in the

control of the individual" *(The Population Explosion [New York: Simon & Schuster, 1990], p. 207).*

7. Ehrlich, *The Population Bomb*, p. 148.

8. "Frontier" or "Cowboy Ethics" and "Lifeboat Ethics," in K. S. Shrader-Frechette, ed., *Environmental Ethics* (Pacific Grove, Calif.: Boxwood Press, 1981), p. 35. The discussion of lifeboat ethics in this book owes much to Shrader-Frechette's analysis.

9. Richard J. Neuhaus, *In Defense of People: Ecology and the Seduction of Radicalism* (New York: Macmillan Co., 1971), p. 188.

10. Shrader-Frechette, *Environmental Ethics*, pp. 37–38.

11. Ibid., p. 38.

12. Neuhaus, *In Defense of People*, pp. 151–61, and Shrader-Frechette, *Environmental Ethics*, pp. 38–39.

13. Shrader-Frechette, *Environmental Ethics*, p. 41.

CHAPTER 7

1. Ben Wattenberg, *The Birth Dearth* (New York: Pharos Books, 1987). See also Ben Wattenberg, "The Birth Dearth: Dangers Ahead?" *U.S. News and World Report*, June 22, 1987, pp. 56–65.

2. Ken Dychtwald and Joe Flower, *Age Wave: The Challenges and Opportunities of Aging America* (Los Angeles: Jeremy P. Tarcher).

3. Harold O. J. Brown, "Not Enough Children," *Christianity Today* 29 (Oct. 18, 1985): 10.

4. Wattenberg, *The Birth Dearth*, pp. 7–10.

5. Ibid, p. 47.

6. Ibid., pp. 65–78.

7. Ibid., pp. 100–15.

8. Data from Russell P. Sherwin, "What Is an Adverse Health Effect?" *Environmental Health Perspectives* 52 (1983): 177–82, and Dychtwald and Flower, *Age Wave*, pp. 25–50.

9. Michael D. Hurd, "The Economic Status of the Elderly," *Science* 244 (May 12, 1989): 659–63.

10. Edward Stockwell and H. T. Groat, *World Population: An Introduction to Demography* (New York: Franklin Watts, 1984), p. 156.

11. Dychtwald and Flower, *Age Wave*, pp. 25–50.

12. J. Gordon Harris, *Biblical Perspectives on the Aging: God and the Elderly* (Philadelphia: Fortress Press, 1987).

13. Lorraine D. Chaiventone and Julie A. Armstrong, eds., *Affirmative Aging:. A Resource for Ministry* (San Francisco: Harper & Row, 1985).

14. Arthur Simon, *Bread for the World* (New York: Paulist Press, 1975).

15. Ron Sider, *Rich Christian in an Age of Hunger* (Chicago: Inter-Varsity Press, 1977).

16. Jonathan and Amos Turk and Karen Arms, *Environmental Science* (Philadelphia: W. B. Saunders Co., 1983), p. 350.

17. C. Dean Freudenberger, *Food for Tomorrow* (Minneapolis: Augsburg Publishing House, 1984), p. 64.

18. Loren Wilkenson, *Earthkeeping: Christian Stewardship of Natural Resources* (New York: W. W. Norton & Co., 1940), pp. 54–56.

19. Allen Hammond, Eric Rodenburg, and William Moomaw, "Calculating National Accountability for Climate Change," *Environment* 33 (Jan./Feb. 1991): 10–15, 33–36.

CHAPTER 8

1. Lester Brown and Jodi Jacobson, *Our Demographically Divided World* Worldwatch Paper no. 74 (Washington, D.C.: Worldwatch Institute, 1986), p. 19.

2. Ibid., p. 21.

3. Ibid., p. 3

4. Fred T. Sai, "The Population Factor in Africa's Dilemma," *Science* 226 (Nov. 16, 1984): 801–6.

5. Ibid.

6. William A. Haviland, *Anthropology* (New York: Holt, Rinehard & Winston, 1985), p. 671.

7. Marvin Harris and H. T. Ross, *Death, Sex and Fertility: Population Regulation in Preindustrial and Developing Societies* (New York: Columbia University Press, 1987), p. 49.

8. Ibid, p. 41.

9. John Wesley, *The Journal of the Rev. John Wesley in Four Volumes*, vol. 1 (London: J. M. Dent & Co., 1907), p. 66.

10. Ibid., p. 74.

11. Sai, "The Population Factor in Africa's Dilemma," p. 802.

12. Ibid.

13. Ibid, p.804.

14. Ibid.

15. William D. Chandler, *Investing in Children*, Worldwatch Paper no. 64 (Washington, D.C.: Worldwatch Institute, 1985), p. 29.

16. Kathleen Newland, *Infant Mortality and the Health of Societies* Worldwatch Paper no. 47 (Washington, D.C. Worldwatch Institute, 1981), pp. 29–30.

17. Ibid., pp. 26–30.

18. Ibid., p 40.

19. Jodi Jacobson, *Planning the Global Family*, Worldwatch Paper no. 80 (Washington, D.C.: Worldwatch Institute, 1987), pp. 19–23.

20. William W. Murdoch, *The Poverty of Nations: The Political Economy of Hunger and Population* (Baltimore: Johns Hopkins University Press, 1980), pp. 49–52.

21. Ibid.

22. Ibid., pp. 202–23.

23. Cimade, Inodep, and Mink, *Africa's Refugee Crisis: What's to Be Done*

NOTES

(London: Zed Books, 1986); Peter Nobel, *Refugees and Development in Africa* (Uppsala, Sweden: Scandinavian Institute of African Studies, 1987).

24. Sai, "The Population Factor in Africa's Dilemma," p. 803.

25. Ibid.

26. Murdoch, *The Poverty of Nations*, p. 63.

27. Jacobson, *Planning the Global Family*, p. 40.

28. Ibid.

29. Ibid.

30. E. Nevis, "Using an American Perspective in Understanding Another Culture: Toward a Hierarchy of Needs for the People's Republic of China," *Journal of Applied Behavioral Science* 19 (1983): 249–64.

31. Jacobson, *Planning the Global Family*, p. 40.

CHAPTER 9

1. Christine Oppong, *Sex Roles, Population and Development in West Africa* (Portsmouth, N.H.: Heinemann, 1987), p. 104.

2. Ibid.

3. Shireen J. Jejeebhoy and Sumati Kulkarni, "Reproductive Motivation: A Comparison of Wives and Husbands in Maharastra, India," *Studies in Family Planning* 20, no. 5 (1989): 264–72.

4. Mohamed R. Joesoef, Andrew L. Baughman, and Budi Utomo, "Husband's Approval of Contraceptive Use in Metropolitan Indonesia: Program Implications," *Studies in Family Planning* 19, no. 3 (1988): 162–68.

5. Mona A. Khalifa, "Attitudes of Urban Sudanese Men Toward Family Planning," *Studies in Family Planning* 19, no. 4 (1988): 236–43.

6. Kaswantale Chibalonza, Chirwisa Chirhamolekwa, and Jane T. Bertrand, "Attitudes Toward Tubal Ligation among Acceptors, Potential Candidates and Husbands in Zaire," *Studies in Family Planning* 20, no. 5 (1989): 273–80.

7. Recent examples, which are written from a conservative perspective and are meant for parents to use in educating children, include Tim LaHaye, *Sex Education Is for the Family* (Grand Rapids, Zondervan Publishing House, 1985) and Connie Marshner, *Decent Exposure: How To Teach Your Children About Sex* (Brentwood, Tenn.: Wolgemuth & Hyatt, 1988). Volumes such as these discourage parents from letting children participate in "secular" sex education programs in the state-run schools. The question of the values taught in sex education is one of worldwide concern for Christians. Until recently, however, many Christians just objected to state-run programs and did not let their children participate. In the last decade Christians have realized that sex education is here to stay and is very necessary. Therefore, if public programs are not suitable, Christian alternatives must be created.

8. Bamikale Feyisetan and Anne R. Pebley, "Premarital Sexuality in Urban Nigeria,"*Studies in Family Planning* 20, no. 6 (1989): 343–54.

9. The Ministry for Population Concerns includes members of several mainline denominations including Presbyterians, Methodists, and Unitari-

ans. As of this writing Carol Benson Holst is director, and their address is P.O. Box 9955, Glendale, CA 91226.

10. Gerry Rogers, *Poverty and Populations: Approaches and Evidence* (Geneva: International Labour Office, 1984), pp. 31–35.

11. Ibid, p. 36.

12. Martin Stockwell and H. T. Groat, *World Population: An Introduction to Demography* (New York: Franklin Watts, 1984), pp. 256–63.

CHAPTER 10

1. Leslie Corsa and Deborah Oakley, *Population Planning* (Ann Arbor, Mich.: University of Michigan Press, 1979), p. 254.

2. Martin Stockwell and H. T. Groat, *World Population: An Introduction to Demography* (New York: Franklin Watts, 1984), p. 230.

3. Corsa and Oakley, *Population Planning*, p. 253.

4. A woman's husband should be informed about the procedures used and should give his full consent. The use of implants near the surface of the skin could elicit an amateur attempt at removal if the husband disapproves. It should be noted that implants can cause abnormal bleeding, and their use may be problematic in cultures that have taboos concerning blood or discharges. The husband may be unhappy if his wife is bleeding frequently and his culture does not permit intercourse when blood is present.

5. Corsa and Oakley, *Population Planning*, p. 254, mentions a program in Ghana that used powdered milk as an incentive for having IUDs inserted. The program's enrollment doubled, and the costs per woman declined.

6. IUDs are not considered acceptable as contraceptives by some Christians on the grounds that they cause loss of a fertilized egg. See Roberg N. Wennberg, *Life in the Balance: Exploring the Abortion Controversy* (Grand Rapids: Wm. B. Eerdmans, 1985), pp. 66–68. Recent medical evidence suggests, however, that IUDs are not abortifacients but that they operate primarily by decreasing the number of sperm reaching the oviduct and by removing unfertilized ova from the female reproductive tract. See Irving Sivin, "IUDs Are Contraceptives, Not Abortifacients: A Comment on Research and Belief," *Studies in Family Planning* 20, no. 6 (1989): 355–59.

7. See Thomas M. Shapiro, *Population Control Politics: Women, Sterilization and Reproductive Choice* (Philadelphia: Temple University Press, 1985), for a discussion of this issue in a United States context.

8. In the Chinese situation, the government is attempting to make education widely available and is protecting peasant land tenure. That is, the government has attempted to deal with basic resource distribution questions. In implementing their population control program, they have also made a "one child per family" policy. Rather than favoring urban intellectuals or Communist party bosses, the program allows rural couples somewhat larger families. The program therefore does not favor the "haves" over the "have-nots." The basic disadvantages of the program are the very small family size it directs (one child), the pressure it places on women to terminate a pregnancy

even if they wish to have the baby, and the possibility of fatal discrimination against female fetuses and infants.

9. Stockwell and Groat, *World Population*, pp. 230–32.

10. Betsy Hartmann, *Reproductive Rights and Wrongs: The Global Politics of Population Control and Contraceptive Choice* (New York: Harper & Row, 1987), pp. 176–85. Recent research indicates that some hormonal contraceptives influence breast milk more than others. See World Health Organization Task Force on Oral Contraceptives, "Effects of Hormonal Contraceptives on Breast Milk Composition and Infant Growth," *Studies in Family Planning* 9, no. 6 (1988): 361–69.

11. Ibid., p. 254.

12. Mona A. Khalifa, "Attitudes of Urban Sudanese Men Toward Family Planning,"*Studies in Family Planning* 19, no. 4 (1988): 236–43.

13. Jane T. Bertrand, Nellie Mathu, Joseph Dwyer, Margert Thou, and Grace Wambwa, "Attitudes Toward Voluntary Surgical Contraception in Four Districts in Kenya," *Studies in Family Planning* 20, no. 5 (1989): 281–88.

14. Hartman, *Reproductive Rights and Wrongs*, pp. 197–228.

15. Ibid.

16. IUDs have probably been incorrectly considered abortifacients; see note 6.

17. It should be noted that if a women's rights stance is taken concerning abortion, this assumes that the needs of the mother take precedence over those of the child. In the developed world this is usually not a matter of competition for critical resources, such as food. An extension of this thinking to the developing world, however, returns us to the historic strategy of protecting the interests of the mother rather than the interests of the infant in times of resource-related stress. This makes sense in stressed environments because a motherless child will probably die, whereas a childless woman may not. Ironically, one of the major reasons for accelerated population growth in the developing world is that women still want large families. Christianity has long fought the concept that parents may do as they wish with their children, although as mentioned in chapter 4, the stance of Christendom has often been hypocritical.

18. Leonard Glantz, "Is the Fetus a Person? A Lawyer's View," in William B. Bondeson, H. Tristan Englehardt, and Stuart F. Spicher, eds., *Abortion and the Status of the Fetus*, Philosophy and Medicine, vol. 13 (Dordrecht, Netherlands: D. Reidel Publishing Co., 1983), p. 116. In the United States any person has full rights under the law; therefore, it is legally necessary to deny personhood if one does not wish to give a "human" of any sort full legal rights. The opposite is not the case. Something that is not a person is not stripped of all rights but may have certain limited rights, as long as they do not override those of human "persons." For further reading on the philosophical aspects of this issue, see Michael F. Goodman, *What Is a Person?* (Clifton, N.J.: Humana Press, 1988).

19. It may seem to the reader by this point that I am taking no stand on abortion. This is not because of disinterest in the issue, but because it would

require much too much space in a volume on another, albeit related, topic. I personally believe that the fetus is a person and that his or her interests must be fully considered. The purpose of this volume, however, is not to argue this point but to deal with abortion specifically as it relates to population issues. The reader who would like to know more about the ethics of abortion from a Christian perspective is referred to Michael Gorman, *Abortion and the Early Church* (Downers Grove, Ill.: Inter-Varsity Press, 1982); Ronald Sider, *Completely Pro-Life: Building a Consistent Stance on Abortion, the Family, Nuclear Weapons, the Poor* (Downers Grove, Ill.: Inter-Varsity Press, 1987); Robert Wenberg, *Life in the Balance: Exploring the Abortion Controversy* (Grand Rapids: Wm. B. Eerdmans, 1988); or one of the many discussions available in the medical ethics literature.

20. John Ankerberg and John Weldon, *When Does Life Begin? And 39 Other Tough Questions about Abortion* (Brentwood, Tenn.: Wolgemuth & Hyatt, 1989), p. 151.

21. R. C. Sproul, *Abortion: A Rational Look at an Emotional Issue* (Colorado Springs, Colo.: Navipress, 1990).

22. George Grant, *Grand Illusions: The Legacy of Planned Parenthood* (Brentwood, Tenn.: Wolgemuth & Hyatt, 1988), p. 29.

23. Ibid.

24. F. LaGard Smith, *When Choice Becomes God* (Eugene, Ore.: Harvest House, 1990), p. 200.

25. Josh McDowell, *The Myths of Sex Education* (San Bernardino, Calif.: Here's Life Publishers, 1990), p. 123.

26. Ibid., p. 122.

27. Ibid., p. 59, and William R. Grady, Mark D. Hayward, and Junichi Yagi, "Contraceptive Failure in the United States: Estimates from the 1982 National Survey of Family Growth," *Family Planning Perspectives* 18, no. 5 (1986): 200–209.

28. Grady, Hayward, and Yagi, "Contraceptive Failure in the United States," p. 204.

29. Stanley K. Henshaw and Jane Silverman, "The Characteristics and Prior Contraceptive Use of U.S. Abortion Patients," *Family Planning Perspectives* 20, no. 4 (1988): 158–68.

30. Deborah A. Dawson, "The Effects of Sex Education on Adolescent Behaviors," *Family Planning Perspectives* 18, no. 1 (1986): 162–70.

31. Bamikale Feyisetan and Anne R. Pebley, "Premarital Sexuality in Urban Nigeria," *Studies in Family Planning* 20, no. 6 (1989):. 343–54.

32. See Sider, *Completely Pro-life*.

33. See Hans-Martin Sass, "Responsibilities in Human Reproduction and Population Policy," in Bondeson, Engelhardt, and Spicher, *Abortion and the Status of the Fetus*, for a philosophical discussion of developing a contraceptive ethos.

INDEX